The Politics
of Unemployment

The Politics
of Unemployment

Donald C. Baumer
Smith College

Carl E. Van Horn
Rutgers University

A Division of
Congressional Quarterly Inc.
1414 22nd Street, N.W., Washington, D.C. 20037

Printed in the United States of America

Library of Congress Cataloging in Publication Data

Baumer, Donald C., 1950-
    The politics of unemployment.

    Bibliography: p.
    Includes index.
    1. Manpower policy—United States. 2. Unemployment—United States.
I. Van Horn, Carl E. II. Title.
HD5724.B346   1984   331.13′77′0973   84-14222
ISBN 0-87187-323-0 (pbk.)

To
Elmer and Virginia Baumer
Polly Baumer
George and Audrey Van Horn
Christy Van Horn

Contents

Tables and Figures

Preface

Unemployment has long been a potent and controversial political issue. No national political figure would dare treat the dangers of widespread unemployment or the plight of the jobless in the casual manner prevalent in the early part of this century. Since the political revolution sparked by the Great Depression of the 1930s, presidents and members of Congress have known that the ups and downs of the unemployment rate, the most visible sign of economic well-being, could determine whether they retain power or retire from public life.

The federal government annually pours billions of dollars into financial assistance for the unemployed, job creation measures, and training programs. Yet, deep ideological divisions remain about when and how the government should aid the unemployed. Recently, double-digit unemployment—the highest level in 40 years—has ignited new public fears and fostered higher expectations for government remedies. Unemployment is once again one of the most hotly debated items on the domestic policy agenda.

This book probes into the ever-shifting domain of unemployment programs. It is difficult to imagine a more tumultuous history. During the last decade, federal employment strategies were revised again and again; budgets tripled and then shrank to original levels; five major legislative initiatives added new programs, subtracted others, and restructured existing ones; temporary job creation measures started small, grew to enormous proportions, vanished briefly, and then rose again; administrative responsibilities shifted from federal to local governments and then to states and private sector representatives. As economic trends, political power, and public opinion changed, the nation's arsenal of weapons in the fight against unemployment was transformed in response.

We address two central questions. What does a political analysis of unemployment programs teach us about their design and effectiveness and about future policy options? What does an examination of this period of policy turmoil tell us about American politics?

Our story traces more than a decade of the politics of unemployment and analyzes the formulation, administration, and reformulation of public policies. We are particularly interested in the dynamic relationship between policy making and policy implementation. We want to illuminate the profound influence that public laws, politicians, and politics have on program performance, and we hope to show how all these affect subsequent rounds of policy making.

Chapter 1 examines the political and economic dimensions of the unemployment problem and provides an overview of changing government strategies. Chapter 2 describes the processes and institutions through which ideas are translated into government action. The special circumstances of unemployment programs are contrasted with broader features of the public policy cycle.

Chapters 3 through 6 investigate the last decade of federal employment and training programs in detail. Our analysis of four "seasons" of public policy highlight the unique issues that emerge during a particular era while following persistent themes, such as the struggle among federal, state, and local implementers and the distribution of program benefits.

Chapter 3 covers the first season of employment programs, from 1973 to 1976, and traces the enactment and early years of the Comprehensive Employment and Training Act—a law intended to improve the delivery of federal job training measures. Chapter 4 examines the second season, from 1976 to 1978. This phase was characterized by rapidly expanding jobs programs and experimental youth employment strategies. Implementation problems sprang up almost as fast as the new programs, undermining the system's reputation.

The third season of employment programs is analyzed in Chapter 5. Between 1978 and 1980, policy makers attempted to repair the damaged reputation of federal jobs programs by writing tougher statutes and stepping up federal enforcement. Chapter 6 covers the most recent season of employment and training policy, from 1980 to 1984. The election of Ronald Reagan and other conservative lawmakers ushered in a substantially different policy perspective. But the conservatives could not afford to ignore 12 million jobless Americans or the message delivered by the 1982 congressional election. Congress and the president were forced to endorse new jobs programs for the unemployed.

The observations, analyses, and opinions contained in this book are based on extensive research undertaken by the authors during the last 10 years. Field research was conducted in more than 50 cities and counties across the nation and in Washington. Hundreds of elected officials, professional staff, interest group representatives, and citizens were interviewed and observed in public and private meetings. Our perspective is both "top-down" and "bottom-up." We are familiar with the aspirations and actions of federal officials, as well as state and local implementers. We have tried to convey the "street-level" reality of programs without burdening the reader with anecdote after anecdote. Our study also draws upon a vast literature on unemployment programs available in government documents and consulting reports.

We cannot begin to list all those who helped us. Hundreds of people have given us information and allowed us to interview them. We collaborated with dozens of associates on studies that contributed to our knowledge and understanding. There are, however, several people without whose assistance we could not have completed this book. Randall Ripley, Grace Franklin, and our former colleagues at the Mershon Center of Ohio State University deserve special praise. Under Ripley's leadership, we participated in six research projects funded by the U.S. Department of Labor that were invaluable.

We were fortunate to have splendid research and secretarial support. Susan Massart and Peggy McNutt served ably and diligently as research assistants. Joanne Pfeiffer typed and retyped drafts and made many trips to the copy room. Judy Luckus also pitched in on the typewriter. The Eagleton Institute of Politics supplied generous financial assistance.

Several colleagues at Smith and Rutgers and other institutions read and commented on portions of the manuscript. We especially thank David Ford, William Gormley, Philip Green, Donald Robinson, and Stanley Rothman. Dorothy James, Charles O. Jones, and Randall Ripley, who reviewed the manuscript, provided many valuable suggestions. We also want to thank Joanne Daniels and Carolyn Goldinger of CQ Press for their guidance and encouragement.

Finally, we are most grateful to our families—Polly, Benjamin, and Maggie Baumer and Christy and Evan Van Horn—for putting up with us over the long life of this endeavor.

None of those from whom we sought advice is responsible for any errors that remain in this book. We do hope that their counsel was put to good use.

Donald C. Baumer
Carl E. Van Horn

Unemployment and Public Policy 1

Unemployment is a political issue of the highest order, commanding the attention of elected officials, a wide spectrum of interest groups, and the general public. The unemployment rate—the percentage of citizens unable to find work when they want it—is the single most important signpost of the nation's prosperity. The costs of high unemployment are enormous. A 1 percent rise in the unemployment rate, for example, deprives the federal treasury of $25 billion through lost tax revenues and increased spending in programs such as unemployment insurance, food stamps, and welfare payments.

The costs of unemployment also must be measured in personal and social terms. The unemployed, their families, and the communities most affected by joblessness experience a host of ills. As unemployment spreads, crime, family disintegration, spouse and child abuse, and physical and mental illnesses also increase. The victims of unemployment lose more than jobs; their health, property, and hope for the future are also at risk. As Stephen Bailey, the noted political scientist, observed, the contemporary concern about unemployment

> . . . is but the latest version of man's age-old petition, "Give us this day our daily bread." If attention is now addressed to Washington . . . rather than to heaven, it is only because man has changed his mind about the relative competence of God and government in dealing with pressing economic issues.[1]

Even though politicians and government cannot afford to ignore unemployment, there are sharp disagreements about what role government can or should play in ameliorating the problem. Determining how government should respond to unemployment is not a simple task. The scarcity of objective facts precludes ready solutions. Instead, the remedies proposed by presidents, legislators, party leaders, labor leaders, and economists reflect vastly different definitions of the unemployment situation. The problems and the possible solutions are shaped by political convictions about public and private initiative and by opinions about what the government is capable of accomplishing. Developing strategies to alleviate unemployment is an inherently political process.

Whether and how the federal government should help the unemployed has been one of America's fundamental political conflicts for more than 50 years. During the mid-1980s, the problem of unemployment grips the nation's attention more firmly than at any time since the Great Depression.[2] Politicians and policy analysts search for measures that can guarantee prosperity. American workers are increasingly anxious about keeping their jobs, their homes, and their standard of living. Young people are no longer certain that they have good prospects of getting steady jobs. The long-coveted goal of full employment for all Americans seems impossible to reach.

Attention to and controversy about unemployment have risen in recent years, and predictions about continuing high levels of unemployment suggest that it will remain a central issue of American government and political life for the rest of the century. To understand the politics of unemployment, we will begin by describing the nature and causes of unemployment, how these change over time, and how presidents and Congresses responded in the past. Through this brief review, we will begin to understand the importance of the political lens through which facts about unemployment are observed and evaluated.

Unemployment and Its Causes

In the early 1980s unemployment reached the highest level in more than 40 years. During 1982, 10.8 percent of the workforce was unemployed during one month, more than one American in five was unemployed at some time during the year, and more than four million people could not find work for the entire year.[3] At the peak of unemployment in 1982, 12 million people could not find jobs, and another 2 million people were not counted among the ranks of the unemployed because they had given up looking for work. Unemployment among minority groups was nearly double the national average, and more than half of the minority teenagers could not find jobs.

The upsurge in unemployment during the 1980s must be seen in the context of long-term trends in the nation's workforce. During the 20th century, the nation's worst bout with unemployment came during the 1930s when one-quarter of the workforce was jobless and the unemployment rate remained in the high teens for nearly the whole decade. The rate dipped during and immediately after World War II, but since the 1950s it has been getting gradually higher, as shown by the data in Figure 1-1. During the 1950s and 1960s unemployment averaged around 4.6

Figure 1-1   Average Annual and Peak Month Unemployment Rate for the United States, 1950 to 1983, in percent

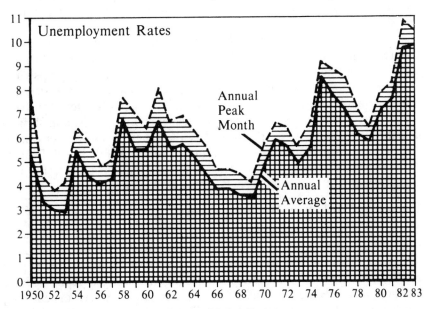

Source: U.S. Department of Labor, Bureau of Labor Statistics

percent; the 1970s saw unemployment climb to an average of 6.2 percent, and the average for the 1980s is already 8.5 percent. The yearly unemployment rate has not averaged less than 4 percent since 1969—a level that was once thought to be the standard for successful employment policy.

Aggregate statistics mask important features about the unemployed. They vary widely by age, education, race, and region. Unemployment hits some groups much harder than others. In January 1984, for example, the nation's overall unemployment rate was 8 percent, but it was 17 percent for blacks, 19 percent among teenagers, and more than 46 percent for black teenagers. Blue-collar workers suffered an unemployment rate nearly three times higher than white-collar workers. West Virginia had the nation's highest jobless rate at nearly 16 percent, while New Hampshire had only 4.3 percent of its citizens out of work.[4]

The official unemployment rate understates the full extent of the problem because it excludes two categories of potential workers: "discouraged workers," who have given up their search for a job even though they want to work, and part-time employees, who would rather work full time. The U.S. Department of Labor estimated that during 1983 more than 1.6

million people fell into the discouraged worker category and that 6 million part-time workers wanted full-time jobs. If these people were included in the calculation, the unemployment rate would be considerably higher than the official level.[5]

Unemployment is caused by many complex and interdependent factors of the national and world economy. How much unemployment there will be and who will be unemployed are determined by upswings and slowdowns in economic activity, long-term changes in the size and composition of the workforce, expansion and decline in selected industries, technological innovations, international trade, energy prices, and shifting demands for workers with specific skills. All of these factors are, or can be, directly or indirectly affected by government policy. While it is difficult to separate causes and effects, it is possible to examine important trends that contribute to the nature and extent of unemployment.

Expanding Workforce, Declining Productivity

Because the unemployment rate is the percentage of the labor force that is jobless, it follows that short- and long-term changes in the size of the labor force have serious effects on the unemployment rate. To be counted as part of the labor force an individual must either have a job or be actively looking for one. Since the mid-1950s, the number of Americans entering the workforce has increased steadily. The number of people working in the United States jumped from 69 million in 1960 to nearly 110 million in 1982. Perhaps more important, the participation rate of adult workers grew from 66 percent in 1960 to 72 percent in 1980. Not only are there more people, but also greater percentages of them are working now than before. These increases reflect important demographic and social changes in American society. The postwar baby boom caused a huge population increase that brought millions of new entrants to the labor force in the late 1960s and 1970s. The labor force participation of women increased from 36 percent in 1960 to 47 percent in 1980, and unprecedented numbers of legal and illegal immigrants also entered the job market.

An expanding labor force has created great pressure on the U.S. economy to generate more jobs—the other side of the unemployment equation. According to the Congressional Budget Office (CBO), a real economic growth rate of 3 to 4 percent (growth in excess of inflation) would be required to lower the nation's unemployment rate 1 percentage point.[6] Real economic growth is determined by the size and productivity of the labor force, but productivity has been declining. Since 1973 the productivity of the nation's workforce has grown at a 1 percent annual average; the growth rate averaged 2 percent between 1965 and 1973 and 3 percent between 1945 and 1965.[7] If the current trends continue, we can expect to witness continued growth in the labor force but only slow to moderate growth in the economy and in productivity. Both trends could lead to relatively high rates of unemployment for the remainder of the century.

Cyclical and Structural Unemployment

Even though the economy has grown significantly, it is evident from the data in Figure 1-1 that progress has not been steady. Cyclical trends in economic activity cause unemployment to rise and fall. Thus, over time, some people are periodically employed and unemployed as the economy prospers or falters. People affected by these swings in the economy are known as the *cyclically unemployed*. As demand for products—automobiles, for example—slackens, some workers in the automotive, rubber, and related industries are laid off. When demand for automobiles rebounds, many workers will be called back to their jobs. Cyclically unemployed individuals' problems are eliminated by an upturn in the economy because these workers are fully prepared to return to jobs in industry.

Even when the economy is healthy, however, millions of Americans remain unemployed either because they lack the skills and education expected by employers or because they held jobs in industries experiencing prolonged economic decline. For these workers, upswings in the cycle of business activity may be insufficient. They are referred to as the *structurally unemployed;* for one reason or another, there is little demand for their skills, at least where they live.

Unlike the cyclically unemployed, the structurally unemployed experience prolonged unemployment or alternating periods of short-term employment and unemployment. Among the structurally unemployed, many are *disadvantaged*—those with little or no work experience, training, or education. A significant percentage of the disadvantaged depend on public assistance. One in three is younger than 21 years of age; many are members of minority groups; others have limited ability to speak and write English. Besides lacking the skills and education demanded in the labor market, many disadvantaged citizens also encounter racial, ethnic, and gender discrimination.

It is difficult to state precisely the size of this group, but a 1980 study released by CBO classified 16 million people as disadvantaged.[8] Most of these people were unemployed or discouraged from looking for work; others were working but earning no more than the federally established minimum for a family in poverty. The disadvantaged population includes high school dropouts; Asian, Mexican, and Latin American immigrants; and others who are poorly prepared to fill available jobs in American business and industry. They remain on welfare, unemployed, or engaged in menial tasks because they do not have the basic education and skills required for most entry-level jobs. Their futures are made even more bleak by the fact that the competition is increasing for unskilled, entry-level jobs.

Without jobs due to plant closings caused by import competition, product obsolescence, or industry decline or relocation, an increasing proportion of the structurally unemployed are *displaced workers*, profoundly affected by changes in the national and international economy.[9] No one knows exactly how large this group of displaced workers is— estimates vary from around 200,000 to 2 million—but this category of unemployed workers poses special problems for public policy.[10] In contrast to the disadvantaged individual, the displaced worker often has a stable employment record in a single industry or trade and relatively few episodes of unemployment. Many displaced workers are white males in their prime wage earning years; they tend to be concentrated in America's older industrial communities in the Northeast and Midwest. At one time, their skills and education were adequate to earn them above average wages in major industries. Now they find themselves without opportunities in a labor market that has changed dramatically since they entered it decades ago.

The U.S. auto industry provides a striking example of industrial decline leading to worker displacement. American automakers have lost significant shares of the domestic and world market. For a host of reasons, ranging from the industry's failure to produce fuel-efficient automobiles fast enough to the high cost of its workforce, more than 270,000 automotive manufacturing jobs were lost in less than 10 years. Some economists predict that further automation of the manufacturing process will eliminate another 200,000 jobs by 1985.[11] The declining auto industry is only one example of an ongoing restructuring in the economy that forces people accustomed to good wages and stable jobs to join the ranks of the chronically unemployed.

Government Strategies for Aiding the Jobless

A staggering array of government policies attempt to address the problem of unemployment. At the broadest level, the federal government's tax and expenditure policies influence aggregate demand for goods and services and have a direct effect on the sectors and groups that have money to spend. Trade policies determine the extent to which goods and services may be exported or imported. Environmental regulations and energy policies have serious effects on selected industries. Monetary policies directly influence many businesses, especially those heavily dependent on the cost of borrowing money, such as the housing industry.

In this book we concern ourselves primarily with government programs designed to help the unemployed either by treating the symptoms of unemployment or by providing jobs or training. The emphasis, therefore, is on governmental spending programs that attack unemployment directly, rather than on broader policies and strategies that indirectly affect the overall level of unemployment in society.

Over the past 50 years, there has been no shortage of government strategies to help unemployed Americans. Beginning with the New Deal of President Franklin D. Roosevelt, which pumped billions of dollars into temporary jobs for people affected by the Depression, right through to the Job Training Partnership Act of 1982, which funds training services for unemployed low-income individuals, federal lawmakers have proposed and enacted dozens of measures to ease unemployment. Since fiscal year 1975, federal spending on unemployment insurance, temporary jobs, and training programs averaged around $20 billion per year.[12] In 1983, a year with extraordinarily high unemployment, federal aid for the jobless cost more than $36 billion. Though only a small fraction of the total federal budget—nearly $850 billion in 1983—unemployment programs constitute a significant portion of the budget reserved for purposes other than pensions, health care, and national defense.

Just as people experience unemployment for diverse reasons, so do government programs aid the different categories among the unemployed with a variety of remedies. Generally, federal assistance for unemployed citizens can be grouped into two categories: programs for the cyclically unemployed—people who temporarily lose their jobs because of declines in economic activity—and programs for the structurally unemployed—people who suffer chronic unemployment because their skills are not demanded by employers.

The rationale for cyclical unemployment measures is that the government should soften the blows delivered by economic downturns and help the unemployed maintain their standard of living until the private sector rebounds and rehires the workers. Rather than ignore the unemployed and force them to skip house and car payments and lose their possessions, policy makers argue that government should offer some form of temporary aid.

Within the broad category of cyclical unemployment programs, many approaches have emerged from Washington over the years. Generally these policies have been of two distinct types: *income support* and *job creation* programs. Income support measures provide partial and temporary replacement of the unemployed workers' prior wages or salaries. The principal income support program, known as the unemployment insurance system, is financed jointly by employer contributions made on behalf of employees, by state revenues, and by federal grants and loans to state governments where the system is administered.

Job creation programs, in which the federal government underwrites the cost of temporary jobs in state and local governments or on public works projects, are another weapon against cyclical unemployment. Proponents of federal jobs programs believe it more efficient and effective to improve the level and quality of public services in communities than to let the unemployed idly collect unemployment benefits.

Federal programs for the structurally unemployed are based on the belief that the chronically unemployed will remain jobless unless they become more competitive in the labor market. These measures are intended to help the long-term unemployed acquire skills that may lead to jobs produced by an expanding economy. The primary beneficiaries of structural unemployment programs are the disadvantaged—people with low incomes, minorities, and others with limited education, training, or work experience. Displaced workers also may benefit.

Because of the mismatch between the skills found among the unemployed and the skills sought by employers, policy makers argue that the government should sponsor training programs, provide remedial assistance, and offer employers incentives to hire the long-term unemployed. People who drop out of mainstream educational and training institutions are thus afforded a second chance to obtain the education and skills necessary to become productive members of society. In theory, aid for the structurally unemployed may reduce the costs of public assistance and other government income-transfer programs, develop a better-trained workforce for employers, and lessen suffering caused by crime and other ills associated with a permanent underclass.

Early Federal Aid for the Unemployed

Direct and sustained federal intervention on behalf of the unemployed dates from the 1930s.[13] Before then, unemployment was not considered a government problem. The variety of approaches, different target groups, and changing appropriations, shown in Table 1-1, indicate that federal policy toward the unemployed has shifted and expanded dramatically over the past five decades. Federal involvement has been intense and extensive at some times and rather limited at others; the problems of different categories of unemployed people were recognized and addressed through public laws; remedies were tried and abandoned or modified.

Federal aid for the jobless was spurred by a national and world economic crisis during the 1930s and by the election of President Roosevelt and a Congress committed to government action. Lawmakers sought measures that would maintain consumer demand, alleviate human suffering, and quell the social unrest accompanying the nation's highest recorded levels of unemployment. With one American in four out of work, Roosevelt's emergency relief measures whizzed through Congress, putting in place temporary jobs programs, short-term financial assistance, and other humanitarian aid for the jobless and poor.[14]

The president and Congress initiated unprecedented job creation programs that put people to work on conservation and public works projects. Although diverse in approach and beneficiaries, each Roosevelt-era jobs program had a common purpose—aiding the unemployed while providing a public benefit. The Public Works Administration, for example, gobbled up more than $3 billion during its lifetime, generating several hundred thousand jobs for builders of highways, dams, roads, public buildings, and other large-scale and enduring public works projects. The companion Works Progress Administration hired more than 8 million unemployed workers on small-scale, labor-intensive projects, at a cost of more than $11 billion.

The public works projects were designed to aid any unemployed person able and willing to work. Concern for the special problems experienced by structurally unemployed individuals had not entered the policy debate. The emergency public works projects were phased out during World War II, but the New Deal experience left a widespread impression with the public and government leaders that the federal government could successfully generate useful temporary jobs during periods of severe economic distress.

Unemployment Insurance

The principal legacy of Depression-era policy making was the establishment of unemployment insurance.[15] Although temporary jobs programs come and go and remain highly controversial today, the nationwide unemployment insurance system continues uninterrupted after more than 50 years. Deeply imbedded in the American welfare state, unemployment insurance, like Social Security pensions and health care benefits for the elderly, has become one of a handful of government "entitlements" that politicians are loathe to alter, except to extend benefits and make them more generous.

The cost of unemployment insurance fluctuates with shifting economic conditions, and the system's price tag has been growing ever higher as the duration and amount of benefits increase and the eligible workforce expands. In 1950 federal grants to states for unemployment payments were less than $200 million. In the 1970s annual expenditures on unemployment insurance averaged nearly $10 billion. By 1983, with more than 5 million unemployed workers receiving benefits, the cost had ballooned to $33 billion.

Unemployment insurance enjoys enduring support because it benefits a wide cross section of society. Everyone from blue-collar laborers to a laid-off bank vice-president is eligible for assistance. The size of a worker's "unemployment check" varies by states and according to the prior work experience and wages, but the average unemployed worker

Table 1-1 Major Federal Programs to Aid the Unemployed, 1932–1984

Program	Years of Operation	Estimated Expenditures	Description	Target Group
Relief and Construction Act	1932-1933	$300 million	Public construction projects; first public works program	Unemployed
Civilian Conservation Corps	1937-1943	$3 billion	Temporary jobs in national parks and forests	Unemployed youth
Civil Works Administration	1933-1934	$950 million	Temporary jobs on small-scale public works projects	Unemployed
Public Works Administration	1933-1943	$3 billion	Temporary jobs on large-scale public works projects, such as roads and dams	Unemployed and veterans
Wagner-Peyser Act (U.S. Employment Service)	1933-present	No estimate available	Initially referred workers to PWA projects; evolved into nationwide service for matching job openings with applicants	Employed and unemployed job applicants
Works Progress Administration	1935-1942	$11 billion	Temporary jobs on small-scale projects for community betterment	Unemployed
Social Security Act (unemployment insurance)	1935-present	$170 billion (1950-1983)	Partial and temporary income support; length and amount of benefits vary by state and by prior experience and wages of worker	Unemployed, laid-off from regular jobs
Area Redevelopment Act	1961-1965	$280 million	Grants and loans to help attract industry and to train or retrain workers	Unemployed residents of economically depressed regions
Public Works Acceleration Act	1962-1963	$843 million	Temporary jobs on federal public works projects	Employed and unemployed job applicants in areas of high unemployment

Program	Years	Amount	Services	Target Group
Manpower Development and Training Act	1962-1974	$3.6 billion	Vocational training programs	Initially, unemployed workers displaced by automation; later, low-income youth and adults
Economic Opportunity Act	1964-1974	$6.5 billion	Vocational training, part-time jobs, remedial education	Principally, low-income youth
Emergency Employment Act	1971-1974	$2.3 billion	Temporary jobs in state and local government services	Unemployed
Comprehensive Employment and Training Act	1973-1983	$60.5 billion	Training; part-time and full-time jobs; and other employment services (See below for details.)	Long- and short-term unemployed and low-income (See below for details.)
Title I (changed to Title II in 1978)	1973-1983	$18 billion	Comprehensive employment and training services, including vocational training, and part-time work experience	Initially, the unemployed and low-income; after 1978, only long-term unemployed and low-income
Title II (changed to Title IID in 1978)	1973-1981	$9.6 billion	Temporary jobs in state and local government and in the private nonprofit sector	Initially, the unemployed; after 1978, only long-term unemployed and low-income
Title III	1973-1983	$3.2 billion	Training and part-time work experience	Long-term unemployed, Indians, migrants, veterans, and youth
Title IV—Job Corps (revised from the Economic Opportunity Act)	1970-1983	$3.6 billion	Residential training and remedial education programs	Low-income, unemployed youth

Table 1-1 (Cont.) Major Federal Programs to Aid the Unemployed, 1932-1984

Program	Years of Operation	Estimated Expenditures	Description	Target Group
Title VI (Emergency Jobs and Unemployment Assistance Act of 1974 and Emergency Jobs Programs Extension Act of 1976)	1974-1981	$14.9 billion	Temporary jobs in state and local government and in the private nonprofit sector	Initially, the unemployed; after 1978, only long-term unemployed and low-income
Title VII (Private Sector Initiative Program)	1978-1983	$825 million	Established private industry councils to carry out employment and training programs	Long-term unemployed and low-income
Summer Youth Employment Program	1973-present	$6.2 billion	Temporary, part-time jobs in government, educational, and community service organizations	Unemployed, low-income youth
Youth Employment Demonstration Projects Act	1977-1982	$5.1 billion	Several experimental training and part-time jobs programs	Low-income youth; high school students or dropouts
Trade Adjustment Act	1975-present	$3.9 billion (1975-1981)	Temporary income support and retraining programs	People unemployed because of import competition
Local Public Works Program	1976-1977	$6 billion	Temporary jobs on small-scale public works projects	Employed and unemployed construction workers

Program	Years	Cost	Description	Target group
Antirecession Fiscal Assistance	1976-1978	$3 billion	Grants to states and communities with high unemployment rates to maintain government services	State and local government employees
New Jobs Tax Credit	1977-1978	$4.1 billion in forgone revenues	Tax credits to businesses hiring new employees	Businesses hiring new workers and unemployed
Targeted Jobs Tax Credit	1978-present	$2.8 billion in forgone revenues	Tax credits to businesses hiring workers from targeted groups of unemployed	Low-income youth, Vietnam-era veterans, ex-convicts, welfare recipients, participants from vocational rehabilitation programs
Job Training Partnership Act	1983-present	$10 billion (1983-1986)	Replaced CETA's vocational training programs; increases involvement of private sector representatives in program planning and operation	Long-term unemployed and low-income
Transportation Assistance Act	1982-present	Up to $71 billion from FY 1983 to FY 1986	Temporary jobs for highway construction and repair	Employed and unemployed construction workers
Emergency Supplemental Appropriations Act	1983-present	$4.6 billion	Temporary public works jobs, social service and community employment, and humanitarian relief; added funds to more than 40 existing federal programs	Employed and unemployed

Sources: *Employment and Training Report of the President; Budget of the United States;* and *Congressional Quarterly Almanac.*

received a weekly check of $115 for 32 weeks during 1983. In states with extremely high unemployment, laid-off workers could obtain payments for more than a year.

Unemployment insurance sometimes is derided as "middle-class welfare" because its beneficiaries are typically not poor and have stable employment records. To keep their benefits they are merely required to report that they are awaiting recall to a regular job or that they have searched for suitable jobs within their occupational field.[16] Unlike public assistance for low-income people, unemployment insurance contains no expectation or requirement that only those who need assistance will receive it. Moreover, many people feel they are entitled to an unemployment check. But laid-off workers in states with high unemployment receive benefits equal to the amount their employers paid into the system in one month or so. After that, and for up to 65 weeks in some states, they will be benefiting from taxes levied on other employers and from federal grants. Despite the enormous scope and costs of unemployment insurance, fewer than half of the unemployed were receiving this kind of assistance at the peak of the 1981-1983 recession. Self-employed workers, people who worked for short periods of time, part-time workers, and those who had exhausted their benefits all fell outside the system.

Following World War II an economic boom absorbed returning servicemen, and thousands of women who had worked in factories dropped out of the labor force to raise families. Unemployment receded as a major national issue after the passage of the "GI Bill," which educated returning servicemen, and the Employment Act, which put the federal government on record as being concerned with unemployment and established a council of economic advisers to the president but authorized no specific spending programs to reduce joblessness.[17] Episodes of high unemployment during the 1950s failed to provoke federal legislation to expand programs for the jobless. Except for vocational training for Korean War veterans, the federal government expressed little tangible interest in the plight of the unemployed beyond the continued partial funding of unemployment insurance.

The War on Poverty

The political fortunes of government unemployment programs took a dramatic turn during the 1960s. When unemployment reached 8 percent in 1961, President John F. Kennedy—the first Democrat in the White House in eight years—and a Congress controlled by Democrats found the case for temporary jobs programs compelling. The Public Works Acceleration Act of 1962 authorized nearly a billion dollars for building and maintenance projects in communities experiencing high and sustained levels of unemployment.

The problems of the chronically unemployed also were deemed worthy of federal government involvement. The severe hardships of economically depressed regions were addressed by the Area Redevelopment Act of 1961 that channeled job training and industrial revitalization grants into the nation's poorest states and communities. Soon after, some workers who lost their jobs because of automation could obtain retraining assistance through the Manpower Development and Training Act of 1962. Spending on these experimental programs remained modest, however. In 1963 federal training programs cost only $64 million.

President Lyndon B. Johnson's War on Poverty gave unemployment programs an enormous boost. As national policy makers "discovered" new categories of structurally unemployed citizens, new programs multiplied. Employment and training programs were latched onto as a potential remedy for breaking the "culture of poverty." Lawmakers hoped that job training could be effectively joined with health, education, and social services to help people escape debilitating cycles of chronic unemployment and indefinite public assistance.

Throughout the 1960s many different employment and training measures were authorized by federal lawmakers and administered by public and private organizations.[18] The principal legislation—the Manpower Development and Training Act and the Economic Opportunity Act—housed more than a dozen programs for high school dropouts, inner-city youth, delinquents, welfare recipients, and older workers. These different measures had in common an emphasis on aiding disadvantaged citizens with limited education, skills, and experience.

Employment and training programs acquired image problems during the 1960s. Unlike unemployment insurance or public works projects that benefit a cross section of unemployed Americans, War on Poverty programs were aimed at the poor, minorities, and residents of depressed urban communities. The participants made no financial contribution to their programs. Most were not even taxpayers, and many had never worked. From the standpoint of some critics, the War on Poverty rewarded undeserving people whose chronic unemployment was of their own making.

The community organizations that operated many of the War on Poverty programs also contributed to the image problem. Because Johnson and many members of Congress did not have much faith in either the ability or the commitment of state and local governments to serve low-income people, new mechanisms were established for channeling funds from federal agencies to poor people. It became common at this time for the federal government to fund community-based organizations directly, thus bypassing state and local elected officials. Some of these community groups employed political activists who criticized the local officials. In a few cases, federal funds helped underwrite protests by the poor against the policies and practices of local governments. Politicians at all levels of government reacted negatively to these developments. Soon mayors and county executives demanded more control over the planning and operation of War on Poverty measures.[19]

Despite harsh criticism, training and employment services for long-term unemployed and low-income individuals have continued uninter-rupted since the Johnson administration. However, spending on training programs for the chronically unemployed has been considerably smaller than for job creation programs or unemployment insurance. During the 1960s, annual expenditures were consistently less than a billion dollars; during the 1970s, job training programs for the disadvantaged averaged around $2 billion per year.

Types of Employment and Training Programs

The legacy of the War on Poverty was a large, diverse, and uncoordinated set of programs aimed at serving the many needs of the chronically unemployed. The different categorical programs operating in the late 1960s and early 1970s are best thought of in terms of the basic approach they embodied. *Vocational or skill training* programs taught low-income people trades, such as carpentry, welding, auto mechanics, and cooking, in an effort to make them more competitive in the labor market. Technical classes typically lasted from six months to a year and usually were complemented with instruction in basic math, reading, and other courses that led to a high school diploma, which many participants lacked.[20]

For many of those with little job experience, however, vocational training was thought to be inappropriate. Consequently, *work experience* programs that offered part-time jobs in public and private nonprofit organizations to low-income youth or others often were funded by the federal government. A typical work experience program employed high school students for 10 to 20 hours per week after school hours in minimum wage jobs. During the summer months, the number of hours, participants, and work sites often were expanded. Ideally, youthful workers acquired good work habits while earning a modest wage.

Another structural employment program focused on the other side of the equation by offering an incentive for employers to hire low-skilled, low-income workers. Businesses that hired people (who were not expected to be quite up to the normal standards) received partial wage subsidies. This approach, known as *on-the-job training,* usually gave private employers about one-half of the trainees' wages for up to six months. The employer was compensated for costs associated with training a "marginal" employee, and a previously jobless individual gained stable employment with the business.

As experience with federal job training programs mounted, pressure began to build in Washington for something more than remedial training for the unemployed. Large Democratic majorities in Congress were concerned about steadily rising unemployment and the severe fiscal problems experienced by many cities in the Northeast and Midwest. A new form of temporary full-time jobs program—*public service employment*—offered a way to support local government services with federal tax revenues and to engage the unemployed in productive tasks. Unlike the public works projects of the 1930s and 1960s, public service employment funds could not be used to purchase supplies, equipment, or other materials needed to complete building, sewer, or road projects. Indeed, public service employment programs usually required that 90 percent of the funds appropriated be used for paying the wages of workers who could be hired by state and local governments or by private nonprofit agencies. Public service employment offered politicians a direct method for aiding distressed individuals and communities.

The first new-style public jobs measure to be enacted was the Emergency Employment Act of 1971 that provided nearly 200,000 jobs in state and local government agencies between 1972 and 1974. This initial experience with a large public service jobs program showed that local governments were capable of creating many worthwhile jobs quickly. However, permissive entrance standards allowed state and local elected officials to hire mostly nondisadvantaged individuals to fill the positions funded by the program.[21] This first round of public service employment was of little value to the low-income, long-term unemployed.

The Comprehensive Employment and Training Act

The patchwork of federal employment and training measures was reordered under the Comprehensive Employment and Training Act of 1973 (CETA), which transferred administrative responsibility from the federal government to state and local officials.[22] From 1973 to 1983 CETA was the centerpiece of American public policy for the unemployed. Its programs were the only unemployment measures that sought to help the chronically unemployed obtain steady jobs. The law's public service employment components were the largest federal job stimulus measures in existence at the time and the only ones focused on helping the long-term unemployed. CETA accounted for practically all the discretionary spending and for a large chunk of overall spending on unemployment programs during the late 1970s and early 1980s.

CETA changed dramatically during its life span as appropriations of more than 60 billion federal dollars were spent to train millions of unemployed people and create millions of temporary jobs. During CETA's first year, state and local governments spent $2.7 billion on training and jobs programs; spending more than doubled two years later, tripled by 1979, and returned to original levels by 1982 (Table 1-2).

The fluctuating funding levels reflected Congress's shifting objectives. CETA was formally amended several times. Public service employment programs were added in 1974 and 1977, modified in 1978, and eliminated in 1981; major programs for youth, veterans, migrant workers, and senior citizens were added; and the entire law underwent comprehensive reform in 1978 and 1982. Initially, CETA's principal mission was training the chronically unemployed for private sector jobs. Within months after enactment, however, Congress grafted large "emergency" jobs components onto CETA to counter the effects of the recession of 1974-1975. Over the next few years, CETA ballooned from subsidizing approximately 100,000 jobs to more than 725,000 jobs in 1978-1979.

CETA's public service employment programs were large and visible, but they were only part of the job creation programs in existence during the 1970s and early 1980s. Indeed, public works and public service employment programs were enacted and abolished with dizzying frequency (Table 1-1). Spending on temporary jobs programs averaged roughly $4 billion per year between 1971 and 1983. Under the presidency of Jimmy Carter the cost of temporary employment measures skyrocketed to an annual average of $13 billion between 1977 and 1979. In 10 years more money was funneled into job creation than had been spent in the entire history of federal unemployment programs.

As policy makers grew unhappy with large-scale public service employment they decided to give CETA an additional mission involving the private sector. The private sector initiative program, created by CETA's 1978 reauthorization, called upon CETA prime sponsors to establish private industry councils, made up primarily of people in business, to advise local employment and training agencies on how to improve the effectiveness of their programs and procedures. The Targeted Jobs Tax Credit of 1978 represented a new strategy for helping the chronically unemployed, but it was also part of the new private sector direction imposed on CETA. Like on-the-job training, it directed its incentives and rewards toward employers who could receive a tax credit for hiring chronically unemployed individuals who fell into any one of several categories of need.[23]

Adding another dimension to enormous growth and frequent change was the law's complexity. CETA was supposed to streamline employment and training programs that President Richard Nixon characterized as "overcentralized, bureaucratic, remote from the people they mean to serve, overguidelined and far less effective than they might be in helping the unskilled and disadvantaged."[24] Initially, the law consolidated roughly 17 separate programs previously administered by more than 50,000 educa-

Table 1-2 Appropriations for CETA and JTPA, Fiscal Years 1975 to 1985, in millions of dollars

Program	CETA									JTPA		
	1975	1976	1977	1978	1979	1980	1981	1982	1983	Oct. 1983 to June 1984[b]	1984[c]	1985[d]
Total	3,743	6,339	8,053	8,125	10,290	8,128	7,740	3,895	3,990	2,794	3,605	3,610
Comprehensive training[e]	1,819	2,302	2,481	2,268	2,361	2,922	2,821	1,925	2,409	1,560	2,079	2,063
Special youth[f]	175	184	1,274	417	1,238	1,492	1,636	1,204	622	415	578	600
Summer youth[g]	473	528	595	756	785	609	839	766	824	725	725	724
Public service employment	1,275	3,325	3,703	4,684	5,905	3,105	2,444	0	0	0	0	0
Dislocated workers	0	0	0	0	0	0	0	0	135	94	223	223

[a] Includes transition quarter when fiscal year shifted from July 1 through June 30 to October 1 through September 30.

[b] Estimated for the transition year—October 1, 1983, to June 30, 1984. JTPA program year runs from July 1 to June 30.

[c] Estimated for the JTPA program year, July 1, 1984, to June 30, 1985.

[d] Proposed by President Reagan, second JTPA program year, July 1, 1985, to June 30, 1986.

[e] Includes: programs for native Americans, migrants and seasonal workers, veterans; the private sector initiative program; and research and demonstration programs.

[f] Includes: Job Corps, Youth Employment and Training Programs; Youth Community Conservation and Improvement Projects; and Young Adult Conservation Corps.

[g] Temporary, part-time jobs for low-income young people during the summer months only.

Sources: Employment and Training Administration, U.S. Department of Labor, and *Budget of the United States*.

tional and community organizations under contracts with federal agencies. The new law made more than 450 "prime sponsors" (which, for the most part, were state or local governments with 100,000 or more residents) responsible for the program.

Consolidating programs and eliminating direct federal involvement did little to simplify things. Instead, the complexity was pushed to another level. In 1980, for example, 471 prime sponsors with 30,000 employees spent more than $8 billion through 50,000 private and public agencies and enrolled 3.6 million people in a dozen distinct job and training programs.

Not surprisingly, CETA was very controversial. Although it initially enjoyed bipartisan support—Nixon called it "one of the finest pieces of legislation to come to my desk this year" [25]—five years later, during its first reauthorization, CETA was attacked even by former supporters. By 1978, liberal members of Congress, like David Obey, D-Wis., called CETA "the second most unpopular program in the country, after welfare." [26] The law's history has been likened to roller-coaster rides, stormy Atlantic crossings, and bulging pork barrels. A vivid image of CETA was captured by a reporter in the *New York Times:*

> The programs under the seven-year-old Comprehensive Employment and Training Act, like well-traveled suitcases, have acquired quite a collection of scratches, baggage tickets, and unsightly bulges. They have been battered by scandals and abuses and jolted as the political and ideological course of the act has shifted from destination to destination. They have been crammed, emptied, and crammed again at a cost of $51 billion since the legislation setting up CETA . . . was signed. . . .[27]

The Reagan Period

Shortly after his election in 1980, Ronald Reagan singled out CETA's public service employment program for termination. Following the president's lead, Congress eliminated temporary job creation measures from the 1982 budget. Within little more than a year however, Congress again enacted public works employment programs—the Transportation Assistance Act of 1982 and a $4.6 billion employment generating appropriation in 1983.

Even the less controversial training programs were in jeopardy during the first two years of the Reagan administration. A federal *job training* program was eventually maintained by changing CETA's focus and name, but employment and training programs might not have survived had it not been for the extremely high unemployment rates in 1982. The Job Training Partnership Act (JTPA), which replaced CETA in 1983, emphasized the importance of skill training and private sector job placement in federal efforts to aid the structurally unemployed. The new law excluded public service jobs, revised program guidelines, and shifted principal management authority from local governments to a shared power arrangement between governors, local elected officials, and private sector representatives.

Currently a complex set of federal programs aids the unemployed. Training programs for low-income youth, adults, and displaced workers are available through JTPA. Temporary income support is provided to the unemployed through unemployment insurance. Employers can receive federal tax credits for hiring long-term unemployed and disadvantaged workers under the targeted jobs tax credit. Several hundred thousand construction workers are engaged in federally funded road repair and building projects through public works jobs bills. In 1983 combined spending on unemployment programs exceeded $36 billion.

Formulating Unemployment Programs

National policy toward the unemployed emerges from a complex mixture of political and economic events, public opinion, perceptions of the unemployment problem, and opinions about what the government can and should do about it. Our brief retrospective on federal government strategies suggests that governmental responses to unemployment are determined by politicians' answers to four fundamental questions:

Under what conditions should the government help the unemployed?
Who among the unemployed should be helped?
What strategies are most effective for helping the unemployed?
How much can the government afford to spend on unemployment programs?

Perceptions about the effectiveness of past unemployment programs help politicians answer these questions and often blur traditional ideological divisions. In the turbulent politics of unemployment, bipartisan support for particular approaches may swiftly turn into bipartisan repudiation.

When Should Government Help?

Although most federal lawmakers consider programs for the unemployed to be within the legitimate scope of government activity, controversy arises over *when* government help is appropriate. At what level of unemployment should the federal government take action? Evidently the answer to this question changes over time. In 1950 the unemployment rate reached 7.8 percent, but there were no emergency jobs programs. In 1971 and 1974, with unemployment at 6.6 percent and 6.7 percent respectively, however, Congress enacted "emergency" job creation measures.

Partisanship and ideology are very important in explaining the timing of federal action. Spending on job creation and training programs for the unemployed expands and contracts with the changing composition of Congress and party control of the White House. Democrats favor broad unemployment measures; Republicans are less supportive of government solutions. Unemployment insurance has not been affected by partisan changes, however, because spending in this entitlement program depends on the number of eligible people filing claims, which, of course, varies with the overall rate of unemployment.

Clearly the government's response to unemployment depends on more than just partisanship and ideology. When a majority of Congress fears that a failure to address unemployment will bring negative electoral consequences, then action is forthcoming. Legislators of both parties recognize the potentially disastrous electoral repercussions of high unemployment and a bad economy.

An example of this political calculus can be found in the reaction of Republican lawmakers to emergency jobs programs in 1982 and 1983. Before the congressional elections, Republicans in the House of Representatives and Senate condemned jobs bills sponsored by the Democrats, even though unemployment had passed the 10 percent mark. Losses by more than two dozen incumbent Republicans and close calls for many others brought about substantial attitude adjustments. Republicans read the returns as proof that the electorate had become concerned about continuing high levels of unemployment. Voters may have been influenced by extensive media coverage of soup kitchens for the poor and long lines of people applying for jobs. The election results created a climate in Congress that was much more favorable to the enactment of temporary jobs programs.

The perceptions and ideological outlooks of elected officials are especially important in the politics of unemployment because the unemployed are not well organized as a voting bloc or an interest group.[28] Compare the political influence of the unemployed with that of Social Security recipients, for example. The 36 million people receiving old-age pensions are quite effective in getting and enriching their benefits. Dozens of interest groups, from the American Association of Retired Persons to the AFL-CIO, lobby on behalf of Social Security recipients. No one questions the "right" of retired people to receive government benefits, and nearly everyone sympathizes with senior citizens—people whose station in life is inevitable and whose reliance on government support is virtually universal.

Unemployed people experience a very different political reality. Their voting power is weak, their claim to governmental assistance is widely questioned, and their lobbying forces pale in comparison to other interest groups. They are dependent on the empathy of other voters, but many people think "it can't happen to me," or "it's their own fault," so there is limited incentive for them to help the unemployed.

Lawmakers' opinions about when government action might be appropriate also is shaped by past experience and future expectations. Following the Depression and World War II, the consensus among national policy makers for more than 20 years was that the rising tide of economic recovery would lift all boats. Government employment and training measures were considered unnecessary except in extreme cases like the Depression. As unemployment rates crept upward during the 1960s and 1970s, those advocating government intervention succeeded in establishing training programs in 1962 and temporary jobs programs in 1971. After that it was considerably less difficult to extend and expand the federal commitment to the unemployed. If government officials are willing to intervene when unemployment is around 4 percent, then more government action is likely when unemployment exceeds 6 percent, and so on.

The issue of "politically acceptable" unemployment levels dominates the debate over government action. According to many economists, there is a level of unemployment—referred to euphemistically as "full employment"—at which government sponsored job creation programs are not only unnecessary but actually counterproductive.[29] Because the unemployed include people who are between jobs or taking a break from work, government help is not required for a substantial portion of them. Moreover, some economists argue that stimulative government spending—such as jobs programs—ignites inflation as the economy approaches full employment. Four percent was the widely accepted economic definition of full employment during the 1950s and 1960s. By the 1970s, however, some economists argued that a 6 percent unemployment rate constituted full employment. In practice, politicians apply varying definitions of politically acceptable unemployment.

Who Should Be Helped?

People experience unemployment for diverse reasons. Some are unemployed because they want to be. They move in and out of the labor market, or change jobs frequently, or quit jobs that could last much longer. Others desperately need jobs to support themselves and their families but cannot find work despite their best efforts. Government policy makers must draw the line somewhere and decide who "deserves" government aid. Should the government retrain unemployed Ph.D.'s? Do unemployed minority teenagers who drop out of high school deserve another chance? What should government do about older workers who lose private sector jobs after 30 years service?

Presidents and Congresses have provided conflicting answers to these and other questions about the scope of unemployment programs. Who receives government help is controlled partly by contemporary policy fads.

Minority teenagers consistently have had extremely high unemployment rates, yet this problem went "unrecognized" until the War on Poverty. Now, however, government sponsored training for low-income youth seems permanently established in the portfolio of unemployment programs.

Displaced workers have come in and out of fashion in the minds of policy makers. During the early 1960s the Manpower Development and Training Act was designed to serve those who had been displaced by automation. Soon the emphasis shifted away from these workers, however, and the urban poor became the principal focus of government policy. People have always lost jobs because of industrial decline and restructuring, but it is only during the last few years that government retraining programs for displaced workers began cropping up again. The displaced worker problem has been rediscovered and urgent government action proposed.

Controversy also exists over which unemployed groups should receive top priority. Given that all unemployed workers will not receive aid—a point to which we shall return momentarily—government policies inevitably single out special categories of the unemployed. But definitions of the "truly needy" periodically change along with political preferences. Depression-era programs served the unemployed on a "first come, first serve" basis. War on Poverty and CETA training aimed at the long-term unemployed, the disadvantaged, and minorities. Public service employment programs, fashioned during the 1970s, initially hired the recently unemployed worker but later were restricted to serving the poor and chronically unemployed. Unemployment insurance helps only the recently unemployed. Public works projects, such as those supported by the Transportation Assistance Act of 1982, assist employed and unemployed construction workers. The Targeted Jobs Tax Credit mainly benefits employers and only secondarily and indirectly the unemployed. The choice of which groups should participate in these programs has profound political implications.

What Should Be Done to Help?

Closely related to the issue of who should benefit is the question of what remedies are best suited for different categories of people. Inevitably, decisions about what to do are tied up with preferences about whom to serve. Public works construction projects require skilled laborers, so inexperienced workers and women are seldom hired. Temporary income support measures are fine if the worker is already part of the labor force but of no benefit to someone who has never held a job. Employment tax credits may help unemployed people who already have skills to obtain jobs more quickly but are less useful to individuals with little or no training.

The remedies may not neatly match the problems of the unemployed and may strike only a glancing blow at root causes. Consider displaced workers, for example. Is it more effective to provide partial income replacement, retraining programs in new industries, or relocation assistance so they can move to places where the private economy is vital? Do any of these strategies arrest industrial decline? What is most effective for cyclically unemployed people who are likely to regain their jobs? Should unemployment insurance be given without requiring beneficiaries to engage in retraining or public works projects? For the low-income, long-term unemployed a plethora of approaches has been suggested. But is it more effective to upgrade their skills and education, to match them with employers looking for entry-level workers, or to provide government funded jobs?

Reliable knowledge about which strategy works best for particular groups of unemployed people unfortunately is scant.[30] But, even if it were abundantly available, lawmakers would still confront difficult political choices and hold deep-seated biases about the scope of government activity. The question of what is politically feasible places constraints on potential remedies. Suppose, for example, that the U.S. Department of Labor advocates policies that encourage people to relocate from Michigan to Texas. Clearly, this idea raises the ire of Michigan's elected officials and the families and friends of those who must relocate. Most would no doubt prefer to see their state's economy revitalized. There are implications for Texas, as well. Can the state handle a large influx of people? Will its schools and other facilities be overburdened? Within contemporary boundaries of political feasibility, the particular mix of programs available at any given moment is based on perceptions about what seems to work best.

How Much Can the Government Afford?

Federal government spending on unemployment programs has grown substantially, but erratically, over the past 15 years (Figure 1-2). Reflecting changing budget and economic priorities, the relationship between unemployment program spending and the unemployment rate varies greatly. From 1969 to 1976—an era of Republican rule in the White House and Democratic control in Congress—unemployment expenditures grew along with rising unemployment. Unemployment insurance, an "entitlement" program whose expenditures are determined by the number of eligible unemployed, accounted for more than two-thirds of all spending during this period, thus explaining why spending mirrored unemployment rates. From 1977 to 1980—with Democrats in charge on Capitol Hill *and* at the White House— spending on employment and training measures increased sharply as programs multiplied, even though

Figure 1-2   Government Expenditures for the Unemployed, 1969-1983

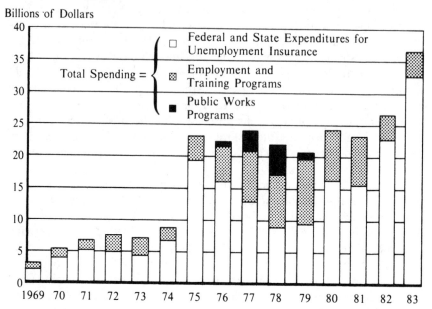

Billions of Dollars

Sources: *Employment and Training Report of the President; Statistical Abstract of the United States;* U.S. Department of Labor, Bureau of Labor Statistics

unemployment gradually declined. By 1979 only half of the spending was consumed by unemployment insurance; the remainder was allocated to temporary jobs programs and remedial training. In 1981 and 1982—when Republicans captured the White House and the Senate—discretionary expenditures plummeted, even though unemployment rates rose rapidly and thus kept total spending at high levels. By 1983, however, job creation programs had come roaring back.

Government sponsored unemployment measures are considerably less extensive in the United States than in other industrialized nations. In the United States, the functioning of the labor market is considered primarily a private sector matter. In other countries, such as Great Britain, West Germany, and Sweden, government plays a much more active and central role.[31] In Sweden, for example, if the private sector does not provide enough jobs, the government considers it a legitimate policy objective to provide substitute employment through government incentives to the private sector, public sector employment, or the encouragement of shorter working hours and part-time employment.[32] Nothing approaching this level of government intervention in the labor market has ever been applied in the United States.

Despite the enormous scope and cost of U.S. unemployment programs, they never serve more than a small fraction of the jobless. In 1983, for example, fewer than half the unemployed were receiving unemployment benefits. At its peak, CETA supported jobs sufficient to reduce the unemployment rate by less than 1 percentage point under optimistic assumptions. The Job Training Partnership Act was scheduled to serve about 700,000 unemployed workers during 1983-1984, but more than 16 million were eligible for assistance. Far from being universal, the nation's unemployment programs aid only a portion of the unemployed and are never large enough to reduce unemployment substantially.

Because the resources to fight unemployment are limited, constraints are placed on the amount "invested" in any one person. On the average, government training programs spend around $3,000 per individual, public service employment programs cost around $10,000 per year for each job, public works jobs cost about $30,000 per year, and unemployment insurance costs approximately $3,300 per person.

With regard to the disadvantaged, the amount spent on each individual raises a fundamental question: can six months or a year of training significantly alter their employment prospects when other institutions, with more money and longer "treatment" periods, were unsuccessful? Unavoidably, short-term unemployment measures are bound to achieve only partial success. This marginal rate of success may help explain why government employment and training programs are controversial and plagued with poor reputations. While a 50 percent success rate may be highly laudable, it seems rather meager to the average observer. Unemployment programs are not dealing with a cross section of society, but rather with those who experience severe difficulties in getting and keeping jobs. For many, the magnitude of their problems far exceeds the potency of the government intervention.

Conclusions

Clashes over unemployment policies and programs are now regular and prominent in the American political scene. Unemployment received little attention during the 1950s and early 1960s, but, as unemployment rose during the 1970s and 1980s, it captured greater attention in elections and policy dialogues. If predictions about the long-term and deeply embedded nature of the unemployment problem are correct, then the politics of unemployment are likely to remain high on the nation's agenda for years to come.

Government sponsored remedies for the unemployed spark intense controversy because they raise fundamental questions about the role of government in society. Unemployment measures are created, expanded, revised, and eliminated with great frequency and urgency. Changes in partisan and ideological balances in Congress and the White House, the attitudes of the president and leaders of Congress, the mood of the public, and the health of the economy all affect the debate over unemployment. With the exception of unemployment insurance, which has survived for 50 years, no unemployment programs command broad and sustained support among elected officials or in society. What government should do on behalf of the jobless remains a divisive and vexing policy question.

While broad political and economic conditions determine basic strategies for assisting the unemployed and cause frequent change, specific policies are shaped by past experience. Perceptions of success and failure with earlier government interventions strongly influence the content of new proposals. Policies that enjoy good reputations, such as unemployment insurance, are less vulnerable than unpopular policies when the political and economic environment is transformed. Government strategies that have poor or mixed records, such as public service employment, frequently are abandoned when political and economic change erodes their base of support.

To understand how and why government addresses unemployment, one must examine the public policy process. Fortunately, systematic inquiries about public policies have grown enormously in recent years and have produced many insights. Before scrutinizing the politics of unemployment more closely, it will be helpful to outline a general framework for describing and explaining the formulation and implementation of public policies in the American system.

Notes

1. Stephen K. Bailey, *Congress Makes a Law: The Story Behind the Employment Act of 1946* (New York: Columbia University Press, 1950), 3.
2. *Gallup Poll Report,* September 1982, 6-7. In 1982 the public ranked unemployment as the single most important problem facing the nation for the first time since 1937. Throughout the late 1970s and early 1980s the "high cost of living" or "inflation" was considered most important. Before that, issues of war and peace were mentioned most often by respondents.
3. The data for 1982 are taken from the Labor Department's annual survey on work and joblessness, as reported in *National Journal,* Aug. 20, 1983, 1754.
4. As reported by the Bureau of Labor Statistics, "Employment Situation January 1984," *News U.S.D.L,* 84-44, Feb. 3, 1984, and "State and Metropolitan Employment and Unemployment," *News U.S.D.L.,* 84-121, March 20, 1984.

5. Some economists argue that the official unemployment rate overstates the extent of unemployment by 1 to 1½ percent compared with rates reported during the 1950s and 1960s. Since then welfare registration requirements and other demographic changes may have contributed to this increase. For an excellent discussion of the factors that might inflate unemployment figures and a critique of this viewpoint, see Paul O. Flaim, "The Effect of Demographic Changes on the Nation's Unemployment Rate," *Monthly Labor Review*, March 1979, 13-22.
6. Congressional Budget Office, "Strategies for Assisting the Unemployed" (Congressional Budget Office, Washington, D.C., Dec. 8, 1982, Photocopied).
7. See *Employment and Training Report of the President* (Washington, D.C.: GPO, 1981), 17.
8. Congressional Budget Office, "Strategies," 48.
9. See Robert Beauregard, Carl Van Horn, and David Ford, "Governmental Assistance to Displaced Workers: An Historical Perspective," *Journal of Health and Human Resources Administration* 6 (Fall 1983): 166-184.
10. Congressional Budget Office, "Strategies," 59.
11. Bureau of Labor Statistics, *Employment and Earnings* 30 (December 1983): 42 and 58.
12. Data on expenditures come from the *Employment and Training Report of the President* (initially entitled the *Manpower Report of the President*), issued annually.
13. For historical reviews, see Ewan Clague and Leo Kramer, *Manpower Policies and Programs: A Review, 1935-1975* (Kalamazoo, Mich.: W. E. Upjohn Institute for Employment Research, 1976) and John A. Garraty, *Unemployment in History* (New York: Harper & Row, 1978).
14. For excellent discussions of the Roosevelt programs, see Harold Ickes, *Back to Work* (New York: Macmillan, 1935); Nels Anderson, *The Right to Work* (New York: Modern Age Books, 1938); and Arthur MacMahon et al., *The Administration of Federal Work Relief* (Chicago: Public Administration Service, 1941).
15. For a good overview of the unemployment insurance system, see Saul J. Blaustein, *Jobs and Income Security for Unemployed Workers* (Kalamazoo, Mich.: W. E. Upjohn Institute for Employment Research, 1981).
16. Phil Keisling, "Reform Jobless Benefits," *New York Times,* Jan. 23, 1983, E21.
17. Bailey, *Congress Makes a Law.*
18. For histories of this period in employment and training policy, see Garth Mangum, *MDTA: The Foundation of Federal Manpower Policy* (Baltimore: Johns Hopkins University Press, 1968) and Stanley H. Ruttenberg and Jocelyn Gutchess, *Manpower Challenge of the 1970s* (Baltimore: Johns Hopkins University Press, 1970).
19. There are many good accounts of the politics and policies of the War on Poverty. We suggest James L. Sundquist, *Politics and Policy* (Washington, D.C.: Brookings Institution, 1968); Daniel P. Moynihan, *Maximum Feasible Misunderstanding* (New York: Free Press, 1969); and Robert H.

Haveman, ed., *A Decade of Federal Antipoverty Programs* (New York: Academic Press, 1977).

20. This type of vocational training should not be confused with the vocational education provided by the school system in every state. Although the training itself may be similar, federally funded vocational training programs serve mainly high school dropouts or older adults, while regular vocational education programs serve in-school youth.

21. Sar A. Levitan and Robert Taggart, *The Emergency Employment Act* (Salt Lake City: Olympus, 1974).

22. The best accounts of CETA's legislative history may be found in Roger H. Davidson, *The Politics of Comprehensive Manpower Reform* (Baltimore: Johns Hopkins University Press, 1972) and Sar A. Levitan and Joyce K. Zickler, *The Quest for a Workable Federal Manpower Partnership* (Cambridge: Harvard University Press, 1974). For an excellent account of CETA's implementation, see Grace A. Franklin and Randall B. Ripley, *CETA: Politics and Policy, 1973-1982* (Knoxville: University of Tennessee Press, 1984).

23. The categories of unemployed targeted in the legislation were: Vietnam-era veterans, low-income youth, ex-convicts, public assistance recipients, and those referred to employers by vocational rehabilitation agencies. The tax credit gave employers a 50 percent credit against their federal tax obligations for the first $6,000 of wages paid to target group employees during their first year of employment and a 25 percent credit on the first $6,000 of their second year's wages.

24. Richard M. Nixon, "Manpower Revenue Sharing Message," *Weekly Compilation of Presidential Documents,* March 8, 1971, 419-422.

25. Quoted in Charles Culhane, "Revenue Sharing Shift Set for Worker Training Programs," *National Journal Reports,* Jan. 12, 1974, 52.

26. Quoted in "Major CETA Jobs Program Extended Through Fiscal '82," *Congressional Quarterly Weekly Report,* Nov. 4, 1978, 3185.

27. Ronald Smothers, "CETA Cutbacks Leaving Thousands Unemployed," *New York Times,* April 11, 1981, 1.

28. See, for example, Murray Edelman, *The Symbolic Uses of Politics* (Champaign: University of Illinois Press, 1964).

29. See, for example, Irving H. Siegel, *Fuller Employment with Less Inflation: Essays on Policy and Statistics* (Kalamazoo, Mich.: W. E. Upjohn Institute for Employment Research, 1981).

30. Although a great deal of academic research has been funded by the U.S. Department of Labor, especially since 1964, consensus within the academic community over which strategies are most effective has begun to gel only recently. For a summary, see Robert Taggart, *A Fisherman's Guide: An Assessment of Training and Remediation Strategies* (Kalamazoo, Mich.: W. E. Upjohn Institute for Employment Research, 1982).

31. See, for example, Arnold J. Heidenheimer et al., *Comparative Public Policy* (New York: St. Martin's Press, 1975).

32. Fritz W. Scharpf, *Economic and Institutional Constraints of Full Employment Strategies: Sweden, Austria, and West Germany, 1973-1982,* Interna-

tional Institute of Management, Labor Market Policy Discussion Papers, IIM/LMP 83-20 (Berlin, West Germany); Andrew Zimbalist and Howard Sherman, *Comparing Economic Systems: A Political-Economic Approach* (New York: Academic Press, 1984).

The Policy Process 2

Our overview of unemployment programs stressed that broad political and economic trends and politicians' perceptions, ideologies, and opinions about the efficacy of earlier remedies shape governmental action. This chapter places unemployment policy in a broader context and discusses how public policies are formulated and implemented. By looking generally at the policy process, we hope to distinguish what is unique and what is typical about the politics of unemployment.

The policy process is extremely complex and constantly in flux. Employment and training policy, for example, is made up of dozens of diverse government strategies that disburse billions of dollar annually. A plethora of interest groups, professional staff, and elected officials participates in the formulation and implementation of unemployment programs. Federal, state, and local governments and both profit-making and nonprofit private organizations are involved. Since the War on Poverty era, the number of programs serving the unemployed has exploded and contracted, objectives have multiplied and shifted, and political controversy has been a constant companion.

To make sense of this confusing and shifting terrain we need some general theories about how the policy process works. Fortunately, research and writing undertaken by political scientists yield some general propositions and concepts that help describe and explain the public policy process in the American political system. The central objective of this chapter is to lay out a framework for understanding public policy and to locate unemployment policy and programs within it.

The Policy Cycle

Generally, political scientists regard "public policy" as authoritative government actions that state an intention to do something or to be guided by some principle. The most common public policies are laws adopted by

Congress and signed by the president or decisions promulgated by the Supreme Court. The Clean Air Act and the Supreme Court decision on abortion in *Roe v. Wade* are obvious examples. The first announced guidelines for cleaning up and regulating the air we breathe; the latter affirmed a woman's constitutional right to seek an abortion.

Varied types of governments—federal, state, and local—and many agents within governments—legislatures, executive officials, courts, and bureaucracies—make public policy that affects the distribution of benefits in society and governs our public and private behavior. Public policy encompasses everything from a congressional declaration of war to city zoning ordinances. Public policies that affect unemployment may be found in congressional statutes, such as the Job Training Partnership Act (JTPA), in Federal Reserve Board decisions governing interest rates, and in Labor Department rulings about safety standards in the operation of steel plants.

The critical actions and processes that shape public policy can be grasped better by separating them into several distinct, but related, phases or stages. Political scientists divide up and delineate the "policy cycle" in many ways, but most recognize the critical importance of five stages: issue definition and agenda setting, policy formulation and adoption, policy implementation, evaluation, and termination.[1]

The division of the policy process into stages provides an organizational framework for describing and explaining public policy. It is important to bear in mind, however, that these phases are not predictable and immutable paths through which all policies flow. Some policies are formulated but never adopted by Congress. Others are adopted but not implemented. Many policies are never evaluated or terminated. Nevertheless, the concept of a policy cycle helps us think about how public policies evolve from an idea to legislation to concrete services and perhaps to oblivion. Such an analysis also illuminates how the results of one phase shape future actions and results. The discussion of phases in the policy process is not intended to imply isolated activities, but to highlight actions that influence what takes place later on. Indeed, we are particularly interested in demonstrating the dynamic relationship that exists between policy formulation and policy implementation.

Issue Definition and Agenda Setting

At any given moment American society is literally teeming with conflicts and problems that may have political implications. Yet only a few issues receive governmental attention. There are no given problems.[2] The process by which problems are selected for governmental action is extremely important. In fact, the struggle for establishing the policy agenda may be more important than the policy-making process because fundamental issues and alternatives often are defined at the selection stage. The process by which issues are created, defined, and brought to the attention of authoritative decision makers is commonly referred to as "issue definition and agenda setting."

Political issues arise when conflicts or problems in society are considered seriously by government institutions. Which problems are considered depends in large part on the political and economic conditions present at the time. Take the issue of air and water pollution, for example. Throughout most of the nation's history these problems did not concern government officials. But during the 1960s the consequences of pollution were widely publicized in scientific reports and the media and recognized by elected officials. Large groups mobilized and demanded federal legislation. Some key legislators and the president were drawn into the fray, leading to passage of the Clean Air Act of 1970 and the Clean Water Act of 1972.

Immediate and visible events affect the issue creation process. In the summer of 1983 a bridge on Interstate 95, a highway connecting New York City with New England, collapsed. A portion of the roadway fell into a Connecticut river, killing three motorists and injuring three others. Because this bridge was crossed by 100,000 commuters every day and millions every year, the issues of bridge safety, government inspection, and repair programs instantly became important political problems on the agendas of governors and the Federal Highway Administration.

Other problems may take a long time to gain attention on the government agenda.[3] The question of whether public school teachers should receive extra pay for meritorious service was hotly debated during 1983. This idea had been around for decades, but it worked its way into the national limelight after a highly publicized education commission report, the president, and his political rivals started discussing "merit pay." Thus, depending on the prevailing political and economic conditions and the play of events, policy issues can be born in an instant or take many years to emerge.

Of particular significance in the development of political agendas and policies is the struggle by opposing sides to define issues. Consider the bitter debate over abortion. "Pro-life" groups strongly believe that abortions amount to taking a human life and fervently seek governmental action forbidding medical practitioners from performing them. "Pro-choice" groups believe just as strongly that women should have the right to decide whether to terminate a pregnancy and that government institutions should not interfere with that decision. For the pro-life groups, the issue is defined as a matter of life and death over which the government should exercise control to protect the unborn. For pro-choice groups, the issue is defined as a woman's right to choose how to deal with pregnancy;

government should therefore guarantee freedom of choice.

In most cases a small number of especially interested citizens wage the issue definition battle, attempting to convince elected officials and the public that their view of the problem is more accurate. The side that succeeds in having its definition accepted has a decided advantage in subsequent stages of the policy process. Indeed, the definition of alternatives has been properly called the supreme instrument of political power.[4]

In any policy debate, there is usually disagreement over two fundamental questions. What are the root causes of the problem *and* what aspects of the problem, if any, require governmental action? Contemporary debates over unemployment illustrate the issue definition contest quite well. Many Republican and conservative lawmakers blame high unemployment on overregulation of the private sector, excessive government social welfare spending, and high taxes that inhibit industrial development. Democrats and liberals often explain high unemployment rates by pointing to foreign competition, overseas corporate investments, and the lack of adequate government training and jobs programs. Clearly, quite different conclusions follow from these points of view about the proper role of government in shaping economic growth. Gains made by one side or the other in defining the causes of unemployment have major policy implications. When definitions change, alternatives are redefined by elected officials, and policy remedies may change radically or even disappear.

At any given time, a wide range of issues is on the agendas of the president and Congress. Consider issues before Congress in late 1983. Congress weighed matters such as export subsidies, farm loan repayment deferrals, the defense budget, Social Security reforms, natural gas pricing, heating aid for the poor, the status of the U.S. Commission on Civil Rights, the confirmation of a new secretary of the interior, U.S. military involvement in Lebanon and Central America, and an invasion of the Caribbean island of Grenada. Obviously, some issues, such as the defense budget, receive almost continuous attention; others, such as natural gas pricing or public works proposals, are considered only from time to time. Still others, such as military interventions and confirmation hearings, are one shot affairs.

One of the most striking features of the governmental agenda is the large amount of time that is taken up with recurring problems, such as the budget, and with events over which elected officials have little or no control, such as international crises. This means that many issues are crowded out by other matters that cannot be ignored. Indeed, most of the items on the agendas of policy-making institutions are reconsiderations of policies and programs that have been around for several years. The struggle for the "discretionary" agenda is therefore made more intense.

Routes to the Agenda

Many factors determine which efforts to secure agenda status succeed, including the nature of the issue, the power and prestige of supporting and opposing groups, and the effectiveness with which political symbols and the media are manipulated.[5] People promoting items for agenda consideration can employ public or private strategies. A public strategy involves an effort to define an issue in a way that appeals to the general public, to aggregate interest group support, and to attract positive media attention. The basic idea is to "expand the scope of conflict" by drawing as many groups and individuals as possible into the debate.[6] Politicians find it difficult to ignore issues that arouse the public. The environmental and the nuclear freeze movements are classic examples of a few groups with intense feelings successfully blazing a public path to the agenda.

The private route to the government agenda is favored by politically powerful groups and individuals who take advantage of cooperative relationships with those in government to have their concerns addressed. Not only is it unnecessary for such groups to go public, but also it may be advantageous for them to minimize controversy by avoiding public debate on matters of concern to them. The agendas of Congress, the bureaucracy, and federal regulatory agencies are crammed with special interest issues that are decided with little discussion or debate. Many of these issues have minor significance for the public; others are quite important. Legislation containing favorable tax provisions or awarding lucrative government contracts to one or several private companies or localities are classic examples of items that may attain agenda status without widespread public awareness.

Biases in the Process

While the American political system offers many opportunities for getting matters on the agenda, it also imposes many obstacles or veto points. Governmental institutions and individuals occupying central roles are not neutral; rather they tend to favor certain kinds of issues and groups over others. Therefore, various biases are introduced into the agenda-setting process. Among the more important biases are the traditions and procedures of the policy-making institutions, the preferences of policy makers, and the unequal power of those who participate in the political process and those who don't.

The established practices of Congress, bureaucratic agencies, the courts, and the White House shape the way policy demands are presented and determine how they are received. For example, the Supreme Court does not alter its rulings in response to public demonstrations, but Congress may take up matters in response to widespread public protests. Policy-making institutions develop procedures that other participants must master if they want to receive consideration. It is essential to know the rules of the game and to have experience in playing. The politically organized have an advantage in the agenda-setting process because they understand the rules and have access to decision makers. This allows them to be more successful in defining issues and bringing them to the government's agenda.

Individual policy makers—the president and members of Congress— have a good deal of discretion during agenda setting. They can either promote or discourage policies from getting governmental consideration. In some cases, presidents and legislators select issues that interest them and their supporters and put them on the agenda. The Ford administration's campaign to immunize the population against the possible outbreak of swine flu in 1975 is a memorable example of issue creation and policy action orchestrated by elected officials with little or no public or interest group demand. Moreover, political officials can stall or kill consideration of issues they would rather not address. Powerful committee chairpersons and legislative leaders often are successful in resisting the attempts of others to have issues considered by Congress. For many years, key members of the House and Senate were able to block consideration of civil rights legislation, for example.

The process of narrowing down the immense realm of social interaction and conflict to those few issues that government authorities can deal with seriously is one of the key steps in policy making. Issue definition and agenda setting have enormous influence on the rest of the policy process.

Clearly, the unemployed are disadvantaged at the agenda-setting stage of the policy process. They lack money, organization, leadership, and access to policy makers via private channels. These weaknesses are manifested by the fact that government unemployment programs are frequently attacked and revised by elected officials.

Policy Formulation and Adoption

The real or perceived demands of interest groups and the public and the preferences of elected officials may be translated into authoritative government prescriptions during the policy-making process. Policy making is best thought of as consisting of two stages—*formulation* and *adoption*.[7] Once a problem reaches the institutional agenda, a plan or strategy for resolving the problem is formulated by the governmental and nongovernmental participants. In some cases, an alternative reached by compromise is then adopted by formal vote of Congress or by a decision within an executive branch agency or independent commission. The distinction between formulation and adoption serves to emphasize that many alternatives formulated by interest groups, congressional committees, and government agencies are never adopted as public policies. While the formulation stage often involves a small number of participants and proceeds in relative obscurity, the adoption stage usually encompasses a much larger set of actors and a broader audience.

Characteristics of the Policy-making Process

Perhaps the best way to understand policy making is to identify its underlying characteristics and then consider the implications. Political scientists generally agree on the following characteristics of American public policy:

Policy Making Is Protracted and Complicated. Students of American government quickly learn that a bill must overcome many hurdles on its way to becoming a law. Majority support must be obtained in committees, subcommittees, and on the floors of the House and Senate. Conference committees formed from the two bodies also must agree on each detail of the legislation. Failure to maintain a majority at any stage can derail a bill, as can the inability to override a presidential veto. The number of participants can be quite large and spread across Congress, the executive branch, and a variety of groups representing private and public interests. This creates many opportunities for decisions or "nondecisions."

Policy making involves much more than simply formulating and adopting proposals and then moving on to the next issue. Most government policies also must survive an annual budget process in which a new set of actors and interests shapes policy objectives and allocates resources. Finally, many programs are periodically reformulated through amendments and reauthorizations, thus adding yet another layer of complexity.

Policy Making Is Continuous. Because of the large number of participants and opportunities for redefining policy, the process is ongoing. Statutes, funding levels, and regulations undergo constant modifications. People who lose at one stage of the process appeal to the next stage. For example, interest groups that cannot thwart legislation in the House of Representatives can appeal to senators or to the president. Legislators who fail to win approval for specific language during the bill-drafting stage may have their preferences endorsed by the bureaucracies overseeing the program.

Careful attention to continuous policy making is particularly important because it is unlikely that government will explore many new policy domains in the coming years. With limited money available, government officials and interest groups will be preoccupied with refining, extending, and revamping existing laws. Perhaps more than many other policy areas, employment and training policy has been subjected to a constant barrage of major alterations—changes that profoundly shaped implementation and performance.

Policy Making Is Fragmented.   American public policy is formed by many participants and institutions within and outside government, each with independent interests, responsibilities, and power bases. Several features of the political system's structure and practice contribute to policy fragmentation, including the sharing of power among the executive, legislative, and judicial branches; the division of power among federal, state, and local governments; the overlapping of jurisdictions and responsibilities in congressional committees and executive branch agencies; pervasive interest group participation; weak political parties; and numerous opportunities for policy making in authorizations, appropriations, reauthorizations, and oversight. Overall, these characteristics fragment policy making both across institutions and levels of government and within single institutions like Congress.

A great deal of policy formulation occurs within subdivisions of the political system known as subgovernments.[8] Subgovernments typically include a congressional committee or subcommittee with jurisdiction over a policy domain, an executive bureau charged with administering programs, and interest groups that have a stake in the programs. Found in areas as diverse as agriculture, education, transportation, and employment policy, subgovernment members exchange political support for benefits without encountering much opposition. Interest groups provide financial support and information to members of Congress; they also supply information and political support to the agencies responsible for the programs. Members of Congress provide funds and authority to executive agencies, and the agencies deliver benefits to interest group members.

Subgovernments vary greatly in the control they exercise over the policy process. The proposals of some subgovernments are rarely modified in larger policy-making arenas. Bills formulated by the veterans' subgovernment, for example, are nearly always adopted by Congress with only minor modifications. In other policy areas, subgovernment recommendations are drastically revised as they move through the process, and they often fail to gain adoption. Generally, subgovernments are more effective when their actions are routine, noncontroversial, and politically popular. Highly contentious matters that raise ideological questions are likely to foster widespread debate and undermine subgovernment hegemony.[9]

Government sponsored unemployment programs usually engender controversy, receive widespread public attention, and divide members of Congress and interest groups along partisan and ideological lines. Conflict within the subgovernment is high, and consensus, even when reached, is seldom strong. The employment and training subgovernment (Table 2-1)

Table 2-1 The Changing Employment and Training Subgovernment

1974	1984
Congressional Committees	
House	
Education and Labor Carl E. Perkins, D-Ky., chairman	No change
Subcommittee on Manpower, Compensation, Health, and Safety Dominick Daniels, D-N.J., chairman	Subcommittee on Employment Opportunities Augustus Hawkins, D-Calif., chairman
Senate	
Labor and Public Welfare Harrison Williams, D-N.J., chairman	Labor and Public Welfare Orin Hatch, R-Utah, chairman
Subcommittee on Labor Harrison Williams, chairman	Subcommittee on Employment and Productivity Dan Quayle, R-Ind., chairman
Executive Branch Agencies	
U.S. Department of Labor, Manpower Administration	U.S. Department of Labor, Employment and Training Administration
Principal Interest Groups	
Client	
Jobs for Progress NAACP National Urban League Opportunities Industrialization Center	Same groups, plus National Organization for Women
Labor	
AFL-CIO American Federation of State, County and Municipal Employees	No change
State and Local Government	
National Association of Counties National League of Cities U.S. Conference of Mayors	Same groups, plus National Conference of State Legislators National Governors' Association
Business Groups	
Little or no participation	Business Roundtable Committee for Economic Development Conference Board National Alliance of Business National Association of Manufacturers U.S. Chamber of Commerce

is relatively weak.[10] But this subgovernment has played an important role in determining the size and content of federal programs for the jobless during the 1970s and 1980s.

Policy Making Varies with the Issue.   Every policy-making episode is unique, but it is possible to group public policies together because they share several common features. The most widely used categorization of public policies was developed by Theodore Lowi, who argued that the policy process differs according to whether the policy under consideration is distributive, redistributive, or regulatory.[11]

Distributive policies confer government subsidies on private individuals or groups. Public works projects (dams and bridges), agricultural subsidies, and tax credits for businesses are examples. *Redistributive* policies use public authority to transfer benefits from one group in society to another. The term usually refers to transfers that assist the less well off at the expense of the better off, but transfers can operate in the opposite direction. Federal job training programs are classic redistributive policies because revenues from income and other taxes are used to provide services for the unemployed poor. *Regulatory* policies restrict the activities of private individuals or firms on behalf of the public interest. Occupational health and safety standards, minimum wage laws, and consumer product safety rules are typical examples.

Distributive policies are likely to be formulated within subgovernments and enacted with little opposition because subgovernment constituents benefit without others in society realizing immediate or obvious disadvantages. In contrast, trade-offs between winners and losers are clear in redistributive policies. Hence, controversy is widespread, and subgovernment control over formulation and adoption is greatly restricted. Regulatory policies are also controversial because it is usually clear that certain groups stand to gain or lose from their adoption. Naturally there is an incentive for politicians and interest groups to try to make policies appear distributive to avoid conflict and to gather support more easily at each stage of the policy process.

Implications for Public Policy

These broad characteristics of the policy-making process have implications for the nature of public policies. The process just described leads to three important observations about public policies.

Public Policies Change Gradually.   The protracted and continuous process of policy making and the fragmentation of decision making in Congress and the executive branch mean that most policies address problems in small manageable steps. The style and substance of public policy is incremental.[12] Change occurs gradually in a political system that fragments power and offers participants many opportunities to veto or water down policy proposals. Policy issues are rarely considered comprehensively, nor is change likely to be radical.

Under these circumstances, future policy directions often are governed by past decisions. Participants find that the compromises reached by their predecessors serve as useful guides. Because policy makers want to avoid controversy and conflict during a drawn-out process, the most prudent and politically feasible strategy is to seek modest changes in current policy rather than risk rejection of a new approach. Opposition from others is less likely when changes from the status quo are minor and therefore do not threaten other vested interests.

As with any general pattern, there are exceptions. Occasionally public policy departs radically from past practice either by involving the government in matters heretofore left to the private sector or by substantially increasing or reducing the resources devoted to a particular problem. Landmark legislation, such as the Social Security Act, which guaranteed government support for retirees, or the Civil Rights Act of 1964, which forbade discrimination against minorities and other groups, represented major change, as did the vast increase in temporary jobs programs during the 1970s. According to Charles Jones, these unusual, but significant policy changes typically occur when a well-organized and vocal public unites and demands government action and/or when policy makers achieve a temporary consensus around unprecedented proposals.[13] When this happens, incremental decision making is cast aside and policy makers engage in what Jones labels, "speculative augmentation." They pursue major changes and speculate that the bureaucracy will be capable of handling the increased responsibilities or resources effectively. Not surprisingly, such policies are difficult to implement.

Public Policies Are Often Vague.   Many public laws contain ambiguous statements of broad objectives. Statutes may contain no more than general aspirations that a majority of Congress and the president can endorse. The task of translating aspirations into practice is delegated to government administrators, state and local elected officials, and private organizations. The more controversial and visible the policy domain, the more likely that legislative language will be fuzzy.

The propensity of Congress to enact vague and sometimes internally contradictory legislation is understandable when one reflects on the characteristics of the American political process. The policy-making process is characterized by attempts to reconcile competing claims of interest groups and policy remedies as well as the divergent preferences of policy makers. The resulting compromises produce policy statements that majority coalitions can support. At each stage of the process, the number of people who must agree to legislative language gets larger and the demand for broad, general statements increases. The broader the language—and the less redistributive its intent—the larger the group that can reach consensus.

Ambiguous laws also serve the interests of members of Congress and the president. By avoiding explicit policy objectives and delegating hard choices to federal administrators, politicians not only gather broader support for legislation but also give themselves leeway to blame federal agencies for failures in carrying out legislative intent and to take credit for correcting faults through constituent case work.[14] The preference for policy ambiguity is reinforced strongly by elected officials' goals. Although they have many personal, policy, and institutional goals, most constantly seek positions that will enhance their prospects for reelection.[15] Legislation that appeals to broad political constituencies is preferred.

The interests of other participants in the political process also may be advanced by vague laws. Despite the problems these laws cause, executive branch agencies often prefer ambiguous policy statements because such statements enhance the agencies' power to define the real meaning of policy. State and local officials and interest groups also support open-ended policy statements because they gain discretion over program administration.

Once again, an important caveat must be noted here. Policies are not always ambiguous, and even muddled policies do not remain that way forever. In fact, successive reconsiderations of public laws often yield very specific policies as legislators, interest groups, and the bureaucracy reach agreement both on what they want to achieve and how to go about accomplishing it.

Public Policies Are Often Poorly Designed.   Many public laws are endorsed without Congress and the president ever carefully defining or understanding the problems the laws are supposed to address.[16] Consequently, many public laws are poorly fashioned to achieve their objectives. An underlying reason for this troublesome condition is that the demands and characteristics of the political process are frequently at odds with methods that might yield more effective public laws.

The interest groups, government administrators, and members of Congress who initiate policy making may desire sound and effective public laws, but several obstacles stand in their way. For instance, they must achieve majority support at successive stages of the legislative process. The interests of legislators, who may not share the initiators' desire for sound policy or their perspectives on the problem, must be accommodated. Moreover, the interest groups or legislators who perceive a need for government intervention may not be sure how to translate their aspirations into concrete, workable policy. They may not know how to solve problems like deficient reading ability among poor youngsters or chronic unemployment. Those crafting policy remedies may have little or no understanding of the issue or contact with the people they are trying to help. Finally, policy makers may make false assumptions either about the problem itself or the capacity of federal, state, and local bureaucracies to treat it effectively.

Several scholars take this line of reasoning one step further. David Mayhew argues, for example, that many poor public laws are created because members of Congress and the president are more interested in taking positions and claiming credit for helping those who demand government action than they are in the effects that public laws generate in society.[17] Congressional votes are monitored carefully by interested segments of the public; organizations calculate member ratings from a handful of key votes. Members of Congress are thus rewarded or punished for their issue *positions,* not according to whether the laws they adopt solve or ameliorate public problems. If laws are subsequently judged ineffective, then Congress can easily blame the bureaucracy and obtain additional rewards from those seeking corrective action.[18] In short, members of Congress may ignore important policy design issues, not because they don't know better, but because it is in their interests to do so.

All this is not to say that policy formulation and adoption are unimportant. Rather it suggests that policy makers, in an attempt to satisfy demands and take credit, often enact policies that are long on goals, but short on the means for carrying them out. According to Murray Edelman, a great deal of policy making is designed to quell politically aroused groups by passing symbolically reassuring legislation that may not confer many tangible benefits.[19] It also implies that poorly organized groups, such as the unemployed, are less likely to hold elected officials accountable for the effects of public laws and are therefore more likely to obtain poorly designed and symbolic policy from Congress. Conversely, well-organized groups that monitor the impacts of public laws are likely to be more successful in obtaining policies that confer tangible benefits.

Policy Implementation

The fact that Congress often adopts poorly designed public policy as it gropes toward politically acceptable remedies has obvious and immediate consequences for administrators who carry out legislative intent. Laws are based on assumptions about the delivery of public services or the regulation of individuals, and these assumptions are tested when federal, state, and local administrators attempt to put the law's provisions into practice. The process of moving from policy statement to concrete programs is referred to as policy implementation, which is defined by Donald Van Meter and Carl Van Horn as "those actions by public and private individuals (or groups) that are directed at the achievement of objectives set forth in prior policy decisions." [20]

Observers of the implementation process invariably report that there is a gap between the assumptions and expectations written into public laws and how federal, state, and local implementers actually perform. The step from policy goal to public service is problematic. The gap between policies and the delivery of services, between assumptions and reality, appears in two forms, according to Paul Berman.[21] The first of these is called the "macro-implementation" problem—the translation of national policy objectives into local programs. The central question is how successful federal agencies and Congress are in convincing local administrators to follow national objectives when implementing a program. The second gap between policy and results is labeled the "micro-implementation" problem—the relationship between objectives and results at the delivery level. Here the problem shifts from one of the federal government trying to mold local attitudes and behavior (the macro-implementation problem) to one of organizational capacity at the delivery level. Can local administrators and service providers carry out their responsibilities effectively and efficiently? Implementation failures of both types are common occurrences on the public policy scene.[22]

Consider the implementation problems associated with enrolling people in federal employment and training programs, for example. Federal statutes set forth guidelines about the characteristics of people who should be allowed to participate in federal jobs programs, but these statements are not self-enforcing. First, the federal government must ensure that the law's basic standards are followed by the several hundred state and local governments that carry them out—a macro-implementation problem. Then, state and local program managers must ensure that their staffs and subcontractors conform to the law's intent when deciding who gets into programs—a micro-implementation problem. The potential for deviation from the original legislative objectives, for the appearance of a gap between intentions and what actually happens, can easily appear at any link along the chain of decisions that eventually result in a person entering a program or receiving a temporary job.

Fifty years ago, students of American politics drew sharp distinctions between politics and administration. The two were characterized as separate activities conducted by people with different motivations and training. Politics was a world of give and take, of conflict and compromise. Administration was a world of neutral competence where management science and planning would ensure the rational delivery of public services; programs would be free from the influence of tawdry political considerations. Although this concept of a division between politics and adminstration still holds normative appeal for some, it was abandoned long ago by scholars of politics because it did not realistically portray the behavior they observed.[23]

In fact, policy implementation is first and foremost a political process. During implementation, competing interests continue the struggle over the allocation of resources and benefits. Like other political phenomena, the results are influenced by broad political and economic trends and the power and skills of the participants. Given the characteristics and the end products of the policy-making process—continuous interaction among interest groups, the bureaucracy, and elected officials and vague and poorly designed statutes—it is understandable that policy implementation would be both difficult and politically charged. Many laws are enacted to appease disparate groups seeking benefits from government. But legislative compromises containing ambiguous policy prescriptions place enormous burdens on implementers because their actions confer or withhold tangible benefits.

Mapping Policy Implementation

Unlike the policy formulation and adoption stage, where action is concentrated in a few prominent political institutions, the implementation stage takes place in thousands of organizations and state and local governments spread across the country. Decisions and events that shape policy implementation are not neatly recorded. What is needed, therefore, is a general guide to the landscape so that one can follow the broad patterns.

Although it is impossible to capture the complexity of policy implementation in simple diagrams, Figure 2-1 depicts the key relationships and conditions that influence the process. The model highlights the conditions, institutions, events, attitudes, and relationships that shape program implementation. Generally, the delivery of public services is a product of the interaction among *policy standards and resources,* the *national policy environment,* and the *local policy environment.* Taken together these factors help us understand the political relationships, the program expenditures, and the distribution of benefits that constitute *program performance.*

Policy Standards and Resources. Previously we emphasized that a gap exists between the law and the performance of program administrators. Although some deviation from legislative intent is predictable, the guidelines and the amount of money appropriated strongly shape the implementation process. The statute and regulations governing the program influence federal, state, and local officials, provide a focal point for program decisions, and establish criteria by which the political community judges progress. The objectives and procedures contained in the law and its regulations help explain the delivery of public services.

Two dimensions of policy standards deserve special attention. First, it is important to examine how clearly legislative goals are stated, whether they contradict one another, and how precisely they guide administrators. Implementers examine laws for direction and intent, but if they find none or if they are confused by competing objectives, then consistent public service delivery is unlikely to occur.

Second, public laws legitimate numerous goals, but many of these goals are destined to receive little or no attention during implementation. Some will be important at one time and unimportant at another, while others remain central throughout the law's history. Therefore, it is essential to determine a law's leading objectives and trace how these change over time because the priorities and actions of implementers are directly affected by the prevailing policy goals. Our review of unemployment programs demonstrates that policy objectives shift frequently as changing political and economic conditions encourage policy makers to reconsider problems and remedies.

Money and the manner in which it is distributed also shape policy implementation. Budget decisions translate legislative aspirations into concrete terms. Many public laws announce ambitious goals but provide paltry sums for their realization. The federal budget process is also unpredictable. Administrators often must plan next year's programs without knowing when they will receive funds or how much they will have to spend. Moreover, financial resources expand and contract as policy makers articulate new goals and as broader government fiscal conditions dictate.

The National Policy Environment.   While the law provides a foundation for implementation, the national policy environment determines which aspects of the law receive principal attention, the degree to which priorities change over time, and the messages that "street-level bureaucrats" receive from Washington.[24] Many of the key participants in the national policy environment are the same people who dominate policy formulation and adoption. These may include administrators from the federal agency responsible for overseeing the policy; congressional committees, subcommittees, and, occasionally, individual members or the entire Congress; the White House staff, the Office of Management and Budget, and (very rarely) the president; and the national interest groups concerned most directly with the policy area. These actors affect the process by commenting upon and drafting regulations, by pressuring federal agencies to administer the law in accord with their preferences, and by intervening on behalf of favored constituents.

Two activities of national-level actors are particularly significant— the communication of policy and its enforcement. Because public policies are subject to varying interpretations, communication between participants in the implementation process is complex and difficult. Federal administrators may distort legislative intent either intentionally or unin-

Figure 2-1 A Model of Policy Implementation

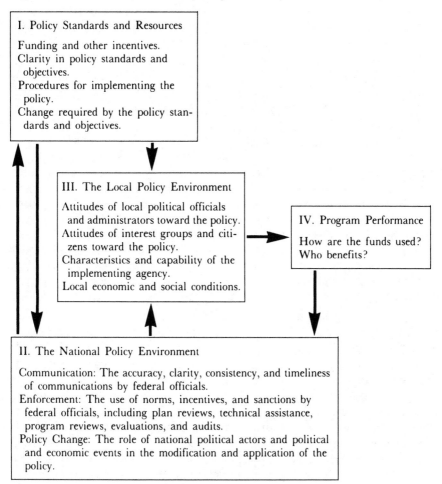

I. Policy Standards and Resources

Funding and other incentives.
Clarity in policy standards and
  objectives.
Procedures for implementing the
  policy.
Change required by the policy standards and objectives.

III. The Local Policy Environment

Attitudes of local political officials
  and administrators toward the policy.
Attitudes of interest groups and citizens toward the policy.
Characteristics and capability of the
  implementing agency.
Local economic and social conditions.

IV. Program Performance

How are the funds used?
Who benefits?

II. The National Policy Environment

Communication: The accuracy, clarity, consistency, and timeliness
  of communications by federal officials.
Enforcement: The use of norms, incentives, and sanctions by
  federal officials, including plan reviews, technical assistance,
  program reviews, evaluations, and audits.
Policy Change: The role of national political actors and political
  and economic events in the modification and application of the
  policy.

tentionally or render contradictory interpretations of the statute at
different times. Conflicting messages also may flow from diverse sources
within the federal establishment or from Congress and the White House.
A good deal of what goes on during policy implementation depends on the
accuracy, clarity, consistency, and timeliness with which policy objectives
and directives are communicated to implementers. If messages are fuzzy or
contradictory, administrators are sure to follow diverse procedures and
concentrate on different priorities as they deliver public services.

The implementation of federal programs typically requires joint
efforts by public and private agencies at the national, state, and local

levels. Federal agencies rarely deliver services directly. Instead they rely on state and local governments to carry the administrative burden. Federal agencies are responsible for enforcing the law, but there is no clear hierarchy in the system that allows these officials to command compliance from state and local officials. There is, furthermore, a natural tension between national goals and state and local preferences. The federal government presses for the attainment of objectives embodied in federal statutes, but state and local implementers may resist to protect local interest and prerogatives.

Lacking direct power over the stewards of federal objectives, national-level officials must employ other means to exert influence over implementers' behavior. Federal overseers often appeal to local officials' sense of appropriate professional norms; provide technical assistance and political support; require elaborate prior assurances from grant recipients; conduct on-site audits, program reviews, and evaluations; and threaten to withhold or actually withhold funds from offending agencies and jurisdictions. How well federal administrators play the enforcement game, and toward what end, are important determinants of program performance.

Political conditions affect the administration of public policy. Major political upheavals, such as the election of a president, turnover in the control of Congress, or changes in its composition, affect not only who makes policy but also the priorities that implementers are asked to pursue. Ronald Reagan's election in 1980, for example, ushered in a substantially less aggressive federal role in the regulation of various forms of environmental pollution.

Economic trends and how they are perceived and interpreted by the public and elected officials also influence implementation. For example, high unemployment rates during 1977 led Carter administration officials to press local implementers to hire people rapidly under CETA-funded public service employment programs. More generally, shifts in economic indicators, such as unemployment, inflation, the gross national product, and the federal budget deficit, affect national priorities and the path of implementation in many areas of policy.

The Local Policy Environment.   Public policy objectives finally get translated into concrete services in the local policy environment. The attitudes, actions, and capabilities of local implementers, along with the political and economic environment, ultimately determine whether policies succeed or fail.

Consider the typical intergovernmental program structure. A law dealing with community development, for example, is enacted by Congress and assigned to the Department of Housing and Urban Development (HUD). HUD issues regulations governing the expenditure of program funds, intended beneficiaries, and reporting requirements. Funds are distributed by formula to hundreds of cities and counties throughout the country. Administrators in these jurisdictions make the major program decisions—what kinds of community development programs they would like to have, where within the community the projects should be undertaken, what organizations and agencies should receive contracts to render services, and what kinds of people should benefit. Although the degree of local discretion varies considerably from one law to the next, local program administrators almost always make important choices.

The local political environment is a microcosm of the national policy environment. Within any city, county, or state, there are many organizations and individuals with a stake in programs, each holding different expectations, goals, demands, and power. Employment and training program administration, for example, involves the following: governors, mayors, county officials, and private sector advisory groups who establish local policy; an administrative staff to carry out policies; contractors, such as vocational schools and community organizations, to provide services; program enrollees and their advocates; and other interested observers, such as the local media. Accommodating all the different view points of this menagerie and balancing their concerns and demands is extremely challenging.

The attitudes of elected officials, professional staffs, citizens, and interest groups about the objectives contained in the national statute play a central role in explaining the course of local implementation. Responses to national objectives vary across states and communities and within communities. Take civil rights policies, for example. During the 1960s many southern governors and other elected officials opposed the objectives embodied in federal laws that sought to guarantee the rights of minorities. Many southern communities resorted to a variety of legal and illegal tactics to avoid carrying out these laws. Less dramatic examples occur on a day-to-day basis, but local officials who *disagree* with national policy objectives and procedures or who prefer alternative strategies strongly shape public policy.

The success of national policies also depends on the capability of state and local governments. State governments may be willing to carry out national objectives but incapable of doing so either because professional staffs are poorly trained or because financial resources are insufficient. Not to be overlooked is the fact that federal statutes may require administrators to accomplish tasks that are unrealistic for the amount of time and money allotted.

Economic, political, and social conditions are other important aspects of the local policy environment. Perceptions of need for the services offered by the program are particularly important. Communities experiencing high unemployment are likely to be more vigorous than relatively affluent ones in undertaking government sponsored jobs programs. A community that has suffered environmental hazards in the past is more likely to take environmental regulations seriously. States, cities, and counties under severe fiscal pressure will gobble up federal funds and dispense them more quickly than financially healthy jursdictions.

Program Performance.   The interaction of laws, the national policy environment, and the local policy environment determine "program performance." Public policies have both proximate and ultimate effects. The distribution of program services and the extent to which programs serve intended beneficiaries are typical examples of proximate effects or program performance. The ultimate effects of public policies, often termed "program impacts," measure whether long-term changes in behavior or conditions result from effective policy implementation.

An example from education policy helps illustrate this distinction. Remedial education programs for low-income youngsters have proximate and ultimate objectives. The product of policy implementation is the delivery of reading programs to educationally disadvantaged children—the proximate objective. Giving children better reading programs may or may not have salutory effects on their reading ability, the ultimate objective. In other words, perfectly implemented programs can meet their proximate objectives, but fail to accomplish their ultimate objectives. In the case of reading programs, it may be that improved reading classes and materials are simply insufficient to improve a child's cognitive reading skills. Policy evaluations can focus on proximate effects, ultimate effects, or both.

Evaluation

Evaluations are judgments, both formal and informal, about the success or failure of public policies. Policy makers assess existing policies to consider changes in their scope, objectives, and funding levels and to contemplate new policy initiatives. Administrators and political officials base their evaluations of public policy on newspaper articles, constituent letters, personal experiences, staff papers, audits and investigations, and research reports. Evaluative information runs along a continuum from the systematic and objective to the nonsystematic and impressionistic. Presidents, members of Congress, and senior political officials use both types of information, but the nonsystematic variety tends to be more influential.

Systematic evaluations are conducted by professional cadres of evaluators located in federal agencies, universities, or private research organizations. Within the federal establishment, the Office of Management and Budget in the executive branch, the Congressional Budget Office and the General Accounting Office in the legislative branch, and other organizations produce reams of carefully researched studies about public policies and their consequences. Though the approaches differ, the more systematic inquiries follow research practices developed by social scientists. The central purposes of systematic studies are to make the most objective, reliable, and valid observations possible about public policies.

Nonsystematic information is introduced into the policy process through newspaper and magazine articles, television programs, testimony at congressional hearings, letters from angry or grateful constituents, public meetings, and private conversations. As examples, a constituent has trouble obtaining a Social Security check and reports his or her frustration to a member of Congress; or CBS's *60 Minutes* airs an exposé on fraud in a government health care program; or the *Washington Post* reports delays on sewer construction projects. Although the evidence may be inconclusive and unrepresentative, nonsystematic inquiries affect policy makers' judgments about government programs.

The rigor of systematic evaluations is appealing, but complicated problems often undercut their utility.[25] It is difficult to measure program performance and impact. Suppose you wanted to discover whether food stamps improve nutrition within the eligible population. You would have to monitor the eating habits of people before and after they received food stamps, track a similar group of people who did not receive them, and compare the outcomes. Not surprisingly, many systematic studies do not yield unequivocal answers about whether public policies work.

The fact that policy makers pay less attention to systematic studies of programs than to other information also is explained by the demands of the policy process. Fundamental decisions about the nature and scope of government policies are shaped by political and economic events. After a bill is enacted, legislators, administrators, and interest groups focus on the efficiency, fairness, and timeliness of administrative actions. They are primarily concerned with the short-term rather than long-term results. After all, ultimate effects are difficult to gauge, and policy makers may not be around long enough for these effects to materialize.

The policy makers' objectives are to refine policy and deliver services that produce more political benefits than costs. Consequently, they rely on "implementation images" when assessing statutes. These images are formed in a variety of ways—complaints; the media; earnest, but perhaps unrepresentative, testimony on Capitol Hill; and evaluation reports.[26]

Systematic evaluations can be important. They influence the policy debate, especially when a series of respected studies supports or undermines a public policy. Political officials are wary of making assertions that are squarely at odds with research findings. Systematic research does not eliminate political judgment and bias from the process, but it can be a potent weapon during battles over the content of public laws.

Termination

If policy cycles worked perfectly, we would observe the regular demise of public policies when the problems they were created to address were resolved. Indeed, policies occasionally disappear: New Deal public works programs were terminated during World War II, and the price controls on crude oil, developed after the 1973 Arab oil embargo, were eliminated in 1981. A much rarer occurrence is the disappearance of a bureaucratic agency that has delivered services over a period of time. Still the Community Services Administration was abolished when the Reagan administration and Congress decided it no longer had a viable mission.

There are many reasons why policies live through cycles of issue creation, policy making, implementation, and evaluation. First, programs usually are more successful in treating the symptoms of problems than they are at curing them. The provision of adequate health care, the reduction of poverty and hunger, the maintenance of roads and bridges are not problems that can be overcome or resolved.

Second, public policies designed to ameliorate one problem often generate new problems or the original problem changes in unforeseen ways. Efforts to eradicate poverty during the 1960s started simply, but, as policy makers "discovered" new causes of poverty, programs multiplied. As policy implementation proceeds, new problems are dealt with in subsequent rounds of policy making, reauthorization, and appropriations.

Third, the political strength of policy formulators and program beneficiaries helps public policies endure. Policies sustain and reinforce relationships among bureaucratic agencies, interest groups, and legislators that are based on mutual self-interest. Each participant acquires skills both in serving *and* using the other partners to gain benefits. Programs may continue, regardless of whether they effectively treat the problems, because support from powerful groups assures their survival.

A classic example of political survival is the so-called "impact aid" education program. Originally enacted during World War II, the program provided supplemental federal assistance to school districts affected by heavy concentrations of the military. The rationale was that local taxpayers should not be burdened with the costs of federal policy decisions. Gradually, the number of school districts receiving "impact aid" grew to the point where practically every community got some assistance. Despite attempts by presidents from Harry Truman to Jimmy Carter to eliminate it, the program continued, securely supported by a strong coalition of local school administrators and members of Congress.

Occasionally, a new policy is created to govern an established policy domain by terminating an existing law and replacing it with a new one. In the employment and training field, for example, the Manpower Development and Training Act of 1962 and portions of the Economic Opportunity Act were replaced by the Comprehensive Employment and Training Act of 1973 that was in turn supplanted by the Job Training Partnership Act of 1982. Both of these new authorizations contained significant changes for the policy area while leaving other aspects virtually unaffected. The termination of a specific law does not necessarily mean that the political interests and policy concerns served by the policy will be dismantled.

A Dynamic Process

At this juncture, it seems useful to stress a point we made at the beginning of this chapter. The division of the policy process into five stages—issue definition and agenda setting, formulation and adoption, implementation, evaluation, and termination—highlights the activities within each phase and demonstrates that public policies follow common paths. It provides an analytical framework for understanding the complexities of the policy process.

Each stage of the process is related to the others. Choices made at the agenda-setting stage influence policy formulation. The policies adopted by lawmakers shape policy implementation. Experiences during implementation affect evaluations, which in turn may lead to program termination or, more likely, to new rounds of formulation and implementation. The policy process is both dynamic and circular.

Unfortunately, policy making and policy implementation are often treated as isolated, sequential events.[27] The process is presented in snapshots. Congress makes a law, then the bureaucracy carries it out. But policy making is continuous and evolves while a law is being implemented. The formulation of policy is not a story once told and then forgotten. Moreover, people who set agendas and make policy—members of Congress, presidents, interest groups, and agency administrators—also are intimately involved in policy implementation and evaluation.

Looking at the employment and training policy domain is an excellent way to examine the policy cycle. Although federal programs for the jobless are more ambitious and controversial than most public policies, they nonetheless illustrate many facets of the policy process that appear with striking frequency in American politics. To highlight these facets, the last decade of employment and training programs will be divided into four "seasons." During each season, a changing political and economic climate yields new policy agendas, objectives, and implementation experiences. The chapters that follow examine how the ebbs and flows of national politics shape unemployment programs and how implementation problems encountered during one season influence policy evaluations and subsequent policy formulation.

Notes

1. The notion of stages of the policy process has been used by many students of public policy. See Charles O. Jones, *An Introduction to the Study of Public Policy*, 3d ed. (Monterey, Calif.: Brooks/Cole Publishing Co., 1984) and James E. Anderson, *Public Policy-Making*, 2d ed. (New York: Holt, Rinehart & Winston, 1979). The term policy cycle also has been used before. See Judith V. May and Aaron B. Wildavsky, eds., *The Policy Cycle* (Beverly Hills, Calif.: Sage Publications, 1978).
2. See Jones, *An Introduction*, Chap. 1.
3. Roger W. Cobb and Charles D. Elder, *Participation in American Politics* (Baltimore: Johns Hopkins University Press, 1972), 84-85.
4. See E. E. Schattschneider, *The Semi-Sovereign People* (Hinsdale, Ill.: Dryden Press, 1975), Chaps. 1 and 2.
5. Cobb and Elder, *Participation in American Politics,* 82-170.
6. Schattschneider, *The Semi-Sovereign People,* Chap. 1.
7. This distinction and similar terms appear in Jones, *An Introduction,* and Anderson, *Public Policy-Making.*
8. For a full discussion of the subgovernment concept, see Randall B. Ripley and Grace A. Franklin, *Congress, the Bureaucracy, and Public Policy,* rev. ed. (Homewood, Ill.: Dorsey Press, 1980).
9. Ibid., 1-28.
10. Lance deHaven-Smith and Carl E. Van Horn, "Subgovernment Conflict in Public Policy," *Policy Studies Journal* 12 (June 1984).
11. Theodore Lowi, "American Business, Public Policy, Case Studies, and Political Theory," *World Politics* (July 1964): 677-715.
12. The seminal discussion of incrementalism may be found in Charles E. Lindblom, "The Science of Muddling Through," *Public Administration Review* (Spring 1959): 79-88. See also Aaron B. Wildavsky, *The Politics of the Budgetary Process* (Boston: Little, Brown & Co., 1964).
13. See Charles O. Jones, *Clean Air* (Pittsburgh, Pa.: University of Pittsburgh Press, 1975), Chap. 7.
14. Morris P. Fiorina, *Congress: Keystone of the Washington Establishment* (New Haven: Yale University Press, 1977).
15. David R. Mayhew, *Congress: The Electoral Connection* (New Haven: Yale University Press, 1974).
16. See Jones, *An Introduction,* Chap. 1.
17. Mayhew, *Congress: The Electoral Connection,* 52-61.
18. Fiorina, *Congress: Keystone of the Washington Establishment.*
19. Murray Edelman, *The Symbolic Uses of Politics* (Champaign: University of Illinois Press, 1964).
20. Donald S. Van Meter and Carl E. Van Horn, "The Policy Implementation Process: A Conceptual Framework," *Administration and Society* (February 1975): 447.
21. Paul Berman, "The Study of Macro- and Micro-Implementation," *Public Policy* (Spring 1978): 157-184.

22. By now the list of implementation studies is overwhelming. Of the major studies, we offer the following selective list: Eugene Bardach, *The Implementation Game: What Happens After a Bill Becomes Law?* (Cambridge: MIT Press, 1977); Jones, *Clean Air;* Jerome T. Murphy, *State Education Agencies and Discretionary Funds* (Lexington, Mass.: D. C. Heath & Co., 1974); Randall B. Ripley and Grace A. Franklin, *Bureaucracy and Policy Implementation* (Homewood, Ill.: Dorsey Press, 1982); Daniel A. Mazmanian and Paul A. Sabatier, *Public Policy and Implementation* (Glenview, Ill.: Scott, Foresman & Co., 1982); and Carl E. Van Horn, *Policy Implementation in the Federal System* (Lexington: D. C. Heath & Co., 1979).

23. See Norton E. Long, "Power and Administration," *Public Administration Review* (Autumn 1949): 257-264; and Herbert Kaufman, "Emerging Conflicts in the Doctrines of Public Administration," *The American Political Science Review* (December 1956): 1057.

24. The term "street-level bureaucrats" was introduced by Richard Weatherley and Michael Lipsky, "Street-Level Bureaucrats and Institutional Innovation: Implementing Special Education Reform," *Harvard Education Review* 47 (May 1977): 196.

25. There is an extensive literature on the utilization of evaluation research by policy makers. See Carol H. Weiss and Michael J. Bucuvalas, *Social Science Research and Decision-Making* (New York: Columbia University Press, 1980).

26. See, for example, Randall B. Ripley, *Congress: Process and Policy* (New York: W. W. Norton & Co., 1978) or Roger H. Davidson and Walter J. Oleszek, *Congress and Its Members* (Washington, D.C.: CQ Press, 1981).

27. For studies that incorporate the longitudinal approach, see Jones, *Clean Air;* Michael Kirst and Richard Jung, "The Utility of a Longitudinal Approach in Assessing Implementation: A Thirteen-Year View of Title I, ESEA," in *Studying Implementation,* Walter Williams, ed., (Chatham, N.J.: Chatham House Publishers, 1982); and Grace A. Franklin and Randall B. Ripley, *CETA: Politics and Policy, 1973-1982* (Knoxville: University of Tennessee Press, 1984).

The Ambiguity of Reform 3

The Comprehensive Employment and Training Act (CETA) of 1973 was carefully crafted to garner political support from Congress, the president, local government officials, and community groups that operated training programs. Because all their different views had to be accommodated, the law was necessarily ambiguous. Dozens of controversial policy issues were either left fuzzy or ignored. Participants in the process knew that total victory in the legislative arena was not only impossible but also unnecessary. During implementation there would be ample opportunity to pursue causes lost in Congress and to clarify issues left vague by the statute. Embedded in the political disagreements and compromises that produced CETA were the seeds of an implementation struggle that grew quickly following its passage.

Compromise and Ambiguity

Considerable consensus existed about some matters during the debate that preceded CETA's enactment. Congressional hearings and presidential statements reveal substantial agreement over the need for and purpose of federal employment and training programs. Since the early 1960s, Democrats and Republicans had supported federally funded training for low-income, unemployed people, thus affording a "second chance" to people who were unsuccessful in mainstream educational institutions. Consensus also had developed around the need to overhaul existing employment and training measures. The existing administrative structure, often characterized as a "mess" or an "administrative nightmare," was not producing effective and efficient services for the unemployed. Policy makers agreed that programmatic reorganization and regrouping was in order.

Despite areas of consensus, important political differences remained. Interest groups, members of Congress, and the Nixon administration desired reform, but they disagreed over what to do. Democrats and Republicans also were sharply divided over the value of federally subsidized job creation programs. The policy disputes were resolved temporarily in the statute—employment and training programs were consolidated and public service employment (PSE) measures were funded—but underlying differences survived and caused problems after enactment. The legislative compromise sent conflicting signals to implementers, and competing viewpoints were pursued during implementation by Congress, the Labor Department, and state and local government administrators.

The different political ideologies, interests, and constituencies of the Democratic and Republican parties were reflected throughout the debate over CETA, which dragged on between 1969 and 1973. Democrats doubted the Nixon administration's commitment to aiding low-income, unemployed Americans. Some even suspected that the administration really wanted to dismantle the fledgling network of programs. After all, they reasoned, the Economic Opportunity Act and other employment and training programs had emerged during the heyday of Lyndon Johnson's War on Poverty. With large majorities in the House and Senate, Democrats were willing and able to block proposals that did not preserve the essence of Johnson's programs.

Republicans, led by Nixon, sensed that the War on Poverty programs were vulnerable because of widespread perceptions that they were ill-managed and unsuccessful. The Democratic majority might not allow programs to be terminated, but a major overhaul was possible. The White House proposed legislation to revamp existing programs, expand the number of people eligible for service, and shift administrative responsibility away from the federal government.

The administration's original proposal was part of an ambitious strategy designed to devolve power and responsibility from the federal level to state and local levels—a long-cherished Republican ideal. Under the president's New Federalism initiative, as it was known, several "special revenue sharing" programs would consolidate and decentralize grant-in-aid programs in manpower, education, transportation, and other policy domains. Existing job training programs would be folded into an omnibus block grant earmarked for use by state and local officials. The president and his supporters argued that their approach would encourage innovative programs and coordinated service delivery. They maintained that state and local decision makers were better suited to design and oversee strategies for helping their jobless residents. Reducing the federal presence and increasing local control would bring about better management and results.

Congressional Democrats were willing to accept some degree of decentralization and some program consolidation, but they wanted to ensure that public service employment programs enacted in 1971 continued under the new legislation. The battle lines between Democrats and the Republicans were drawn. Program strategies and partisan politics were inextricably linked.

Decentralization

The administration's proposed decentralization of employment and training programs struck at the heart of congressionally centered subgovernments. Giving more responsibility to state and local elected officials would inevitably reduce the power of members of Congress. Cherished relationships with the bureaucracy that help members win reelection might be upset; potential rivals in congressional districts—mayors and county officials—would be handing out more jobs and contracts and, therefore, commanding more political clout. The decentralizing thrust of Nixon's New Federalism made some members nervous and wary.

As passed in 1973, CETA enhanced the power of state and local elected officials by making more than 450 state and local units of government responsible for the design and implementation of employment and training programs. In this sense, the Nixon administration and the Republicans succeeded. But congressional Democrats succeeded in vesting primary authority in local, rather than state, governments, and they thwarted the "no strings" approach favored by the administration through the imposition of several restrictions. Not only were state and local governments required to submit elaborate plans to regional Department of Labor officers, but also federal agencies were responsible for monitoring the progress of the programs. Each jurisdiction administering a CETA program also was required to establish a citizen advisory council composed of representatives from a variety of organizations, including many that had received direct federal funding in previous years. Elected officials had final authority, but they might face entrenched interests on their advisory councils. The law established competitive relationships between federal and local officials and among local actors.

Program Consolidation

The debate over how to consolidate or "decategorize" job training programs again illustrates how politics influenced program design. Republicans wanted to wipe the slate clean of federally mandated narrow gauge programs, a move that would enhance local flexibility and, in their view, produce more effective programs. Republicans also knew that consolidation probably would undermine community organizations created by the War on Poverty. Democrats wanted to protect successful "categorical" narrow purpose federal grant programs and were not content to see community organizations and programs perish.

The law left the matter decidedly unclear. With the exception of the Job Corps and a few programs for special target groups, specific federal programs lost their protected status. State and local governments were expected to fund programs of "demonstrated effectiveness" but were not required to fund any specific agency or group. Under Title I, the law's training provision, "prime sponsors," usually state or local governments with at least 100,000 residents, could establish new programs falling into any one of five categories: classroom training, on-the-job training, work experience, public service employment, or supportive services, such as transportation to and from work. Things could continue pretty much as they were before CETA, with the same local agencies providing identical services, or they could change a great deal. The legislation offered opportunities for reform, but by no means determined the results. Changes would either occur or not occur during implementation. (For a summary of CETA Titles, see page 63.)

Who Will Be Served?

The Nixon administration wanted state and local officials, the prime sponsors, to select the enrollees for their programs. Previous federal categorical programs were assailed for containing strict definitions of eligibility. Democrats expressed grave reservations about open-ended entrance standards. They feared that, without specific provisions, poor people would receive less assistance than before because state and local officials would lavish benefits on more politically potent constituents.

The administration won the first round of the eligibility debate, and CETA was passed with rather broad entrance requirements. Title I, which initially contained the bulk of the funds, required that a person be unemployed for just seven days to be eligible for assistance. While the law emphasized helping the unemployed poor, it nevertheless made many nonpoor citizens eligible for services. In fact, approximately 27 million people, or about 25 percent of the adult workforce, became eligible for the CETA program. Because only a fraction of those people—perhaps two million— could possibly be enrolled, state and local operatives would have wide discretion about whom to serve.

The formula for allocating funds among 450 jurisdictions also helped determine which applicants would be selected. During the categorical era of the 1960s and early 1970s, local organizations and communities applied to the federal government for competitive project grants. The "winners" were those who could negotiate the federal maze with superior technical skills and political clout. CETA altered the game. Funds were allocated by a *formula* based on the local population, unemployment rate, and

The Comprehensive Employment and Training Act of 1973 at a Glance (Public Law 93-203)

Title I: *Comprehensive Services:* authorizes employment and training programs for the unemployed, underemployed, and economically disadvantaged. Programs are administered by prime sponsors, which are cities and counties of 100,000 or more residents, and by combinations of cities and counties. State governments are the prime sponsors for the remaining communities. Funds are allocated according to each area's prior year's funding, the number of unemployed, and adults in low-income families.

Title II: *Public Service Employment:* provides funds to prime sponsors and Indian reservations to establish full-time temporary jobs in governmental and private nonprofit organizations. Funds are allocated to areas experiencing substantial unemployment, defined as 6.5 percent for three or more months.

Title III: *Special Target Groups:* provides for nationally administered programs for native Americans, migrant and seasonal farmworkers, youth, and other groups.

Title IV: *Job Corps:* authorizes the Department of Labor to operate the Job Corps, a program of residential training centers for disadvantaged young men and women.

Title V: *The National Commission for Manpower Policy:* establishes an advisory group of department secretaries and private citizens to identify goals, evaluate programs, and make recommendations to the president and Congress.

Title VI: *Emergency Jobs Program:* provides funds for the creation of full-time temporary jobs in the public sector. Funds are allocated to prime sponsors and Indian tribes based on the number of unemployed, the unemployed in excess of 4.5 percent, and the unemployed living in areas with substantial rates of unemployment. (This program was authorized by the Emergency Jobs and Unemployment Assistance Act of 1974, Public Law 93-567, which amended CETA.)

number of people living in poverty. All areas of the country were *entitled* to a slice of the pie. Big cities with established programs, grant-seeking capability, and high concentrations of minority residents no longer captured a disproportionate share of money, but congressional Democrats inserted a "hold-harmless" clause that eased the transition. No matter what the formula indicated, a city obtained at least 90 percent of the previous year's allocation. Over time this hold-harmless clause diminished in significance.

Public Service Employment (PSE)

No issue generated more partisan controversy than the public service employment program. Experience with War on Poverty programs combined with rising levels of unemployment convinced many liberal Democrats that *job training* programs were insufficient. They proposed that the federal government provide jobs for individuals unable to find work in the private sector. With the enactment of the Emergency Employment Act of 1971, Congress had established the first significant temporary jobs program since the New Deal era. Democrats hoped to expand public jobs programs under CETA.

Nixon and other Republicans regarded public service jobs as anathema. They charged that jobs programs interfered with the private sector's capacity to create "permanent" employment and hurt private employers looking for entry-level workers. Nixon had vetoed employment and training reform legislation in 1970 because of a public jobs component that, according to him, would lead to "dead-end jobs in the public sector." [1] He had signed the Emergency Employment Act of 1971 because of what many policy makers viewed as an alarmingly high 6 percent unemployment rate. In 1973 Republicans were particularly reluctant to support public service employment programs because the unemployment rate was hovering around 4 percent, which gave them an advantage in the political debate.

CETA essentially split the difference between Democrats and Republicans. A PSE program was established under Title II, but its $600 million budget was less than half the budget for the training programs under Title I.[2] Title II PSE programs were authorized only in communities with chronically high unemployment rates—defined as 6.5 percent or higher. But the Democrats succeeded in having temporary job creation listed as an allowable activity under Title I, so PSE programs could be established anywhere in the country.

Sharp increases in the number of jobless Americans during 1974 and 1975 altered PSE's political fortune. In little more than a year, the unemployment rate climbed from 5 percent to 9 percent—the highest level in more than a dozen years. Democratic and Republican members of Congress called for federal action to ease unemployment. Their efforts brought about the passage of the Emergency Jobs and Unemployment Assistance Act, which President Gerald Ford reluctantly signed in December 1974. This new component of CETA, known as Title VI, added $2.5 billion for temporary jobs and expanded federal unemployment insurance coverage.

This jump in spending on job creation programs fundamentally transformed CETA, which had been in operation for only six months. The federal government had moved beyond aiding the structurally unemployed and was now helping those thrown out of work because of fluctuations in the nation's economy—the cyclically unemployed. Job creation, rather than job training, became the most important and costly component of CETA. Federal and local officials could no longer concentrate on improving delivery systems and refining training programs; they were now responsible for combating joblessness.

Following CETA's implementation is like watching a play in which the actors know the topic and their roles but have no script. Instead, the actors make up their lines as the performance unfolds.

The Federal Role: Weak and Inconsistent

By granting state and local governments the principal authority for employment and training programs, subject to significant ongoing federal supervision, CETA created tension between local officials and federal overseers. CETA made chief elected officials responsible within their community, and it was clear from the outset that the 450 jurisdictions would employ different political and organizational strategies to administer the law.

The Labor Department's central staff issued regulations and other directives, giving some concrete meaning to the law's general goals. For example, the law made "economically disadvantaged" people eligible for services, so the department issued regulations governing eligibility and specifying the evidence necessary to verify it for individual applicants. The department was not always precise in its definitions, however, nor did it clarify much of the new law's language.

Labor Department officials assumed new and complex roles under CETA. During the pre-CETA era, the department's officials had managed more than 50,000 contracts with education agencies, community organizations, state and local governments, and private institutions. Each contract was submitted, approved, and subsequently audited by federal officials. Under CETA, the department reviewed "comprehensive" plans submitted by states and communities, provided technical assistance as requested, and monitored program performance. These new tasks were not only more demanding but also contradictory. The department was both guru and traffic cop, administering help *and* punishment to local officials.

The Labor Department's 10 regional offices handled the liaison with the nation's 450 prime sponsors, reviewing plans, collecting information on performance, and, on occasion, prescribing corrective actions. Day-to-day interpretations of federal policy were dispensed by the department's regional field representatives. These individuals determined whether prime sponsors had conducted their CETA affairs in accord with congressional and departmental interpretations of the law and its priorities. With a few hundred federal overseers, it is not surprising that the exercise of federal influence varied widely and the connection with congressional intent was often tenuous.

In general the department's behavior during CETA's early years can be characterized as weak and inconsistent. Labor officials rarely intervened in local decisions, and monitoring and technical assistance were unambitious and ineffectual. Moreover, the department was reluctant or unable to clarify the law's unresolved policy disputes. Prime sponsors generally fended for themselves and did as they pleased. For some jurisdictions, the Labor Department's "hands-off" approach was appropriate and beneficial, but for many others its passive stance slowed the development of more effective employment and training programs.

The department's failure to aid and oversee local CETA programs was the cause of later problems. The law instructed prime sponsors to establish "comprehensive" delivery systems to eliminate the duplicative network of programs that lawmakers had criticized. Although the department was expected to aid prime sponsors in improving service delivery, it offered no guidance on how jurisdictions might reform programs and had no vision of what a "comprehensive" system might look like. One local staffer characterized the situation: "In order to be able to give technical assistance you have to know more than the fellow you are giving it to. Unfortunately, in the case of R/DOL [regional offices], they don't know any more than we do." [3]

The matter of who would be enrolled in CETA programs also was largely unaffected by the Labor Department. This passive posture was consistent with the Nixon administration's view that localities should determine their own needs, but the department did not even hold localities to their own definitions. Prime sponsors were required by regulation to submit an analysis of the "universe of need" in their communities, but the department seldom compared the characteristics of need—race, sex, education, income—identified in the annual plans with the characteristics of those actually served.

Department officials did not encourage effective citizen participation. In practice, the department required local officials to have little more than a "paper" advisory body. During their first annual assessment, federal field representatives generally were uninterested in the role and influence of councils on local decisions. For example, one field representative concluded that a CETA advisory council had significantly influenced programs in a city where the council had never met. The department frequently approved plans from cities and counties where advisory bodies were denied the opportunity to review plans or give advice on local strategies.

The department placed a high priority on assembling information about CETA operations, but it was never clear that they knew how to use this information. Prime sponsors were required to report about enrollments, expenditures, and placements on a regular basis. Although the department insisted on timely reporting, it seldom used the information to initiate corrective actions in jurisdictions that were lagging behind planned performance levels.

In fact, the department's entire monitoring effort often appeared to be an elaborate number manipulation game. The department defined "satisfactory performance" as a prime sponsor's ability to meet planned enrollment, expenditure, and placement targets. If a city's plan said 100 individuals would get jobs by midyear and they did, then performance was satisfactory. No independent assessment was made as to whether 100 placements was an artificially low goal. Even more important, prime sponsors freely adjusted their planned goals *during the year* in light of their actual experience. Thus, if a prime sponsor feared that it would not place 100 people by midyear, it would adjust its plan downward and thus ensure "satisfactory" performance. Prime sponsors quickly became adept at playing the numbers game.

Inconsistency on the part of the Labor Department was a source of great frustration for prime sponsors. Following the enactment of the Emergency Jobs and Unemployment Assistance Act in late 1974 and in response to pressure from Capitol Hill, the department insisted that prime sponsors rapidly expend PSE funds by hiring people as quickly as possible. Local officials were told to establish ambitious enrollment targets and warned that funds left unspent after six months would have to be returned to the federal government. Throughout the spring of 1975, local jurisdictions were judged by their ability to achieve their planned expenditure and job creation levels. Between January and June, enrollments in old and new PSE programs rose by nearly 200,000.[4] But, in May the department's tactics suddenly were changed. Threats to reallocate unused money were rescinded, and prime sponsors were ordered to spread out their allocations by carrying some of the money into the next fiscal year. Many local elected officials and administrators felt abused by this abrupt policy reversal.

The actions and inactions of the Department of Labor during CETA's early years reflected the policy environment in which it functioned. The law offered scant guidance on the department's proper role; central policy issues were subject to varying interpretations. Legislative ambiguity encouraged conflict over the definition of national policy and the department's role. Moreover, an economic recession during CETA's first year created the perfect formula for a contentious and shifting national policy environment. Because no consensus existed on critical policy matters during the law's initial implementation, department policies were often hasty reactions to cues from Congress or the White House. The federal government was inconsistent, confused, and generally ineffective.

Congress was a principal cause of instability in the policy environment. It was in response to pressure from Capitol Hill that the Labor Department urged prime sponsors to waste no time in hiring public service workers in 1975 and, by implication, to shortchange other aspects of CETA. Congress wanted PSE jobs injected immediately into the ailing economy but was insensitive to the shock that such rapid expansion would administer to the newly formed and still evolving CETA organizations. Later, however, when unemployment eased a bit, Congress failed to appropriate public jobs funds in a timely manner, which forced the Department of Labor to put the brakes on a rapidly expanding program.

Given this volatile policy environment, federal administrators were loathe to take strong stands on controversial matters. Department officials were uncertain that their positions would be upheld by their political superiors and ultimately by Congress. The department gave prime sponsors mixed signals on how to proceed because they were getting conflicting and changing messages from Congress, interest groups, and the White House. In the absence of clear direction from political officials and lacking relevant experience for managing a program like CETA, the Department of Labor fell back on traditional bureaucratic imperatives: spend money and keep records. In this way, the department hoped to demonstrate "progress" without doing anything very important or controversial.

Prime Sponsor Politics

Like many other laws, CETA was vague enough to garner majority support in Congress and, therefore, insufficiently clear to give implementers needed direction on many policy issues. There was no simple routine for implementing CETA, and the Labor Department was of little help to bewildered program managers. CETA was bound to cause a minor revolution. State and local officials had to adjust quickly to the new era of job training programs; along the way, turmoil and frustration were inevitable byproducts. Before CETA, mayors and county officials had been involved with the Emergency Employment Act of 1971, but most had no contact with training programs, and the new legislation envisioned a more significant role for these politicians. Even though local governments had anticipated new legislation for more than a year, the shift to local control of the entire employment and training system caught all but a handful of communities unprepared.

Shaky Beginnings

Practically overnight, the 450 new organizations called prime sponsors were established. But giving them a name and responsibilities did not create mature, functioning organizations. There would be a lot of groping before these new organizations learned how to operate effective job training and employment programs. In most of the nation's prime sponsors, new agencies had to be established and people recruited to staff them.

These bureaucracies developed in different ways. State CETA operations could be the responsibility of the governor's office, state labor departments, or departments of economic development and commerce. Local operations were spread around, too, from the mayor's office to the personnel department or to a separate employment department. Added to these relatively simple organizations for single political jurisdictions were more complex prime sponsorships where several jurisdictions formed regional bodies. In these so-called "consortia," administrative authority might be lodged in one of the political jurisdictions, or in a separate public agency reporting to a board of elected officials, or even in a private nonprofit corporation.

The hasty beginnings of CETA had important consequences because governors, mayors, and county executives organized their CETA agencies under assumptions that later proved to be incorrect. When assigning program responsibility to a unit within state or local government, elected officials assumed that CETA would be a relatively small enterprise. Senior CETA staff often were plucked from the middle ranks of larger, more important departments. In many communities, these early choices about program location and staff leadership turned out to be poor because CETA evolved into a larger and more complex program than anyone anticipated.

In addition to setting up an administrative apparatus, elected officials were faced with developing a process for making CETA decisions. Governors, mayors, and county officials had to decide how deeply they would be involved in CETA, who would participate in what decisions, and what role advisory groups would play. Training programs had to be planned, contractors selected, and methods of enrolling people determined. Administrative procedures for collecting data about the local labor market and monitoring fiscal affairs had to be established. Some of these choices carried strategic and political significance, involving the allocation of money and jobs. Others were more technical but no less important to the successful operation of employment and training programs.

Most of the decisions made during the early days of CETA were far from routine; a lot was at stake. In cities and counties where pre-CETA training programs had thrived, a network of community organizations and educational institutions was well established and determined to protect its turf and share of the job training budget. In communities without pre-CETA experience, decision-making patterns and program choices would be worked out from scratch. Whatever the configuration of local job training programs and interests before CETA, the new law demanded new patterns of governance. These patterns, once established, often proved difficult to break. Elected officials had their best opportunity to revise existing program approaches and administrative procedures during CETA's formation in 1974 and early 1975, but many were either unwilling or unable to take advantage of this unique opportunity.

Power Struggles

In general, state and local elected officials responded to their new responsibilities by getting more involved in decision making or by using a professional employment and training staff to exert their will.[5] In virtually all of the 50 prime sponsorships we visited, either the elected officials or their professional staffs dominated CETA politics. This is hardly surprising because the law conferred ultimate authority on elected officials, and the staffs they appointed were the only local actors who occupied themselves with CETA administrative matters on a full-time basis. It is significant that others, such as citizen advisory councils, federal officials, and providers of training services, typically were not influential on CETA matters.

Elected officials participated most actively in decisions involving money, contracts, and jobs, in particular, public service employment programs.[6] In many cities, mayors separated the public jobs program from job training programs so that they could exercise greater control over them.[7] In Youngstown, Ohio, the mayor went so far as to interview and select each of several hundred public service employees funded by CETA. Beyond PSE, elected officials were most concerned with selecting contractors for training programs. Other decisions, such as the mix of services or the overall structure of the system, were delegated to administrators.[8]

CETA advisory councils were influential in shaping training programs in only about a third of the prime sponsors we studied, and the number was even lower when decisions over public service jobs programs were involved. Where councils were important, they helped select training programs, contractors, and program beneficiaries.[9] The councils suffered from liabilities traditionally experienced by citizen advisory groups. It is difficult for the members of advisory bodies to act independently of an administrative staff because they lack either sufficient time or expertise to challenge the staff. More influential councils typically included members representing schools and nonprofit agencies with CETA contracts; these members were knowledgeable and committed to pursuing their interests. For example, an Urban League director serving on a CETA council could be counted on to defend the league's stake in the local system. Councils stacked with representatives of organizations seeking CETA contracts were not "citizen" advisory groups, but rather a collection of vested interests.[10]

It made a difference who controlled CETA decisions. Where elected officials dominated, political calculations were paramount. In some prime sponsorships, contracts for services were awarded on the basis of an organization's political strengths and affiliations, rather than its record of performance. Where contractors sitting on advisory councils made key decisions, the primary concern was that each agency maintain its "fair share" of the CETA budget. If control remained in the hands of administrative staff, funding decisions were based more often on objective performance standards.

To understand CETA politics, one must first look at the behavior of elected officials. Their attitudes about the advantages and disadvantages of delegating authority determined their involvement and in turn the context of local decision making. Elected officials were acutely aware of their time limitations and uninterested in time-consuming matters without electoral payoffs. They carefully weighed the benefits associated with CETA and how much personal involvement was required to get what they wanted out of it.

An elected official's participation also was influenced by local economic and fiscal conditions. In its original form, CETA represented a substantial amount of discretionary funds, and, after the enactment of the Emergency Jobs and Unemployment Assistance Act in late 1974, considerably more money was at stake. This new public jobs program provided a major source of funds that could be used to supplement state, city, or county government payrolls and to provide political patronage. The worse the fiscal condition of the community and the higher its unemployment rate, the more likely were local officials to grasp CETA's potential benefits and become involved in CETA matters.[11] The mayor of Canton, Ohio, described his "discovery" of CETA in early 1975: "When unemployment is low, the manpower division is just another agency. Now it is important because of the unemployment problem. The benefits are spread around and the programs are a political asset." [12]

The power of CETA advisory councils and of contracting agencies was heavily dependent on the attitudes of staff and elected officials about their proper role. Because the law and Labor Department overseers required little more than token activities, councils needed either tangible support from the politicians or a political vacuum before they could influence decisions. The staff and elected officials could create a "rubber stamp council" by appointing overcommitted and/or disinterested members, by conducting boring meetings with no substantive purpose, by withholding information and staff assistance, or by overruling key council recommendations.

Local actors sometimes disagreed about who should exercise control over CETA decisions. But bitter conflicts were rare and confined largely to prime sponsorships where attempts were underway to make radical changes in existing service contracts and relationships. In other communities, CETA activists and elected officials often competed with one another to enhance their power over decisions, but head-on conflict was absent. The authority of elected officials or the administrative staff to determine CETA decisions generally went unchallenged.

The initial implementation of CETA produced a significant degree of decentralization. State and local officials made critical program choices without intervention from the federal government. Accompanying the decentralizing trend was a centralizing trend at the local level. No longer were program choices determined by a loose assortment of contractors sprinkled throughout the community. Nevertheless, local politics ensured that changes brought about under CETA would be constrained by the need to accommodate existing interest groups.

Reforming Employment and Training Programs

Throughout CETA's legislative history most policy makers, program administrators, and interest groups agreed that employment and training programs required a major overhaul. The new law eliminated narrow, inflexible federal job training programs and gave state and local officials authority to restructure services according to local needs and preferences. Although improved program designs were desired, neither the law nor the regulations issued by the Labor Department provided much guidance on how prime sponsors could achieve reform.

Pre-CETA job training programs were criticized because they were fragmented. There were no mechanisms for referring people from one program to another, and many individuals received inadequate or inappropriate services. If a woman happened to walk into a community's Urban League office that offered secretarial training courses, then she either enrolled or got nothing, even though courses at the vocational school across town might interest her more. CETA held out the hope that consolidating programs under one administrative authority would foster "comprehensive" service delivery.

Specifying what a comprehensive delivery system should look like was a very difficult task. What types of services were essential? Which functions should be centralized and which decentralized? What were the best methods of integrating diverse programs? The Labor Department neither answered these questions nor attempted to determine whether prime sponsors had established comprehensive program strategies.

Researchers at the National Academy of Sciences and Ohio State University found that prime sponsors were seldom successful in attempts to integrate service delivery during CETA's early years. In its study, the academy found that only 4 prime sponsors out of 24 substantially reformed their delivery system during the first year. Only 4 additional sites with unified, centralized, and coordinated programs were discovered during the academy's second year study.[13] Ohio State research teams visited 15 jurisdictions selected on the basis of their excellent reputations but found that only 7 had systems that could be regarded as comprehensive.[14]

CETA gave local officials the authority to select contractors to provide training, work experience, and other services to the unemployed. In communities with pre-CETA experience, elected officials could either continue or terminate existing contracts with community organizations, boards of education, and state employment service offices. In communities without program experience, new prime sponsors decided whether to contract with outside agencies or deliver services themselves. Studies of CETA contractors reveal modest changes between 1974 and 1976. State employment service offices were the big losers, experiencing a reduction in their share of funds. Local government agencies created by elected officials for the purpose of running CETA programs were the big winners. Despite dire predictions to the contrary, community organizations and local school districts maintained stable percentages of employment and training contracts under CETA.[15]

Local officials also were responsible for deciding what types of employment and training programs would be funded. Whatever the preexisting mix of services, prime sponsors could, in theory, shift resources from classroom training to on-the-job training to work experience, and so on. Data on CETA's early history indicate some changes in the kinds of programs operated locally (Table 3-1). From fiscal year 1974 (the last pre-CETA "categorical" year) to fiscal year 1976, classroom training and

Table 3-1   CETA Title I Expenditures by Program, Fiscal Years 1974-1976, in millions of dollars and percentages

Program Activity	FY 1974		FY 1975		FY 1976[a]	
Classroom training [b]	$361	42%	$276	32%	$ 524	33%
On-the-job training	145	18	70	8	144	9
Work experience	319	37	375	43	606	38
Public service employment	NA	NA	56	6	171	11
Services	33	4	99	11	145	9
Total	$868	100%[c]	$876	100%[c]	$1,590	100%[c]

[a] Four quarters.

[b] Includes expenditures under 5 percent vocational education grant to governors in fiscal years 1975 and 1976.

[c] May not add to 100 percent due to rounding.

Source: Data supplied by the Employment and Training Administration, U.S. Department of Labor.

on-the-job training programs each declined roughly 10 percent, while work experience programs, public service employment programs (funded under Title I), and supportive services increased. In general, the new strategies for assisting the unemployed emphasized temporary jobs and income maintenance and deemphasized training for private sector jobs.

Overall, the design and operation of CETA training programs and services during fiscal years 1975 and 1976 changed little from programs designed over the previous 10 years. Significant innovations occurred in some communities, particularly where there was no prior experience with training programs. But why was change the exception rather than the rule?

One reason is that the law *authorized* reform; it did not *guarantee* it. Indeed, a probing look behind CETA's rhetoric reveals that the law did not affect the fundamental conditions of the local policy environment. CETA's resources were spread thinly across 450 prime sponsorships. Because many cities and counties received the same or reduced levels of funding as in earlier years, program innovation could be achieved only by taking contracts away from some and awarding them to others. Yet, the law urged state and local governments to consider carefully the merits of existing programs. Moreover, categorical program operators actively participated as members of many advisory councils where funding decisions were debated. Under these circumstances, an elected official's safest strategy was to fund entrenched contractors. With those decisions made, the shape of the system was largely determined.

Wholesale reform also was constrained by the absence of readily available alternatives. The law gave local officials the right to remove classroom training contracts from a board of education, but it did not invent new institutions capable of offering skills training courses. Administrators were forced to live with the available options. Many thought it better to fund programs that were less than perfect than to have no programs at all.

Given such constraints, it would have been difficult for an able and experienced professional staff to design effective and politically salable reforms. But most of the professionals responsible for CETA in 1974 and 1975 were inexperienced. Simultaneously, they were saddled with building new organizations, coping with new responsibilities, and accomplishing institutional and programmatic reform. Within six months, local energies were further diverted by a large public service employment program. One senior Labor Department official recalled: "Public service employment became synonymous with CETA and we forgot about Title I, which is really the guts of the program."

The department did little to encourage local reform. An underlying problem was that neither the department, nor anyone else, could confidently prescribe the best structure for local employment and training systems. For example, local officials were often at a loss in determining the best mix of services for clients or what specific approaches were needed to make their system more effective. The problem of designing programs that help disadvantaged people obtain jobs did not suddenly become easier with CETA's enactment. Prime sponsors groped their way to workable solutions with the same imperfect knowledge and remedies available to their predecessors.

Two countervailing factors promoted modest change under the new regime. First, committed and experienced staff accomplished reform in some communities, especially when supported by local elected officials. Second, high levels of unemployment convinced many local elected officials and staffs that it was appropriate to shift funds away from training programs into temporary public service jobs programs because these were not dependent on a robust private economy.[16]

Public Jobs Programs

State and local officials had important choices to make about their public service employment programs. A host of organizations were eligible to employ federally funded workers; these included state, city, or county agencies; school boards; housing authorities; and private nonprofit organizations, such as the Red Cross or Girl Scouts. During CETA's early years, local officials lavished most of the PSE jobs on their own departments. One study found that three-quarters of the PSE jobs were located in the elected officials' governmental units during CETA's first year and two-thirds during the second year.[17]

Most of the temporary positions required few skills and paid low wages. During 1975 and 1976 nearly 75 percent of the jobs were for unskilled labor and service and clerical workers, and two out of three paid less than $4.00 per hour.[18] PSE jobs differed markedly from the general pattern of local government employment by having fewer people working in education and more people engaged in public works, transportation, parks and recreation, and social services.[19]

Of course, there were exceptions to the general patterns. States, cities, and counties assigned PSE workers to perform virtually every function carried out by government. Some communities hired attorneys and engineers with their federal grants, taking advantage of provisions that allowed localities to use their own funds to supplement the salaries of public service workers making more than $10,000 a year. In some jurisdictions entire departments were staffed with a PSE workforce. Although PSE workers usually occupied low-paying and low-skilled jobs, the exotic examples of PSE-funded lawyers, planners, and Ph.D.'s fostered suspicions in Congress that local officials might be abusing a program intended for the low-income unemployed.

There are several explanations for the way PSE programs took shape. The law did not state clearly where and how to spend funds, so local officials had carte blanche over money intended for public jobs. Governors, mayors, and county executives responded to this windfall first by getting involved in PSE decisions and, second, by steering most of the jobs to state, city, or county governments. However, officials did not want to get locked into services that would be difficult to suspend if the program dried up, so they used PSE for activities that were not considered essential to the operation of their units of government.[20]

Cities and counties experiencing fiscal distress could not afford to keep the PSE workforce out of departments delivering essential services, such as police, fire, and sanitation. Moreover, these jurisdictions were especially likely to allot most, if not all, of their PSE funds to jobs in government departments. Only 3 percent of the PSE jobs went to other government and nonprofit organizations in jurisdictions experiencing severe fiscal pressure. Communities that were in better financial circumstances assigned more than a third of PSE jobs to agencies outside of government.[21]

National policy makers were concerned over the predilection of elected officials to assign PSE workers to their departments. Some members of Congress and Department of Labor officials feared that local officials were *substituting* federal PSE funds for local revenues in violation of legislative intent. If this practice became widespread, PSE's impact on job creation would be substantially diminished because all that changed was the source of funding.

It was hard to enforce regulations prohibiting substitution because to do so one had to assess an imaginary situation: what would a local government have done without CETA funds? Several cities in the Northeast and Midwest laid off municipal workers and then rehired them with federal funds. In Cleveland, Ohio, for example, garbage collectors were given two-week furloughs at one desk, which made them "eligible" for federal public jobs, and then given forms to apply for the city's PSE program at an adjacent desk. Technically, this was not illegal. Cities and counties under genuine fiscal stress could rehire their employees. But large-scale layoffs and rehiring on PSE funds caught the attention of nongovernment organizations, who hoped to garner some PSE jobs, members of Congress, and Labor Department officials, who had the unenviable job of trying to control substitution. The difficulty of this task was compounded by the many subtle forms of substitution, such as using PSE workers to expand a department or filling positions vacated through attrition with PSE enrollees, practices that were nearly impossible to detect. Even though the Labor Department was never able to come up with reliable evidence that local governments were engaging in wide-spread substitution, the perception that the practice was common dominated debates over the design of later PSE programs. Many national policy makers became convinced that PSE money was used either to bail out local governments, which meant that it did not create many *new* jobs, or worse, that it was squandered on ill-conceived, exotic, and unnecessary government services.

Who Benefited?

Framers of the original CETA legislation disagreed over how much discretion local politicians should have over the distribution of public service jobs and training opportunities. Supporters of narrow eligibility criteria wanted programs restricted to the truly needy. They charged that governors, mayors, and county officials were insensitive to the plight of the disadvantaged because, as a group, these people are poorly organized and rarely vote. Supporters of broad entrance standards contended that rigid, federally imposed eligibility criteria constrained local flexibility and reduced program effectiveness and that the insensitivity of local elected officials to the plight of the low-income unemployed had been exaggerated.

CETA articulated broad national goals, urging attention to low-income people and others in need of employment and training services, but leaving federal, state, and local implementers with considerable latitude to determine criteria for selecting program participants. To assess how benefits were distributed one needs to know what share of jobs and services actually were given to the poor, minorities, and other exigent groups. An analysis of the characteristics of people enrolled in CETA programs documents these direct benefits.[22]

Concerns about the probable effect of broad eligibility—that the disadvantaged would not be served—were only partially borne out.[23] According to evidence on the characteristics of people enrolled in programs after the change to CETA (Table 3-2), clients in training and work experience programs were somewhat less disadvantaged. In particular, older and better-educated individuals received more services during the CETA era. In contrast, women were better served by CETA training and work experience programs than they had been before. The changes in client characteristics during this CETA period, from 1974 to 1976, indicate a trend toward less service for the most disadvantaged.

The pattern for public service employment programs was different. During 1974, CETA's only PSE component was Title II. Because it had been justified as a program for the long-term unemployed, we expected that Title II programs would have more disadvantaged enrollees than the Public Employment Program of 1971 (PEP)—a program designed for the recently unemployed. Initially, PSE workers under Title II indeed were younger, less well educated, poorer, and more likely to be females than PEP jobholders. Conversely, minorities held fewer jobs under CETA than under PEP. The PSE client profile changed in 1975 after the Labor Department pushed for rapid increases in Title II enrollments and when the new emergency jobs program, known as Title VI, was added. By the end of fiscal year 1976, PSE workers were noticeably older, better educated, and less poor than the original group of Title II employees.

A casual comparison of the characteristics of people engaged in Title I training programs with those holding PSE jobs reveals significant differences between the two groups. Title I CETA trainees were much more likely to be poor, nonwhite, less well educated, female, and younger than PSE jobholders. Such distinctions between Title I and PSE workers are important for understanding who benefited from CETA. PSE participants received full-time jobs paying around $8,000 per year; Title I programs usually enrolled people in training schools with a small stipend or placed them in part-time jobs at the minimum wage. In short, the more direct and costly benefits were received by a relatively more advantaged group of people, namely, those who were more competitive in the labor market because of their educational backgrounds, age, or work histories.

Another method for getting a handle on program benefits is to compare the characteristics of people *enrolled* with the characteristics of people *eligible to be served* (Table 3-3). We see, for example, that even

Table 3-2 CETA Participant Characteristics, 1974–1976, Compared with Participants in Pre-CETA Programs

Characteristics	Training and Work Experience			Public Service Employment		
	Pre-CETA Programs[a] FY 1974	CETA Title I 12/74[b]	9/76[b]	Categorical Program (PEP)[c] FY 1972–1973	CETA Title II 12/74[b]	CETA Titles II & VI[d] 9/76[b]
Females	42%	49%	46%	28%	35%	36%
Nonwhites[e]	46	46	45	40	35	33
Less than 22 years old	63	65	57	19	25	22
12 or more years of education	34	34	46	74	71	75
Economically disadvantaged[f]	87	81	78	38	48	44

[a] Includes programs funded under the Economic Opportunity Act and the Manpower Development and Training Act.

[b] The rationale for the choice of dates is that December 1974 is the earliest date for which reliable CETA data is available, and September 1976 is the end of the second full year of CETA and the transition quarter that accompanied the shift to a new federal fiscal year.

[c] The Public Employment Program (PEP) was authorized by the Emergency Employment Act of 1971.

[d] Because of the free transfer of Title VI participants into Title II during the summer of 1976, separate figures for the two programs lose all meaning, so only the combined PSE data for 1976 are being presented.

[e] Does not include Hispanics.

[f] A person living in a family with less than the poverty level income or a recipient of cash welfare assistance.

Source: Pre-CETA data from *Employment and Training Report of the President* (Washington, D.C.: Government Printing Office, 1976), 100. CETA data supplied by the Employment and Training Administration, U.S. Department of Labor.

though the trend was away from serving the most disadvantaged in Title I, the enrollees were more disadvantaged than the eligible population as a whole. People enrolled in training and work experience programs were considerably younger, poorer, less well educated, and less likely to be white than those eligible for services. Only in the category of service to women did Title I serve a smaller percentage than was present in the eligible population.

In contrast, public service employment programs were focused less effectively on the disadvantaged population. Women and those with little education were greatly underserved relative to the eligible population for public jobs programs, and the poor were slightly underserved. Minorities, on the other hand, were better represented among PSE workers than in the eligible population.

Radical shifts in the characteristics of groups served by employment and training programs did not materialize during CETA's early years, but there were several noticeable changes. CETA's allocation formula helps account for the patterns of benefit distribution. The formula spread dollars into suburban communities and away from large cities. CETA's programs became available to more whites and to people who were not as poor as those eligible for pre-CETA categorical programs, where service was often restricted to people residing in the inner city.[24] Nevertheless, our analysis of more than 30 jurisdictions strongly suggests that the law's allocation formula did not account for all of the observed shifts in program clientele. For example, many prime sponsors reduced the enrollment of low-income individuals even though their geographical boundaries were identical.[25]

CETA's broad eligibility criteria clearly created opportunities for dramatic changes in the groups served by employment and training programs. Nearly 27 million people, roughly 25 percent of the nation's workforce, were eligible for CETA training programs under Title I, and more than 12 million people were eligible for PSE jobs.[26] Considering that in fiscal year 1976, Title I served 1.7 million people and PSE employed 750,000 people, prime sponsors had great freedom in choosing participants from among those eligible.[27] But, even with such broad discretion, locally run employment and training programs served people similar to those enrolled during the categorical era and, under Title I, served a considerably more disadvantaged group than the eligible population as a whole.

An important explanation for the stability of the client population is the fact that the lineup of program contractors changed very little during CETA. By 1975 the typical CETA contractor had an established clientele based on physical location, reputation with various segments of the community, and years of service. Contractors usually retained the prerog-

Table 3-3 Characteristics of CETA Participants Compared with the Eligible Population, Fiscal Year 1975

Characteristics	Training Programs		Public Service Employment		
			Participants		
	Participants	Eligibles	Title II	Title VI	Eligibles[a]
Females	46%	55%	34%	30%	54%
Nonwhites[b]	45	17	35	29	18
Less than 22 years old	62	22	24	21	23
Less than 12 years of education	61	39	28	25	41
Economically disadvantaged	77	38	48	44	49

[a] Even though the populations eligible for Title II and VI programs were slightly different, these characteristics, in percentage terms, were essentially the same.
[b] Does not include Hispanics.

Sources: CETA data from *Employment and Training Report of the President* (Washington, D.C.: Government Printing Office, 1977), 47. Eligible population estimates from William Barnes, "Target Groups," in *CETA: An Analysis of the Issues*, Special Report no. 23 of the National Commission for Manpower Policy (Washington, D.C.: Government Printing Office, 1978), 79.

ative of choosing enrollees from among the applicants referred to them. Therefore, to make changes in the profile of participants, prime sponsors would have to switch contractors or select participants themselves. Few instituted reforms of this nature.

The situation in public jobs programs was somewhat more open because the 1975 expansion raised enrollment numbers, and state and local governments had to establish and fill many new jobs. Again, the opportunity existed for major changes in the characteristics of jobholders, but only minor changes took place. Overall, stability in the pattern of benefit distribution was more common than change.

If the distribution of program benefits was merely a reflection of demographic characteristics in a given community, then we would expect a close correspondence between people eligible for service and actual enrollees. In fact, detailed analysis of two dozen communities revealed no patterns.[28] Jurisdictions with very similar demographic makeups served vastly different types of people. Other communities with dissimilar eligible populations served similar client populations. Comparisons of the relationship between changing eligible populations and the resulting client populations also failed to reveal systematic patterns. Clearly something more than demographic determinism produced CETA benefit distribution.

More than other factors, the preferences, perceptions, and program choices of administrators and elected officials affected the distribution of jobs and training services to people. In nearly every community we visited, the preferences of the dominant local decision makers shaped CETA's results. State and local officials were free to determine the makeup of the groups of program enrollees, and they exercised their options.

These findings go a long way in explaining the sharp differences between jobholders in the PSE programs and people enrolled in Title I training programs. In most communities, administrators with strong commitments to helping the long-term unemployed and economically disadvantaged made decisions about the enrollees in training programs. Consequently, we observed high rates of service to the economically disadvantaged and only modest changes in relation to the pre-CETA era. CETA administrators carried the War on Poverty's commitment to helping the poor into decisions about contractors and clients.[29]

As always, there were exceptions worth mentioning. Some CETA operatives believed that the employment and training system should move away from the "hard-core" unemployed. To justify this position, they cited declining economic conditions and the expanding pool of eligible individuals who, although unemployed only recently, also were in need of assistance in finding and keeping jobs. In fact, the characteristics of people eligible for programs remained pretty much the same throughout the early years of CETA. Nevertheless, the slight trend away from serving the poor was partially attributable to the *perception* that the recently unemployed should get more assistance.

Elected officials were much more likely to take an interest in public jobs programs and were more concerned with providing good public services than with serving the poor.[30] It is not surprising that elected officials sought the most highly qualified applicants to fill jobs in state, city, and county government agencies. Consequently, public service workers were likely to be less disadvantaged than people enrolled in training programs and better qualified than the eligible population as a whole.

In sum, the law did not impose strict limits on what local officials could do. The Labor Department paid little attention to how jobs and training opportunities were distributed at the local level. Changes in the jurisdictions served by the CETA system and economic conditions had some influence on the types of people served. But local administrators and elected officials were most important in determining the results. Local decisions about whom to serve generally reflected the view that Title I training programs ought to serve the chronically unemployed, low-income population and that public service employment should aid temporarily unemployed workers. This division of employment and training into two camps would have important implications for statutory revisions.

Conclusions

The original version of CETA and its early implementation experiences illustrate the conflict between good politics and good policy. Consolidating employment and training programs and decentralizing authority made sense to most national policy makers, despite the partisan overtones associated with these changes. The reform embodied in CETA attracted wide support precisely because it avoided ideological extremes and assuaged the fears of Democrats, Republicans, and key interest groups. It was a classic example of policy making by compromise and mutual accommodation that characterizes American politics.

Policies that make politicians happy often give implementers fits, however, and this was certainly the case during CETA's first season. The principal cause of disjunction between politics and policy is the ambiguity that inevitably accompanies legislative compromise. The primary way to make conflicting groups believe a law will serve them well (or at least not affect them adversely) is to leave many key policy questions unresolved. The political struggle over who gets what, when, and how is pushed into another forum. Eventually someone defines the vague points of law, and, if policy makers refuse to do it, implementers are forced to resolve questions in one fashion or another. As Martin Rein and Francine Rabinovitz have written:

> One of the consequences of passing ambiguous and inconsistent legislation is that the arena of decision making shifts to a lower level. The every-day practitioners become the ones who solve the lack of consensus through their concrete actions.[31]

Of course, implementers often define laws according to interests that may be at odds with the objectives of some policy makers.

CETA began as a relatively modest measure to straighten out an administrative mess caused by overlapping programs and a detached federal establishment. Its central purpose was to obtain more effective programs by giving increased planning and operational power to state and local elected officials. This transfer of power was accomplished, but not without a host of attendant difficulties that seriously undermined other reform objectives. When vague laws are implemented in the intergovernmental setting, many problems commonly appear: widespread confusion about legislative intent, limited innovation, performance lapses, and unstable policy environments. The Labor Department exacerbated these problems by adopting a "hands-off" posture and by emphasizing procedures instead of performance. One important consequence of this implementation scenario was that the law itself did not greatly influence the course of implementation.

The federal government's retreat from active intervention in the employment and training policy domain meant that program results would be determined primarily by local politics. Shifting the arena of CETA politics from the national to the local level was not a neutral process; the power of certain interests expanded, while that of others diminished. Generally, transferring decisions to the local political arena promoted program stability, but inhibited reform. In most places the same training programs were operated in more or less the same manner before and after CETA.

During CETA's first season we witnessed the gaps between broad policy intentions and actual performance that have been observed in many studies of intergovernmental policy implementation. Federalism complicates social policy implementation, and CETA's brand of decentralization did little, if anything, to uncomplicate matters. Complex bureaucratic networks remained, and it became even more difficult than before to establish accountability for program results. Two prominent studies of implementation failure, Jeffrey Pressman and Aaron Wildavsky's examination of economic development projects in Oakland, California, and Martha Derthick's analysis of the New Towns housing program, emphasize the problems caused by bureaucratic complexity and political accountability during the implementation of intergovernmental policy. Derthick stresses the staunch resistance of local officials to federal initiatives, and Pressman and Wildavsky focus on the complications introduced by extended bureaucratic networks.[32]

CETA's early implementation experience was a bit different from the programs examined in these oft-cited studies. Bureaucratic complexity and local resistance to federal objectives were evident, but the root cause of CETA's problems was that local actors received far-reaching authority but little guidance from the law or federal agencies about how to exercise their authority. In this respect, CETA's implementation was similar to what scholars found in their studies of the Elementary and Secondary Education Act.[33] One of Jerome Murphy's concluding observations captures the dilemma well:

> The price of winning federal reform, then, may well be the appearance of ambiguity. That this was true in 1965 with the overwhelming Democratic majority in Congress underscores the point. This also suggests that typically the implementation phase will be marked not only by standard managerial problems, but also by the more difficult political problems of continually defining a bill's "real" objectives. Hence, passing a law is only a small step toward the achievement of reform. Indeed, if reformers want their goals to be met, then they must somehow be significantly involved in the day-in and day-out battles of implementation.[34]

Capability limitations also contributed a great deal to the implementation problems observed during CETA's first season. Even if the law had been unambiguous and federal guidance decisive, it is not clear that local implementers were capable of developing effective, efficient, and comprehensive systems. It takes time to gain the administrative expertise necessary to accomplish such tasks, yet some localities had little or no experience with employment and training programs before CETA. Many of those that had experience lacked the political will to bring about reform. The advent of large public jobs programs compounded the difficulties of CETA prime sponsors and ensured that reform efforts would be abandoned in all but a few communities. The pressure for expanding public service jobs programs diverted precious energy away from the central reform goals in the law and added uncertainty and instability to the policy environment. This first public jobs expansion was only a small sample of what was soon to come.

====================== **Notes** ======================

1. Quoted in Roger Davidson, *The Politics of Comprehensive Manpower Legislation* (Baltimore: Johns Hopkins University Press, 1972), 66.
2. The $600 million Title II appropriation for fiscal years 1974 and 1975 (to be spent in FY 1975) understates the true magnitude of public service employment. Also available was $240 million in unspent Public Employment Program funds that were to be spent in FY 1975.
3. Carl E. Van Horn, "Implementing CETA: The Federal Role," *Policy Analysis* 4 (Spring 1978): 163.
4. Employment and Training Administration enrollment data show 55,950 Title II participants by December 1974 and 247,572 participants in Titles II and VI by June 1975.
5. See Randall B. Ripley et al., *The Implementation of CETA in Ohio,* Employment and Training Administration, U.S. Department of Labor, R & D Monograph, no. 44 (Washington, D.C.: GPO, 1977), 5-12; William Mirengoff and Lester Rindler, *CETA: Manpower Programs Under Local Control* (Washington, D.C.: National Academy of Sciences, 1978), 50-60.
6. Ripley et al., *Implementation of CETA,* 9.
7. The original Title II legislation designated general purpose units of government serving 50,000 people or more as program agents and gave them administrative authority over Title II and, later, over Title VI programs. PSE allocations also were broken out at the program agent level as well as at the prime sponsor level. Thus, there were statutory reasons for elected officials to treat PSE programs differently from other CETA programs.
8. Ripley et al., *Implementation of CETA,* 5-6; Mirengoff and Rindler, *CETA: Manpower Programs,* 51-53.
9. Ripley et al., *Implementation of CETA,* 7.
10. The Ohio State University study of CETA in Ohio found that 40 percent of the members of CETA planning councils there in 1975 were representatives of organizations receiving CETA funding. See Randall B. Ripley et al., "Progress Report: The Implementation of CETA in Ohio," Employment and Training Administration, U.S. Department of Labor (Washington, D.C.: Sept. 15, 1975, Mimeographed), 81.
11. Donald C. Baumer, "Implementing Public Service Employment," in *The Policy Cycle,* eds. Judith V. May and Aaron B. Wildavsky (Beverly Hills, Calif.: Sage Publications, 1978), 180-182.
12. Quoted in Carl E. Van Horn, *Policy Implementation in the Federal System* (Lexington, Mass.: D. C. Heath & Co., 1979), 75.
13. Mirengoff and Rindler, *CETA: Manpower Programs,* 138.
14. Ripley et al., *CETA Prime Sponsor Management and Program Goal Achievement,* Employment and Training Administration, U.S. Department of Labor, R & D Monograph, no. 56 (Washington, D.C.: GPO, 1978), 26.
15. Mirengoff and Rindler, *CETA: Manpower Programs,* 146. See also Ripley et al., *Implementation of CETA,* 21.
16. Mirengoff and Rindler, *CETA: Manpower Programs,* 120; Ripley et al.,

CETA Prime Sponsor Management, 21-24.

17. Baumer, "Implementing Public Service Employment," 181.
18. Ibid., 182-184.
19. Mirengoff and Rindler, *CETA: Manpower Programs,* 166.
20. Mirengoff and Rindler, *CETA: Manpower Programs,* 164-165; Baumer, "Implementing Public Service Employment," 180-181.
21. Mirengoff and Rindler, *CETA: Manpower Programs,* 164-165.
22. Our analysis of direct benefits stops short of measuring CETA's impact on individuals' long-term employment and earnings potential. Although this information is important in an overall assessment, these outcomes were not very important to Labor Department officials or to members of Congress, at least initially. Little or no reliable data on long-term impact were available to policy makers. The department funded an ambitious project to trace the impact of CETA on participants, but the first estimate isolating the extent to which postprogram earnings were attributable to CETA appeared in 1981— roughly seven years after the program got underway. See Westat, *Continuous Longitudinal Manpower Survey,* U.S. Department of Labor, Employment and Training Administration, Office of Program Evaluation, Net Impact Report, no. 1 (Washington, D.C., March 1981).
23. The participant data presented in Table 3-2 and elsewhere in the book are based on prime sponsors' reports aggregated by the Labor Department. They reflect cumulative enrollments in a program year. Participant data also were compiled by Westat in a continuous longitudinal manpower survey (CLMS). There were few differences between the CLMS data and the prime sponsor data, except the CLMS data consistently showed about a 10 percent lower level of service to the economically disadvantaged and an even greater difference in the percentage of enrollees who were unemployed before entering the program. Again, the CLMS figures were lower. The sponsor data were obtained from applicants during enrollment interviews. CLMS data came from interviews with a sample of participants one to five months after enrollment. Some applicants falsified their income and employment data because these were the primary criteria for eligibility. Some of them may have provided accurate information to CLMS when their eligibility was not at stake. We believe the sponsor data are fully adequate for our purposes, though in a few special instances we utilize CLMS data.
24. U.S. Advisory Commission on Intergovernmental Relations, *The Comprehensive Employment and Training Act: Early Readings from a Hybrid Block Grant* (Washington, D.C.: GPO, 1977), 39; Mirengoff and Rindler, *CETA: Manpower Programs,* 206-207.
25. Donald C. Baumer, Carl E. Van Horn, and Mary K. Marvel, "Explaining Benefit Distribution in CETA Programs," *Journal of Human Resources* 14 (Spring 1979): 182-192.
26. William Barnes, "Target Groups," in *CETA: An Analysis of the Issues,* Policy Report, no. 23 of the National Commission for Manpower Policy (Washington, D.C.: GPO, 1978), 63-101.
27. Mirengoff and Rindler, *CETA: Manpower Programs,* 200.

28. Baumer, Van Horn, and Marvel, "Explaining Benefit Distribution," 183-185.
29. Ibid., 190.
30. Ibid., 190.
31. Martin Rein and Francine F. Rabinovitz, "Implementation: A Theoretical Perspective," (Working paper, no. 43, Joint Center for Urban Studies of MIT and Harvard University, 1977). An abridged version of this paper appears in *American Politics and Public Policy,* eds. Walter D. Burnham and Martha W. Weinberg (Cambridge, Mass.: MIT Press, 1978), 307-335.
32. Jeffrey L. Pressman and Aaron B. Wildavsky, *Implementation* (Berkeley: University of California Press, 1973); Martha Derthick, *New Towns In-Town* (Washington, D.C.: The Urban Institute, 1972).
33. See, for example, Stephen K. Bailey and Edith K. Mosher, *ESEA: The Office of Education Administers a Law* (Syracuse, N.Y.: University of Syracuse Press, 1968).
34. Jerome T. Murphy, "The Education Bureaucracies Implement Novel Policy: The Politics of Title I of ESEA, 1965-72," in *Policy and Politics in America,* ed. Allan P. Sindler (Boston: Little, Brown & Co., 1973), 195.

Public Jobs and Politics 4

The second season of employment and training programs, from the election of Jimmy Carter in 1976 to CETA's overhaul in late 1978, is a fascinating episode of American public policy. Returned to power after eight years of Republican rule at the White House, the Democrats initiated the most ambitious unemployment measures since the Depression. With the nation suffering the highest postwar levels of unemployment, the president and large majorities on Capitol Hill quickly authorized dozens of new programs and appropriated more than $20 billion dollars to combat unemployment. Not since Lyndon Johnson and the legendary 89th Congress had domestic policy expanded so rapidly.

CETA occupied center stage in the Democrats' domestic strategy. Spending on public service employment (PSE) programs grew more than threefold, from $1.5 billion in fiscal year 1975 to more than $4.5 billion in 1978. At its peak, CETA supported three-quarters of a million jobs. Recalling the War on Poverty, Congress enacted a staggering array of employment and training strategies for unemployed young people, older workers, ex-offenders, veterans, migrant workers, and people with limited English speaking ability.

The nation's 450 CETA prime sponsors, still in an embryonic state, implemented these sweeping initiatives. Hundreds of thousands of people obtained temporary full-time jobs; millions of young people and adults received part-time work experience and training services; and state, county, and city governments expanded public services for their residents. As a vehicle for stimulating the economy and rescuing city governments from financial disasters, CETA received high marks from many, especially state and local elected officials.

CETA's successes, however, helped bring about its downfall. The rapid expenditure of PSE funds and the quick expansion of the public service workforce were accomplished at a price. In some communities, ineligible people were hired, and money was wasted on exotic projects; politicians exploited PSE's potential for patronage and used its funds to postpone tax increases. The subsequent disaffection with temporary jobs programs, evident in 1981 when they were terminated, stemmed from the experiences of the PSE expansion period. These disappointing results served to crystalize national policy makers' distrust of large federal government spending programs for the unemployed, helped set the stage for the election of Ronald Reagan and other conservative politicians, and ushered in different remedies for unemployment.

The Nationalization of CETA

The striking transformation of CETA from a modest-sized employment and training measure in 1973 to an instrument of macroeconomic and political policy began in 1975. But it was the election of Carter and the ascendence of liberal Democrats that made CETA a program of the highest national importance for the first time. The CETA system delivered the Democratic party's prescription for the nation's long bout with high unemployment. The rhetoric of local control and program flexibility, heard during the Nixon and Ford administrations, was replaced with demands that local officials follow the national agenda.

During the 1960s federal unemployment programs addressed what were regarded as minor dysfunctions in an economic system that had prospered since World War II. By the mid-1970s economic prosperity no longer seemed assured. An oil embargo, inflation, unemployment, and an urban fiscal crisis, symbolized by the predicted bankruptcy of New York City, beset the nation simultaneously. With unemployment running almost 9 percent in 1975 and more than 7 percent for most of 1976, traditional Democratic pleas for government intervention found receptive audiences. Unemployment could not be managed by the private sector alone or treated as a temporary economic dislocation. Fighting unemployment became a national priority, and control moved back to Washington.

President Gerald Ford and the Democratically controlled Congress had battled over unemployment remedies throughout 1976. The president wanted to phase out federally funded PSE jobs during fiscal year 1977. He successfully resisted the Democrats' effort to double the number of subsidized workers but eventually signed a law extending and revising PSE just before election day. Congress also enacted, over Ford's veto, a $4 billion public works measure that set aside $2 billion for job creation projects and $1.3 billion of unrestricted aid for states and local governments.

Although characterized by the candidates' similarities, the 1976 presidential campaign showcased differences between Republican and

Democratic perceptions of the nation's economic problems and possible solutions. Ford mounted a battle against inflation, threatened to terminate federal jobs programs, refused loan guarantees for New York City, and vetoed public works legislation. Carter emphasized the plight of the unemployed, promising large government employment measures, aid for the cities, and help for young, low-income, and minority citizens.

Because of the close election, Carter was denied a clear mandate for his policy agenda, but he quickly carried out his campaign pledges. A coalition that included members of Congress, the AFL-CIO, minority organizations, and others who had helped "deliver" Carter's victory were determined that the president and Congress enact the kinds of federal unemployment programs scotched under Republican presidents and by earlier Congresses.

Carter wasted no time unveiling a plan for revitalizing the flagging economy. Just a few days after his inauguration, the president proposed a two-year $31 billion economic stimulus package, combining tax cuts and federal spending to spur economic recovery. Under his proposal, spending and job creation programs would be directed to the hard-core unemployed and to communities most hurt by the recession. The package included greatly increased spending on public service employment, public works projects, and youth employment programs. Also proposed were a host of tax rebates and reductions for individuals and businesses.

Within three months Congress gave the president just about everything he wanted and then some. The tax reform package was abandoned, but more than $20 billion in new spending authority for the fiscal 1977 budget remained. In the process of enacting the president's initiatives, Congress raised the ante, doubling his request for PSE jobs, public works, and training programs. Administration officials testified that their proposals contained the highest number of jobs that could be created effectively, but Congress ignored the warning.[1] Public service jobs under CETA would jump from 300,000 in May 1977 to 600,000 six months later. By March 1978, the job level would rise to 725,000.

The transformation of CETA did not stop with PSE. The economic stimulus package appropriated funds for a $1 billion youth program employing 200,000 youngsters in part-time jobs; a $250 million Skills Training and Improvement Program (STIP) for 58,000 young people; a $120 million employment program for 92,000 veterans; $50 million for 15,000 part-time older workers engaged in community service jobs; and $98 million for the Job Corps, Indians, and migrants. When combined with a $2 billion public works measure that supported 300,000 construction workers, the Carter package would employ or train more than 1.4 million people in addition to the 2.5 million enrolled in existing CETA programs.

Less than two weeks after passing the president's economic stimulus package, Congress enacted another major jobs measure—$2.25 billion in emergency grants for states and local governments, known as antirecession aid. Originally adopted over Ford's veto in 1976, the revised law distributed federal aid to areas with high unemployment to help maintain existing governmental services. Antirecession aid was intended to "save" old jobs; PSE was supposed to create new jobs.

The last major component of Carter's employment initiative fell into place with the enactment of the Youth Employment Demonstration Projects Act (YEDPA) in July 1977. Repeating the early success with other jobs bills, the president steered his $1 billion youth proposal through Congress in less than five months. Although appropriations for youth programs were contained in the economic stimulus package, YEDPA was needed to put programs into effect. Added atop the growing heap of programs were the Young Adult Conservation Corps, the Youth Community Conservation and Improvement Projects, the Youth Employment and Training Programs, and several experimental training programs for disadvantaged youngsters. YEDPA, for example, authorized a $100 million demonstration project whereby youth in several cities were *guaranteed jobs* if they remained in school. YEDPA was a grab bag. Unable to choose among the several strategies contained in the House and Senate bills, Congress essentially decided to experiment with all of them.

Thus, in just six months, Carter scored several legislative victories. Democrats had been eager to expand unemployment measures since new domestic policy initiatives were shelved during the Vietnam War. Spurred by the highest unemployment rates in nearly 30 years, a Democratic president and substantial Democratic majorities in Congress finally had seen their dreams come true. The CETA system would lead this dramatic shift in domestic policy. It had been nationalized to wage war against unemployment.

Round Two: 'Fixing' the Problems

Economic conditions and national politics fostered large temporary jobs programs in 1977, but the Emergency Jobs Programs Extension Act of 1976 (EJPEA) had already established the framework for PSE expansion. EJPEA was designed to correct problems that had cropped up during CETA's early years. Because the law's provisions applied only to "new" PSE money (and Congress failed to supply any in 1976), EJPEA had no effect on operations until the economic stimulus funds came on line in May 1977.

The debate over EJPEA centered around two image problems: critics noted the disappointingly small number of low-income jobholders in

CETA public service employment programs and the tendency of local governments to substitute federal funds for local revenue sources. Citing enrollment data, several Republican members of the House Committee on Education and Labor charged that existing jobs programs were not helping the long-term unemployed, the low-skilled, or the disadvantaged. They dismissed PSE as "a holding action for those already equipped to deal with the labor market." [2]

Critics also maintained that public service employment was nothing more than thinly disguised revenue sharing for states and local governments. Academic studies of substitution—the extent to which federal funds replace, rather than supplement, local funds—estimated that anywhere between *half* of the jobs created by PSE to *all* of these jobs were not new. The difference was that these jobs were being paid for by the federal government.[3] Reports that cities and counties were rehiring laid-off workers and supporting up to a third of their workforce with federal jobs funds also provided ammunition for PSE's opponents. Rep. Albert Quie, R-Minn., voiced the complaints of many Republicans when he charged that PSE was "a bailout to the cities and allows them to feign budgetary problems so they can use federal money to pay for their police and firemen." [4]

Democrats in Congress held steadfastly to their belief in the inherent value of federally funded public service jobs. Presenting an extension of the CETA jobs program on the House floor, Democratic representative Dominick Daniels of New Jersey, chairman of the House Subcommittee on Manpower, Compensation, Health and Safety, remarked:

> Public service employment is the most effective emergency solution because it is direct. It hires people. Public service employment yields money in taxes paid by working people, keeps people off welfare and contributes to national productivity.[5]

Responding to strong Republican criticism about substitution, the House Democrats accepted some significant reforms. The House bill set aside two-thirds of all new PSE jobs for short-term positions of 2 to 12 months duration for services that would not otherwise be performed. "Project" PSE would not support existing governmental services. Instead, people without alternative sources of income would be hired for special projects such as neighborhood clean-up campaigns, tree planting, and the winterization of public buildings. Regular, ongoing PSE programs would not be under these restrictions; in fact, prime sponsors were encouraged to rehire local government workers who provided "essential health and safety services" if they had been terminated for "bona fide budgetary reasons." [6] The House Committee on Education and Labor report asserted:

There is nothing contrived about the fiscal crisis of state and local governments. The lay offs that have occurred have been all too genuine. The fact that a small number of these job dislocations have been prevented by the timely use of public service job funds is no cause for alarm.[7]

The Senate preferred a stronger approach to reform. Its bill reserved *all* jobs created above the current level for short-term community improvement projects and for the long-term unemployed poor. Under the existing rules, people were eligible for some PSE jobs after only 15 days of unemployment. The Senate bill set aside jobs for people who were unemployed for 15 weeks or more or for those who had exhausted their unemployment benefits. Even then, individuals could not be hired unless they were already on welfare or their families earned less than 70 percent of the Commerce Department's "lower living standard," about $6,500 for a family of four, in the year prior to enrollment.

During the summer of 1976 House and Senate conferees argued about their differences. House Democrats objected to the Senate's strict eligibility criteria for PSE job openings, fearing that laid-off municipal workers could not be rehired because of the income restrictions. A Labor Department regulation that prohibited local governments from filling more than 10 percent of their PSE jobs with rehired workers also bothered Democrats in the House. But support for stricter eligibility criteria for federal jobs programs was quite broad. It came from Democrats and Republicans in the Senate, from House Republicans, and from President Ford, whose allies threatened that the president would veto any bill that did not direct more aid to the disadvantaged. Sen. Gaylord Nelson, D-Wis., stated the case for tighter enrollment provisions:

I think it's right to give preference to the poor ... and the long-term unemployed in selections for federally subsidized jobs. Otherwise we might just as well take over the cities' budgets.[8]

Eventually a winning compromise was fashioned. House Democrats accepted the Senate's eligibility standards for half of the jobs filled through attrition and all new positions resulting from program expansion. Additional PSE positions were set aside for special projects lasting no more than 12 months. For its part, the Senate agreed to a House provision that explicitly prohibited the Labor Department from imposing a ceiling on the percentage of municipal workers that could be rehired with PSE funds.

This compromise split the public service employment program into two parts. The protected portion, called "sustainment PSE," was defined as the combined Title II and Title VI enrollment as of June 1976, about

320,000 jobs nationwide (60,000 in Title II and 260,000 in Title VI). The 1975-1976 rules governing eligibility and the kinds of jobs that could be supported would apply to this component of PSE, except that half of all the Title VI sustainment jobs vacated after the enactment of EJPEA would have to be filled with people who satisfied new and stricter eligibility standards. The other portion of PSE, called "project PSE," encompassed all the Title VI positions above the sustainment level. All such jobs would have to be part of short-term projects, and the stricter eligibility rules would apply to everyone enrolled in this component of PSE.

The Emergency Jobs Programs Extension Act of 1976 was a classic political compromise. City and county officials could rehire laid-off workers with PSE funds without much fear of penalty. Community organizations, schools, and other nonprofit groups that felt shortchanged by the old PSE programs were guaranteed the lion's share of the new project jobs. Those angered because PSE had "bailed out" some city governments were mollified because the project approach was intended to lessen the replacement of local revenues with PSE funds. Low-income individuals and those representing their interests were promised more federal jobs. Congress successfully achieved a balance between two conflicting objectives—the desire to serve those most in need and the desire to provide public services in distressed communities.

The compromise that satisfied members of Congress, however, was to prove a major headache for implementers. Beyond coping with major changes in the *shape* of PSE, prime sponsors also were responsible for handling massive increases in the federal jobs program. A system that was recovering from the shock of doubling its resources in 1975 was now going to double again. Simultaneously, state and local prime sponsors were implementing a smorgasbord of programs for youth, veterans, and all the others Congress wanted to assist. The original training component of CETA, Title I, now accounted for only 23 percent of the overall program, compared to a 42 percent share in 1975. Seldom had a federal grant-in-aid program expanded so rapidly and changed so dramatically. Given the implementation problems experienced during the early years, heaping more money and programs on the CETA system could be likened to tossing gasoline on a fire.

The Federal Role: Many Goals, One Priority

By 1977 CETA had become a much larger, more complicated, and more important program than the one launched in 1973. CETA's big stakes and new features unsettled established relationships between the federal government and state and local officials. No longer a modest block grant reform, CETA now occupied a central role in a national economic recovery policy. The Labor Department and the nation's 450 prime sponsors would bear the burdens of this new mission.

During CETA's early years, the Labor Department was ineffective in directing implementation along a clear path. Responding to congressional whims, the department often issued confusing and contradictory advice. Nevertheless, it successfully pressured prime sponsors to expand CETA's PSE component rapidly during 1975, and the department's leadership remained confident about its new responsibilities under Carter's economic stimulus program.

The department's policy environment was transformed by Carter's election. He brought to the White House traditional Democratic preferences for strong federal oversight. Carter's desire for quick results from the economic stimulus programs convinced him that the federal government should play a more prominent role.[9] The legislative revisions adopted in late 1976 and in 1977 endorsed a more active role for the Labor Department in planning, monitoring, and enforcing CETA programs. Funding for most of the newly authorized programs for special segments of the unemployed population were allotted by the secretary of labor rather than by a predetermined national formula. To receive funds for youth programs or veterans' training, prime sponsors were required to submit detailed proposals to the department. This process afforded more federal influence over local decisions.

Although a different political environment offered the Labor Department new opportunities for influence, other conditions inhibited dramatic change. Approximately the same complement of federal officials who handled CETA when it was a $4 billion program in early fiscal year 1975 were expected to oversee the $8 billion program in fiscal year 1978. More important, local elected officials and administrators were still in charge of most policy decisions and the programs' day-to-day administration. Now, however, many local officials had become hostile toward the department because they had been "burned" before. They were reluctant to take the department's directives seriously or to respond with dispatch. The department had reversed policies before; it could reverse them again. CETA's great expansion would be played out on a "war-torn" landscape.

Charged with the task of carrying out the economic stimulus program, the Labor Department decided it would, in the words of one local operative, "tell the prime sponsors where, when, and how." The department relentlessly pursued a single mission—put people to work in a hurry! The rapid enlargement of public jobs programs was very complex and full of pitfalls. Instead of helping local officials cope with their task, the department made a bad situation worse by overloading prime sponsors with irrelevant information, issuing contradictory statements, revising positions several times, and generally injecting chaos into the policy system.

During this episode of employment and training programs, unlike others, the federal government had adequate time to prepare for PSE expansion. The Labor Department issued PSE directives to local officials immediately after Carter announced his economic stimulus proposal in January. While it could not predict when or if Congress would appropriate additional funds, the department wanted prime sponsors prepared to "hit the ground running" by the spring of 1977. According to the department's game plan, local administrators would assemble a pool of eligible jobseekers, develop a profile of "unmet community needs," and swiftly place people in useful community projects as soon as Congress made the money available. Prime sponsors received reams of guidelines designed to smooth the transition to the new PSE and a projected weekly schedule for how many people they should hire. The hiring guidelines, though unofficial and later proven false, warned that jurisdictions unable to achieve their job quotas would lose PSE funds.

The orderly process envisioned by department planners evaporated. Congress did not appropriate extra jobs money until May, forcing many prime sponsors to slow down. Prime sponsors complained that the department's instructions either came too late or contained too little useful information, which led to confusion, frustration, and uncertainty. A number of gaffes subsequently embarrassed both the department and local officials. What happened in Albany, N.Y., is illustrative. On May 13, 1977, the mayor's office received a telegram from the Labor Department announcing a six-month PSE allocation of $2 million. The staff received no hiring schedule, but were told to begin employing people immediately. Albany did just that. By the middle of the following week the city had hired more than 350 individuals, about one-third of the 1,000 jobs projected for the first six months. One week later, however, the administrators learned, much to their dismay, that the original allocation figure was wrong. At a briefing in New York City, Albany officials were informed that they would receive $798,000, not $2 million. The city was suddenly forced to put the brakes on its PSE job program or risk exceeding the new expenditure limit.

Some Labor Department actions created bottlenecks, but others eased the way to rapid hiring. For example, the department initially prohibited the use of project PSE funds for enlarging regular governmental services; later it encouraged this practice. At first, regulations stipulated that only people unemployed for 15 consecutive weeks were eligible for PSE projects; later the department permitted the hiring of people unemployed for 15 of the previous 20 weeks. The department reversed itself on financial liability for ineligible workers. It allowed prime sponsors to enroll applicants for 60 days pending verification of the applicant's information. The prime sponsors would incur no financial penalty for mistakes as long as they were corrected within 60 days.[10]

While the department paid lip service to many PSE goals, the only really important goal was rapid expansion, and even this was not consistently and effectively communicated to prime sponsors. Among other things, the department told prime sponsors to hire large numbers of people, generate well-defined short-term community projects, reach people not employed under the old style PSE, involve nonprofit community organizations in project selection and operation, place veterans in 35 percent of the jobs, serve unmet state and local public service needs, and do it all quickly. With the exception of rapid enrollment, these goals were not assigned any order, which made it very difficult for prime sponsors to decide which goals they should emphasize. The results were predictable. Prime sponsors either bogged down in a hopeless effort to comply with every policy whim or ignored them.

Ironically, the PSE expansion effort succeeded while failing. Despite the shortcomings reported above, the nation's prime sponsors exceeded the hiring goals established by the Labor Department. One major study concluded:

> By the start of calendar 1978, the PSE expansion effort could be considered nothing short of an unqualified success in terms of its primary goals; i.e., the rapid hiring of large numbers of long-term unemployed into newly created jobs. . . . There was in place a federal, state, and local manpower delivery system capable of responding quickly and effectively to a new national initiative of major proportions.[11]

But on another level, the PSE expansion was a horrible flop. The frantic scramble to assemble enough projects and process enough applicants to meet hiring goals damaged the program's reputation, and its political support began to erode.

Perhaps the PSE expansion faltered because the law was too complex and ambitious to be implemented without serious problems. But flaws in federal management were not caused solely by a faulty law. Quite simply, program operations were subordinated to political goals. National policy makers wanted quick results. This was an economic stimulus measure, so the faster people were employed, the quicker money would circulate in the economy. But federal officials were not satisfied to stop there. Other goals cropped up as the political agenda changed. For example, the plight of unemployed Vietnam veterans received attention midway through the PSE expansion because the president wanted to placate veterans after he pardoned Vietnam War resisters.

With all the money, logistical obstacles, and federal, state, and local decision makers, some degree of abuse was inevitable. Where there is abuse, or even the hint of it, the media will not be far behind. Journalists throughout the country had no trouble unearthing a plethora of stories about sloppy administration, patronage, officials on the take, and other questionable or fraudulent practices. In some cases there was real abuse; in others, journalists raised its specter where there was none. But, in the end, CETA and federal jobs programs were besmirched.

When the negative publicity became widespread, Congress and the White House ordered a crackdown. In 1978 Secretary of Labor Ray Marshall established a task force on fraud, waste, and abuse to ferret out and punish prime sponsors guilty of misusing the program.[12] Chicago, one of the first cities hit by the department's wrath, was forced to return more than $1 million because of patronage and other violations. In an unprecedented move, the department revoked the prime sponsor status of East St. Louis, Ill., citing persistent violations of the law. Thus, after promoting the rapid PSE buildup and ignoring questions of quality, the national government was now turning around and blaming local officials for abusing the program.

The wish of national policy makers to have it both ways was not unique to CETA.[13] The desire for rapid implementaton of a new program is very strong. When problems emerge, as they inevitably do, the temptation to blame bureaucrats and local officials is irresistible. In mid-1978 an era of tighter federal management had begun, but it would not reach its zenith until the law's reauthorization later that year.

Local Politics and the PSE Pork Barrel

The new Democratic administration and the accompanying change in national policy priorities created immediate and more intense pressures on local elected officials and administrators. Prime sponsors were still feeling their way around the task of administering employment and training programs. They needed a stable environment to progress toward fulfilling CETA's original mission—program reform and comprehensive service delivery. What they got instead was a tidal wave of programs and demands from national policy makers. Along with the added responsibilities came huge increases in appropriations. Spending nearly doubled, from $9.5 billion for the entire CETA system during fiscal years 1975 and 1976 to more than $16 billion during fiscal years 1977 and 1978.

The profusion of objectives and initiatives was more than most prime sponsorships could handle in an orderly manner. Administrative capacity was stretched to the limit and, in some cases, well beyond. With the stakes of the game bigger than ever and the system overloaded with money and responsibilities, local decision making became more contentious and chaotic than during CETA's first season. The system became an ideal breeding ground for politics and disorder.

The politics of implementation changed dramatically during CETA's expansion. The huge influx of money, combined with revised legislative provisions, encouraged more individuals and groups to participate in employment and training matters. Some represented organizations seeking PSE projects and workers; others were advocates for youth, veterans, or other needy groups. As more actors crowded into the CETA arena, political decisions became paramount. Unity and coherence in planning and operations were sacrificed to accommodate those clamoring for a piece of the action.

Public service employment programs had always enticed elected officials, but a vastly expanded program enhanced the fiscal and political payoffs. In many communities, federally funded public service workers became the basis for fiscal stability. With flexible rules governing a large portion of the program, plenty of money, and lax federal oversight (at least initially), local elected officials could not resist involvement in doling out the benefits of public service employment.[14]

Fearing that these officials might abuse their power to dispense jobs, Congress inserted language in the emergency jobs legislation that afforded other groups an opportunity for participation. The statutory language regarding advisory council involvement was strengthened by requiring councils to review PSE project proposals and make recommendations to elected officials. Nevertheless, according to one major study, fewer than half of the jurisdictions engaged their planning councils meaningfully in the selection of PSE projects, and many council members reported that PSE diverted their attention away from other more important CETA policy matters.[15] For some councils, however, soliciting and evaluating PSE project proposals represented a rare opportunity for direct involvement in substantive CETA decisions.

Requirements for "substantial participation by community-based organizations" in PSE project selection proved to be far more significant. Administrators never were clear about what lawmakers intended by this provision, and few included community groups in their early planning for PSE projects. By the time project selection was underway, however, many community organizations had become visible and vocal lobbyists. Drawn by the allure of large PSE grants, organizations submitted proposals for every conceivable aspect of community service. Recalling the period, one official responsible for managing his community's PSE selection process observed: "the crazies came out of the woodwork."

Because the CETA "pork barrel" was big enough to satisfy all, or nearly all, benefit seekers, overt conflict was rare. A more common outcome was bargaining among the large cast of local organizations. Once government staffing and fiscal needs were satisfied by the "sustainment" portion of PSE, most elected officials were willing, or even eager, to dole out PSE monies to others. In many jurisdictions the abundance of funds meant that few if any proposals were rejected. Where the demand for PSE jobs exceeded the supply, bargaining within advisory councils usually diffused potential conflicts. Perhaps only in fiscally distressed areas, where local governments consumed a very large portion of PSE, were local community groups unhappy with their share.

Given unprecedented sums of money, active participation of numerous interest groups, and pressure from the Labor Department for rapid action, it is not surprising that CETA decison making during this period became disorderly. Many local governments circumvented normal procedures for soliciting proposals and letting contracts to fulfill the mandate for rapid hiring. Other jurisdictions became entangled in cumbersome processes that created substantial delays and prodigious volumes of paperwork. Portland, Oregon's, experience represents an extreme example of what went on in the "PSE bazaar":

> After proposals were submitted and screened for legal and technical compliance, they were reviewed and ranked by prime sponsor staff who considered whether they met the definition of "projects," had lasting value, were labor intensive, or had transferable skills. Next, a CETA advisory council subcommittee rated projects in terms of whether they were needed by residents of the community. Finally, city council members rated proposals on whether they were high on the city's list of unmet needs....
>
> Following all the reviews, staff averaged the ratings and—in compliance with local governmental procedures—prepared an ordinance to be adopted by the Portland City Council. While this process assured the applicant agencies an adequate and fair review, it also created an enormous paper flow throughout the entire city. The local PSE manager said it took three to four weeks to consolidate approved projects into contracts for ordinance approval. One of these ordinances included 70 contracts, each of some 20 pages in length. After obtaining signatures from each of three city officials, 20 copies of each of the contracts had to be filed with the auditor's office on Fridays preceding the city council meetings on the following Wednesday. Thus to meet the demands of local regulations, a pickup truck loaded with some 28,000 sheets of paper was at one point dispatched to the auditor's office carrying boxes full of contracts for use in a single council meeting.[16]

The principal criteria for selecting PSE projects became the ease and speed with which they could be established. Other criteria, such as the community's public service needs or the fit between the proposed projects and the needs of the unemployed individuals who might staff them, were given little attention. The Labor Department's assurance that prime sponsors could later correct mistakes made in their initial selections may have encouraged local officials to adopt a casual, sloppy, or even cavalier attitude towards the process. In the words of one CETA administrator, "Title VI [PSE] simply defied us to spend the money responsibly." [17]

The local CETA environment was ripe for abuse and mismanagement. Astute local officials and federal overseers were concerned about the haphazard fashion with which PSE projects were solicited and funded. However, with Congress and the Labor Department pressing for immediate results, local officials felt justified in pushing ahead, despite their reservations. In less than two years, their lack of caution would come back to haunt them.

Frantic Changes, Forgotten Reform

Comprehensive employment and training reforms were buried under the PSE expansion and a mountain of narrow purpose employment and training programs. The policies, resources, and personnel of the CETA system were so unstable and uncertain throughout this period that reforming delivery systems was next to impossible. CETA administrators were fully taxed just coping with the turmoil of their policy environment.

Faced with a large, hastily assembled, and uncoordinated array of unemployment remedies, local administrators were forced to concentrate on institutional survival. Prime sponsor organizations became brokers—allocating funds to diverse organizations, carrying out oversight functions, and collecting basic information—instead of comprehensive planners. Prime sponsors had been transformed into "little Departments of Labor"; important program decisions were either determined in Washington or pushed farther down the line to community organizations and contractors.

The combination of urgent demands for action and a volatile policy environment drained local staff morale. With each new responsibility, local administrators lowered their expectations and resigned themselves to surviving amidst the chaos. Overlooked was the law's original emphasis on helping the structurally unemployed become more competitive in the labor market. The goal of improving the skills and job opportunities of disadvantaged people was overwhelmed by the urge to hire the unemployed on the PSE rolls. CETA evolved into a large-scale income maintenance program, with some overtones of training. Long-term impacts on people's earnings and opportunities for stable private sector employment had been sacrificed for the short-term gains brought by temporary jobs in state and local governments.

The employment and training programs that suffered the most were those designed to foster experimentation. The Youth Employment Demonstration Projects Act, for example, was supposed to test innovative designs. Policy makers hoped to discover better methods for serving disadvantaged youth. These expectations proved totally unrealistic; it was not feasible to develop new ideas and approaches when the staffs' energies were sapped by mounting PSE job projects.

Our description aptly characterizes most jurisdictions, but the behavior of those at the extremes had more influence on policy making. On the positive side were some prime sponsors, consisting of no more than 10 percent of the total, who were fully capable of handling additional money and the experimental programs. In these communities we observed the commendable practices that the Labor Department's leadership and policy analysts were looking for—comprehensive planning, integrated delivery systems, effective training strategies, careful monitoring, and systematic evaluation.[18] When members of Congress and others wished to justify new employment and training measures or greater appropriations, exemplary communities were portrayed as representative of the entire system.

On the negative side, also no more than 10 percent of the total, were jurisdictions that could not cope with additional money and responsibilities. In these communites, abuse, mismanagement, and even criminal conduct were not uncommon. All that is reprehensible about wasteful public spending programs was visible to the casual observer and often castigated by the General Accounting Office, outside evaluators, the Labor Department and, of course, the media.

Many policy makers changed their opinion of CETA during this period. When the PSE expansion began, most of the relevant policy makers regarded the competent prime sponsor as the norm or had no opinion. After the PSE expansion and its alleged debacle, many of CETA's former supporters had revised their positive view and regarded CETA programs as mismanaged and corrupt. Images of the extremes obscured reality and produced policies founded on false premises.

Creating Jobs for the Unemployed

In May 1977 Congress appropriated more than $8 billion for temporary jobs measures through October 1978. State and local administrators were expected to employ 725,000 workers by March 1978. With current enrollments at just under 300,000, they had less than nine months to implement the new "project" concept and to hire 425,000 people. The lion's share of the appropriation, nearly $7 billion, was slated for short-term projects run by governments, schools, and community groups. The balance of the new money was reserved for the older components of PSE, Title II, and the sustainment portion of Title VI. Because these PSE programs had fairly loose entrance requirements and flexible guidelines, hiring people for those jobs was relatively easy.[19] More problematic was creating and filling 340,000 project jobs by the deadline.

After overcoming several false starts, the hiring goal was achieved. By September 1977, PSE enrollment had grown from 300,000 to 553,000. By March 1978 more than 739,000 people were working in federally funded jobs.[20] On one level, the PSE expansion was a smashing success. Billions of dollars were quickly injected into the ailing economy and hundreds of thousands of people were rescued from dependence on unemployment insurance and public assistance. Yet, there were serious costs associated with the single-minded pursuit of the rapid hiring objective. Other missions, such as serving community needs and enhancing the long-term employment prospects of participants, received considerably less attention than they deserved. Quality and effectiveness were abandoned in favor of high enrollments. Many state and local administrators recognized this trade-off at the time but were swept along by a national momentum they felt powerless to resist.

Public Service Employment Projects

The PSE project concept encompassed a potpourri of public service activities during 1977 and 1978. The law specified that projects should serve community needs, employ more than three people, be hosted by a public or private nonprofit agency, and last no longer than 12 months. An overview of PSE projects is presented by Table 4-1.[21] Within local government units, public works, parks and recreation, and social services projects were most common. Typical activities included cleaning up and refurbishing parks, public buildings, and public housing projects. There were unusual projects, too. Albany, N.Y., for example, established a Bureau of Historic Services that conducted archeological investigations in abandoned buildings and vacant city lots. Outside government, in the private nonprofit sector, social service projects were dominant. Counseling services, shelters for the homeless and indigent, and every kind of social service imaginable all were staffed with federally funded workers.

Almost as soon as the PSE projects got underway, critics assailed the program for supporting exotic and useless public spending. Most PSE workers engaged in normal, rather mundane public services, like fixing potholes, but concern over "waste and abuse" was fed by citing projects that subsidized poets and painters or dealt with unsavory social problems such as heroin addiction. The desire for quick results, particularly in communities where dollars were more abundant than good proposals, accounts for many of the questionable projects that provided the raw material for sensationalized accounts of abuse.

Consider the project solicitation and funding process we observed in Pittsburgh. The city mailed announcements of the PSE project fund to

Table 4-1 Title VI Project Employment, by Function and Type of Sponsor, 1977

Function	Total	Type of Project Sponsor Government Agency	Nonprofit Organizations
All functions	100%	100%	100%
Education	18	19	13
Social services	18	8	40
Health and hospitals	5	3	8
Parks and recreation	17	21	9
Creative arts	2	*	7
Public works	23	33	3
Housing	7	4	15
Law enforcement	4	5	2
General administration	2	3	*
Other	3	2	3
Total employment	(326,000)	(227,000)	(99,000)

* Less than 0.5 percent.

Source: Computed from data supplied by the Bureau of Labor Statistics and the Employment and Training Administration, U.S. Department of Labor, as reported by William Mirengoff and Associates, *CETA: An Assessment of Public Service Employment Programs* (Washington, D.C.: National Academy of Sciences, 1980), 147. Reprinted with permission. These are projections of U.S. totals based on a sample of project data summaries collected in the 28 communities covered by this study.

250 community organizations, calling for "practically any kind of activity that leads to human betterment and community improvement." Seventy-five organizations, ranging from the YMCA and the Carnegie Library to the Theatre Express and the Group for Recycling in Pennsylvania, submitted community service proposals of 1 to 100 pages. Each group had one thing in common, however; their proposals received funding. If an organization said it was responding to an "unmet community need," then so be it, and an unmet need was born! As in many communities, Pittsburgh's officials interpreted the Labor Department's message to mean that it was more important to spend money than to spend it wisely. Lamenting the dilemmas posed by the PSE expansion, an official from Illinois remarked: "If we weren't afraid of the possible negative reflections on our program and the impact it might have on our future access to resources ... we might seriously consider sending some of it back." [22]

Although examples of abuse and poor judgment abounded, other projects that *seemed* exotic or wasteful when taken out of context turned out to be appropriate and useful when carefully examined in their home environment. A visit during the spring of 1978 to St. Lawrence County, N.Y., provided an excellent illustration of this phenomenon. In 1978 and 1979 the county spent more than one million federal dollars employing 120 people to cut and trim trees on state forest land. In many areas of the country this project would be regarded as a highly suspect use of public funds because the public benefits and career opportunities offered by tree trimming are not altogether obvious. But St. Lawrence County is not typical of the rest of the country. The management of state-owned forests is important to everyone who lives in this large, poor, rural county in northern New York. The forests generate income from wood harvesting and from tourists who take advantage of their abundant recreational resources. The PSE workers contributed to forest management by trimming and pruning more than 5,000 acres of woodlands. The wood was sold to low-income people at reduced prices to heat their homes. Furthermore, the project's workforce obtained valuable training and experience in a trade that employs many county residents.

Ultimately, judgments about the worth of public services are highly subjective and reflect one's values about the proper responsibilities of individuals and governments in society. The descriptions of "successful" PSE projects, pages 108 and 109, were culled from *CETA Works,* a book prepared by the National Association of Counties. Readers can form their own judgments about the worthiness of these projects. Whatever you conclude, however, this selection amply demonstrates the array of public services crowded under the PSE umbrella during 1977 and 1978.

Job Creation or Substitution?

The Emergency Jobs Programs Extension Act of 1976 attempted to address the criticisms hurled at previous federal jobs measures. Some detractors had asserted that these programs were merely subsidies for city and county government departments because a large number of the jobs would have existed without federal aid. In other words, policy makers worried that federal money might be substituting for state and local government revenues. Because a fundamental purpose of public jobs programs is to create *new* jobs, such shuffling of revenue sources would, if proven true, undermine PSE's unemployment reducing impact.

Several features of the project PSE approach were intended as obstacles to substitution. The 12-month time limit on jobs was supposed to promote turnover and make it more difficult for government managers to balance their budgets with a predictable supply of federally funded employees. Framers of the legislation also hoped that targeting service on the long-term unemployed and welfare recipients would reduce PSE's appeal to officials who might otherwise steer federal jobs into local government departments. By urging greater participation from community organizations, which were generally considered less prone to substitution, it was hoped that a larger proportion of the PSE jobs would truly add to the local economy.

To appreciate fully the potential effect of substitution practices on the utility of job creation strategies, it helps to have a clear picture of the program's potential for *direct unemployment reduction*.[23] Even if one assumes that every job funded under PSE was a new job—a substitution rate of zero—it is clear that PSE was no more than a partial cure for the unemployment problem. The data in Table 4-2 show that the 739,000 PSE workers enrolled in March 1978 represented 12 percent of the unemployed population and thus potentially could reduce unemployment by three-quarters of one percent. But a substitution rate of zero is unrealistic, as discussed below.[24] Therefore the actual direct unemployment reducing effect is somewhat smaller than shown in Table 4-2. However large public jobs programs might have seemed in the abstract, they were no panacea for the unemployment problem.

Public service jobs programs are expensive. At roughly $10,000 per worker, 100,000 thousand jobs cost $1 billion. Consequently, the rate of substitution, or the extent to which new employment is reduced, became a central policy issue. Unfortunately, it is difficult to make accurate determinations of the extent of substitution in PSE programs. Policy analysts are forced to guess what governments and other employing agencies would have done without PSE money. Many incidents of substitution go undetected. Extensive inquiries into government finances are required to determine whether local revenues have been diverted or intentionally not increased because of the availability of federal PSE monies. Nevertheless, policy makers wanted reliable estimates so that they could gauge the impact of job creation programs.

The various techniques for estimating substitution used by government officials and policy analysts yielded predictably different findings. Many economists applied "econometric models" that forecast levels of government employment without public service employment funds. Of course, these hypothetical models were based on many assumptions, including the belief that the need for government services would remain relatively constant. Employment estimates generated by the models were then compared with the actual level of employment. If the actual number of government workers did not exceed the projected level by the number of PSE positions, then substitution had occurred, according to these analysts. Predictive models consistently estimated that after two years of operation 90 to 100 percent of the jobs funded by PSE programs would have been funded from local revenue sources had PSE funds not been available.[25]

Critics of the modeling approach pointed out that the predictions rested on an overly simplistic view of how government employment

Energy Conservation Project, North Plainfield, N.J.

The project was conducted by a staff of CETA enrollees trained by the New Jersey departments of energy and education. They visited homes and small businesses, providing advice on insulation, storm windows, retrofitting doors and windows, and caulking window frames, door frames, wall cracks, vents, utility outlets, and foundation cracks. The project also surveyed churches, public buildings, and homes to assess potential energy savings and conducted periodic weatherization workshops for homes and businesses.

Hupa Oral History Project, Humboldt County, Calif.

The 12-square-mile Hupa Indian Reservation located in Humboldt County is the state's largest Indian reservation. Of the tribe's 2,000 members, the 900 who live on the reservation include many elderly men and women who are the primary resources for the history and culture of the Hupa tribe. Traditionally, the history of the tribe has been passed down orally from one generation to the next, but in recent years, tribal leaders became concerned that, with the death of elderly members, the Hupa history and culture would be lost. To avoid this, tribal members developed a CETA project to write down and tape record the history of the Hupa tribe while those who remember important events are still alive.

Child Poison Prevention, Monroe County, N.Y.

The Monroe County Poison Prevention Project involved federal, state, and county governments, and more than 60 local organizations, in an effort to heighten public awareness of the potential toxicity of many household products and to motivate change in the treatment of these products in the home and marketplace. To change unsafe practices with regard to poisonous products, CETA workers conducted four programs: seminars for groups and organizations having contact with families with young children; the development and introduction of a course on poison prevention for children in the fourth, fifth, and sixth grades; seminars for retailers in three of the area's largest supermarkets; and a five-part series on the use of toxic household products that was published in seven area newspapers.

Vets of Oregon Carpentry Project, Portland, Ore.

The Veterans' Carpentry Project was initiated by a group of Vietnam-era veterans in cooperation with four local agencies and CETA.

. . . Public Service Employment Projects

The program enabled 19 Vietnam-era veterans to receive training as union carpenters while three condemned houses were renovated and put back on the market. All of the trainees have since obtained jobs. Five no longer needed unemployment benefits, three no longer receive AFDC (Aid to Families with Dependent Children), and two have earned high school diplomas.

Resocialization of Psychologically Isolated Older Adults, Montgomery County, Md.

The RPIOA program sought to identify elderly residents who had sustained physically or emotionally impairing traumas (loss of spouse or physical faculties, recovery from a serious illness) and had withdrawn within themselves. The program's purpose was to reacquaint them with normal life. CETA employees were assigned a group of such individuals and took them out for shopping trips, social activities, medical treatment, and social service. They encouraged their clients to read the newspaper and develop other stimulating activities. The staff also provided socialization in the clients' homes and introduced them to neighbors and other isolated persons. The CETA aides formed a quasi-social relationship and acted as a substitute friend or relative until clients were able to maneuver in society and effectively socialize on their own.

Delinquent Tax Review, Vanderburgh County, Ind.

The Vanderburgh County tax assessor's office had a 10-year-old file of individuals and businesses owing an estimated $3 million in past due property taxes and penalties. Four CETA participants were employed to review 30,000 file cards and compile a list to recover a portion of the tax money. After the list was compiled, the four CETA "sleuths"—nicknamed by the local paper—tracked the tax evaders by phone and letter. At the close of the program the CETA participants had been responsible for the collection of more than $60,000. The county is expecting the overall figure to reach $1 million in collected past due taxes as a direct result of the CETA Title VI Special Project. The overall cost of the project to the county was $12,159, thus a profit of more than $47,000 was realized, with more expected in the future.

Source: Joan Amico and Stephen Boochever, eds., *CETA Works* (Washington, D.C.: National Association of Counties, 1979), 6, 38, 44, 89-90, 101, 119. Reprinted with permission.

Table 4-2 CETA PSE Enrollments and Unemployment Statistics

Date	Number of PSE Enrollees[a]	Number Unemployed	Unemployment Rate, percent	PSE Enrollees as Percentage of Unemployed	Percentage Reduction in Unemployment Attributable to PSE
March 1976	369,000	6,944,000	7.6	5.3	.40
September 1977	553,000	6,770,000	6.8	8.2	.55
March 1978	739,000	6,148,000	6.2	12.0	.75

[a] These figures include public service employees funded under all CETA programs.

Source: Computed from data supplied by the Bureau of Labor Statistics and Employment and Training Administration, U.S. Department of Labor, as reported by William Mirengoff and Associates, *CETA: An Assessment of Public Service Employment Programs* (Washington, D.C.: National Academy of Sciences, 1980), 40-41. Reprinted with permission.

changes over time, namely, that it grows in a linear fashion. They also argued that small, but plausible, alterations in the relationships between some variables in the models would produce dramatically different conclusions.[26]

As the substitution controversy raged in Congress, the National Commission for Manpower Policy (now the National Commission for Employment Policy) asked Richard Nathan and his colleagues at the Brookings Institution to study the problem.[27] Because the Brookings study was undertaken during 1977 and 1978 for the explicit purpose of estimating substitution and because its findings were widely circulated among policy makers, we will examine it closely. The Brookings methodology departed from the modeling approaches already described. Instead, a group of experienced analysts visited a sample of communities and, through interviews and a review of documents, attempted to determine the extent to which substitution had occurred. More than 60,000 PSE jobs in 42 cities and counties were classified into job creation or substitution categories.[28] The research, summarized in Table 4-3, estimated that only 15 percent of the jobs would have been paid for out of state, local, or other revenue sources, a finding that was quite significant in policy terms because it was considerably lower than other studies found.

The data in Table 4-3 demonstrate two important points about substitution in PSE. First, the shift to the project design had its intended effect. Substitution rates were uniformly lower in the project portion of PSE. Second, substitution varied considerably by type of employing agency. City and county governments were much more prone to this type of behavior than private nonprofit organizations. Thus project PSE reduced substitution not only because that approach was less amenable to substitution, but also because prime sponsors shifted resources away from government departments and toward private nonprofit agencies.

The Brookings study attracted some criticism, and, not surprisingly, it did not silence congressional skeptics. Most controversial was the classification of "program maintenance" jobs, a label applied in cases where PSE workers staffed existing government services that otherwise would have been curtailed. Brookings's first round of research, during the summer of 1977, found that nearly a third of the sustainment PSE jobs were lumped under the program maintenance heading.[29] This implied that without PSE there would have been very substantial cutbacks in municipal workforces, particularly in large, fiscally distressed cities. But critics argued that it was difficult to know how local governments would have treated revenue shortfalls that threatened vital public services and doubted that large-scale layoffs would have materialized.

Despite the study's detractors, many members of Congress and other policy makers concluded that the new brand of temporary job creation

Table 4-3 Substitution Estimates for Public Service Employment Programs by Type of Employing Agency, December 1977, in percentages

PSE Component	Prime Sponsor Governments		Other Public Agencies		Private-Nonprofit Agencies		All Employing Agencies	
	Substitution Estimate	Percent of all jobs	Substitution Estimate	Percent of all jobs	Substitution Estimate	Percent of all jobs	Overall Substitution Estimate	Percent of all jobs
Sustainment jobs (N=33,413)	23	65	13	25	9	10	19	100
Project jobs (N=28,043)	18	35	11	22	3	43	10	100
All jobs (N=61,456)	22	52	11	23	4	25	15	100

Source: Assembled from Richard Nathan and Associates, *Monitoring the Public Service Employment Program.* National Commission for Manpower Policy, Special Report no. 32, March 1979, 16, 17, 24, and 39.

significantly reduced substitution. They felt confident that most of the jobs sponsored by the federal government were indeed net additions to the workforce and that the legislative reforms had made a difference. Policy gains achieved under project PSE would encourage more policy innovation during CETA's 1978 reauthorization debate.

Who Benefited from the Great PSE Expansion?

In less than two years, from fiscal year 1976 to fiscal year 1978, CETA enrollments jumped to more than 3.3 million, an increase of nearly 800,000. While the public service employment programs accounted for the largest share of the increase, other national programs also grew significantly. Programs authorized by Youth Employment Demonstration Projects Act of 1977 (YEDPA) served nearly a quarter of a million people in 1978, and special assistance also was provided to more than 100,000 Indians, migrant and seasonal workers, and veterans.[30]

One of the most important changes that occurred during this period of employment and training policy was the imposition of stricter eligibility standards on a portion of PSE programs. The Emergency Jobs Programs Extension Act of 1976 established new guidelines for participants hired under the project component of Title VI and for half of the replacement positions under the sustainment portion of this title. Concerned about the apparent lack of attention given to the "truly needy," defined as the long-term unemployed and low-income persons, Congress hoped that the new standards would alter the composition of PSE clientele. The ground rules for the other principal components of CETA, Titles I and II, were unchanged.

The figures presented in Table 4-4 indicate substantial change in the profile of clients served in all three of CETA's major titles during the second season. Most dramatic is the near doubling of the percentage of economically disadvantaged people holding Title VI PSE jobs between 1976 and 1978, a level of service higher than in the training programs under Title I. Because Title VI PSE enrolled nearly five times as many people as Title II PSE during FY 1978, the "average" PSE client was just as likely to be drawn from the ranks of the poor as the average Title I client.

Changes in the characteristics of Title I training program enrollees reflect the impact of transfering youth into the YEDPA programs that became operational in 1977. The establishment of special youth programs accounts for the differences not only in age and education but also in race because youth programs traditionally serve a high percentage of minorities.

At first glance it would appear that the new national standards targeting a large portion of Title VI PSE on the least advantaged were stunningly successful. Before leaping to this conclusion, a few caveats

Table 4-4 CETA Participant Characteristics, Fiscal Years 1976, 1978

| Characteristics | Training Programs | | Public Service Employment | | | |
| | Title I | | Title II | | Title VI | |
	FY 76[a]	FY 78	FY 76[a]	FY 78	FY 76[a]	FY 78
Females	46%	51%	36%	45%	35%	38%
Nonwhites[b]	45	40	39	28	32	34
Less than 22 years old	57	49	22	21	22	21
12 or more years of education	45	52	74	80	74	72
Economically disadvantaged[c]	76	79	47	62	44	81
AFDC recipient	15	16	6	8	6	12

[a] Four quarters.

[b] Does not include Hispanics enrolled in the United States but does include Puerto Ricans enrolled in Puerto Rico, where participants were not classified by race.

[c] The definition of economically disadvantaged used by CETA changed in October 1977 to include persons with incomes between OMB's poverty level and 70 percent of the Bureau of Labor Statistic's lower living standard.

Sources: *Employment and Training Report of the President* (Washington, D.C.: GPO, 1977), 267; *Employment and Training Report of the President* (Washington, D.C.: GPO, 1979), 369.

should be noted. First, and probably most important, the reported income statistics for PSE workers were subject to considerable error, and the enrollment of ineligible people was widespread. Procedures for verifying an individual's income prior to his or her placement into a PSE job were particularly lax during the rush to hire workers. In effect, the Labor Department's policies encouraged careless behavior because prime sponsors were allowed to correct errors up to 60 days after enrollment and were indemnified against liability provided that the state employment service was the referring agency. When the programs were audited, the Labor Department found an ineligible rate of 12 percent among new PSE enrollees, and an independent research contractor, Westat, Inc., came up with a 25 percent error rate.

Second, the change in the definition of "economically disadvantaged" that occurred between 1976 and 1978 diminishes the magnitude of change in service to low-income people. The new definition broadened the category, thus making more people eligible for the program and inflating the difference between the two time periods.

Finally, the age and educational level of the average Title VI client changed very little, a clue that the huge jump in the enrollment of "economically disadvantaged" people may not have signified major changes in the backgrounds of PSE jobholders. Even though the percentage of poor people rose, employing agencies "creamed-off" the best available applicants from low-income groups. Taking all these factors into account, the apparent rise in the enrollment of economically disadvantaged people was probably exaggerated by about half.[31]

The differences among groups participating in the three CETA programs are noteworthy. Title II PSE workers were more likely to be white, to have more formal education, and less likely to be poor than people working in Title VI PSE jobs. By all accounts, Title II funds paid for the most highly prized PSE jobs at this time. People hired under Title II were more likely to work for state or local government agencies, and there were no limits on the duration of their employment, as there were under project PSE. Setting aside the category of economically disadvantaged, the comparison of Title I and PSE clients reveals a pattern similar to that observed from 1974 to 1976. Minorities, women, youth, the poorly educated, and welfare recipients were much more likely to be enrolled in training programs than to be employed in PSE jobs.

The comparison of participants and eligibles shown in Table 4-5 reveals both continuing inequalities and some targeting successes. The inequities are most evident in PSE (especially project PSE) where women, welfare recipients, the poor, and the poorly educated received substantially fewer jobs than their numbers in the eligible population would dictate. This was true despite the increased enrollment of low-income people. The same pattern held for sustainment PSE, although the gap between participants and eligibles was substantially smaller in this portion of CETA PSE.[32] In the Title I training programs, clients typically associated with greatest need—youth, minorities, school dropouts, the poor—were served at a higher rate than they were represented in the eligible population. Except for the shortfall in terms of service to women, Title I continued to be targeted effectively on needy individuals. In contrast, public service jobs were being filled by individuals who, on the average, appeared less needy than the eligible population.

The Significance of CETA Benefit Patterns

What do CETA's enrollment patterns tell us about policy making and implementation? The sharp *increases* in jobs for low-income people experienced during 1977 and 1978 demonstrate that Congress can affect benefit distribution through legislation. The stricter and less ambiguous entrance standards incorporated into the Emergency Jobs Programs Extension Act strongly influenced the behavior of state and local administrators and, ultimately, the composition of the PSE workforce. The

Table 4-5   Characteristics of CETA Participants Compared with the Eligible Population, Fiscal Year 1977

| Characteristics | Training Programs | | Public Service Employment | | | |
| | Title I | | Project | | Sustainment[a] | |
	Partici-pants	Eligibles	Partici-pants	Eligibles	Partici-pants	Eligibles
Females	48%	55%	33%	51%	38%	47%
Nonwhites[b]	45	25	41	34	34	30
Less than 22 years old	51	22	20	20	21	25
12 or more years of education	53	61	70	45	79	60
Economically disadvantaged	64	38	73	93	52	55
AFDC recipients	16	15	15	48	6	12

[a] This includes new enrollees in the sustainment portion of Title VI and all new Title II enrollees. One half of the new enrollees in Title VI were subject to the new and stricter eligibility requirement that applied to all project participants.

[b] Includes Hispanics.

Sources: Partipant data were taken from the *Continuous Longitudinal Manpower Survey*, Westat, Inc., and describe new enrollees in CETA programs during FY 1977. They are, therefore, not the same as the cumulative participant characteristic data reported by the Department of Labor that appear in other tables. The eligible populations are based on *The Current Population Survey*, Bureau of Census data. The figures for Title I participants and eligibles appear in "Target Groups," William Barnes, in *CETA: An Analysis of the Issues* (1978), 79. The figures on PSE participants and project eligibles appear in William Mirengoff and Associates, *CETA: An Assessment of Public Service Employment Programs* (1980), 105, 196. The figures on sustainment eligibles appear in *CETA: Accomplishments, Problems, Solutions*, William Mirengoff and Associates (1982), 314-315. Both Mirengoff works published by the W. E. Upjohn Institute for Employment Research. Reprinted with permission.

experience also illustrates the dynamic nature of the policy process because the images formed during CETA's first phase provoked policy makers to impose the new eligibility standards on a portion of PSE.

PSE's rapid expansion and the greater service to low-income people represent successful "macro-implementation," to borrow Paul Berman's terminology.[33] Central national objectives were, for the most part, carried out faithfully by local implementers. The success was not, however, unqualified. Conflicting signals in the law and from Washington continued to be a problem. Consider, for example, the fact that veterans, women, and welfare recipients all received some attention in national policy directives. Policies urging more jobs for women and welfare recipients never were enforced seriously. In contrast, prime sponsors were told that veterans should receive 35 percent of the PSE project jobs. Veterans eventually obtained 30 percent of the jobs, but actions taken to meet the quotas undermined efforts to hire more women and welfare recipients. Rates of service to women and welfare recipients increased during the 1977-1978 period, but not nearly as much as they would have under different national policy guidelines.

Some prime sponsor directors and staff exhibited hostile attitudes toward the new eligibility criteria. They simply did not believe that Congress or the Labor Department should insist on narrow definitions of need. For instance, we encountered resistance to the low-income standards during a visit to a southern New Jersey county in 1977. Noting that the county's quarterly reports listed all of the enrollees as "economically disadvantaged," we questioned the staff to determine whether this was a true representation. The director settled our doubts when he said: "All the clients are disadvantaged. These are disadvantaged times."

Even more fundamental was the conflict between the desire to hire people quickly to get worthwhile projects underway and the desire to hire the low-income and long-term unemployed. Labor Department officials clearly favored compliance with the numbers of enrollees and amount of expenditures over the targeting objectives. The overriding importance attached to building up the PSE workforce meant that most communities were unable or unwilling to tailor jobs carefully to fit the skills of the less advantaged segment of the eligible population. The staff member in Albany, N.Y., who was responsible for implementing PSE described his agency's dilemma:

> We felt there was a choice between the goals in the PSE project package. On the one hand, you could take a people-oriented approach and build the projects around them. Or you could take an agency-oriented approach and build the people into the agency. We saw a conflict between the two.[34]

Albany opted for a "people" approach, but many prime sponsors were forced into or preferred an "agency" orientation. In some ways this result was preordained by the law's emphasis on useful community projects. Because people with more skills could handle more challenging tasks, they were favored in the hiring decisions. Agencies responsible for carrying out projects were naturally inclined to seek out and hire the best qualified applicants.

The mismatch between Title VI project jobs approved by prime sponsors and the eligible population is obvious in the case of welfare recipients. Blue-collar positions—both skilled and unskilled—accounted for about half of the project jobs. Few women were hired in these positions, and only about 10 percent of the jobs went to people on welfare. But welfare recipients comprised nearly half the eligible population, and 73 percent of the welfare population was female. Clearly, project selection decisions were often insensitive to the needs and abilities of the target population.[35] In short, the stricter eligibility standards were only partially successful because the law contained other goals that pushed prime sponsors in opposite directions.

Despite a more aggressive federal posture, state and local officials exerted the principal influence over hiring decisions. At PSE's peak enrollment levels, there were still more than 10 people eligible for every job, so prime sponsor staffs and employing agencies retained great latitude over who would actually benefit. The hiring procedures typically utilized by local administrators allowed employing agencies to demand skills and educational accomplishments that were relatively uncommon among the eligible population and then gave agency officials the freedom to choose participants from a large number of referrals. Therefore, the hiring process systematically discouraged the hiring of the most disadvantaged, yet program implementers rarely made any attempt to correct the biases present in local PSE systems. Micro-implementation was not nearly as successful as macro-implementation.

Conclusions

During CETA's second season, national policy makers transformed an effort at modest policy reform into an enormous program with clear, but conflicting objectives. The notion of "speculative augmentation," developed by Charles Jones in his study of air pollution policy, characterized the CETA experience during this period.[36] Alarmed by record levels of unemployment and wishing to placate traditional constituencies, a Democratic president and a predominantly Democratic Congress enacted ambitious initiatives. With large coalitions and sufficient institutional power, national policy makers stepped well beyond incremental adjustments, appropriating vast sums for temporary jobs and a panoply of experimental programs for the jobless. Policy makers in Washington speculated that the CETA system could effectively carry out its augmented responsibilities; they didn't examine carefully the potential consequences if their assumptions proved to be wrong. Federal, state, and local administrators were required to implement beyond their capability. Signs of stress and strain were soon evident.

During this episode of policy implementation, politics triumphed over management. To fulfill the political demand for economic recovery, CETA's administrators made a herculean effort to get people hired and spend CETA funds as quickly as possible. But while federal, state, and local officials deserve credit for this substantial achievement, other important policy objectives were foolishly ignored. Comprehensive and careful planning, program innovation and reform, service to the least advantaged, and prudent management practices were compromised or given inadequate attention. Subsequently, CETA received a failing grade from many politicians.

Political evaluations were not, and never are, objective. Symbols, images, and biases crowd out facts and balanced judgments. The inevitable errors and abuse created when a program expands too rapidly in an uncertain policy environment supplied plenty of fuel for the fires of CETA's critics. CETA's image and the reputation of temporary jobs programs were devastated, perhaps permanently, by allegations of widespread corruption and mismanagement. Politicians in Washington joined the chorus of voices condemning CETA and calling for aggressive federal oversight and drastic legislative revisions.

Stepped-up federal enforcement tactics did not silence CETA's foes, but they did succeed in eroding the program's political support even further. Elected officials discovered that complicated regulations and hostile federal officials made CETA programs less appealing. The flexibility and discretion prized by local officials during CETA's early years were fast disappearing. More important, as elected officials became more skeptical about CETA, their political support became less vigorous. Suddenly, federal jobs programs were under attack from various quarters, and few politicians could be counted among the defenders.

The public jobs expansion episode illustrates a paradox of unemployment policy. When the programs are successful, they become expendable. By 1978 the nation's unemployment rate had fallen below 6 percent for the first time since 1974. Although it is impossible to sort out CETA's contribution in a complex economic system, the jobs program certainly made some dent in the unemployment problem. The economic stimulus sought by policy makers had been delivered by the CETA system.

However successful CETA might have been, there may be nothing more politically unpopular and vulnerable than a large, government-funded jobs program operating in the midst of relatively low unemployment. With the perceived need for federal intervention evaporating, the political vultures gathered round CETA. No matter that emergency jobs measures had been enacted in response to alarmingly high unemployment and implemented under adverse conditions. Political memories are short and national priorities change swiftly. In 1978, when CETA faced the court of policy makers, what mattered most was the perception that public funds had been wasted on CETA-funded employment projects. What was once a much needed economic stimulus for a troubled economy was now regarded as a shameful waste of the taxpayers' money.

Notes

1. *Congressional Quarterly Almanac, 1977,* vol. 33 (Washington, D.C.: Congressional Quarterly, 1978), 99.
2. *Congressional Quarterly Almanac, 1976,* vol. 32 (Washington, D.C.: Congressional Quarterly, 1977), 367.
3. The studies of substitution that supported these estimates include: Alan Fechter, *Public Employment Programs* (Washington, D.C.: American Enterprise Institute, 1975); National Planning Association, *An Evaluation of the Economic Impact Project of the Public Employment Program* (Washington, D.C.: National Planning Association, 1974); and George E. Johnson and James D. Tomola, "The Fiscal Substitution Effects of Alternative Approaches to Public Service Employment," *Journal of Human Resources* 12, no. 1 (Winter 1977): 3-26.
4. *Congressional Quarterly Almanac, 1976,* vol. 32, 368.
5. Ibid., 365.
6. Ibid., 366.
7. Ibid., 367.
8. Ibid., 370.
9. Carl E. Van Horn, *Policy Implementation in the Federal System* (Lexington, Mass.: D. C. Heath & Co., 1979), 4-5.
10. The regulations also stipulated that if a prime sponsor had an arrangement with the state employment service office or welfare office to verify the income of program participants, the prime sponsor then was not financially responsible for enrolling ineligibles. This was an obvious inducement for prime sponsors to reach such agreements. For a discussion, see William Mirengoff & Associates, *CETA: An Assessment of Public Service Employment Programs* (Washington, D.C.: National Academy of Sciences, 1980), 47-48.
11. MDC, *The Planning and Implementation of CETA Title VI PSE Expansion Projects Under the Economic Stimulus Program of 1977,* Report to the Employment and Training Administration, U.S. Department of Labor, June 1978, 4.
12. *Congressional Quarterly Weekly Report,* April 1, 1978, 805.
13. See, for example, Morris P. Fiorina, *Congress: Keystone of the Washington Establishment* (New Haven: Yale University Press, 1977), 71.
14. See, for example, Mirengoff, *CETA: An Assessment,* 54-55, 158-163.
15. Ibid., 55, 159.
16. MDC, *The Planning and Implementation of CETA Title VI,* 98.
17. Ibid., 61.
18. For a full discussion of some exemplary approaches to the planning and management of CETA programs during this era, see Randall B. Ripley et al., *Area-Wide Planning in CETA,* Employment and Training Administration, U.S. Department of Labor, R & D Monograph, no. 74, (Washington, D.C.: GPO, 1979), 69-104.
19. In the spring of 1977, when the expansion began, Title II enrollment was

roughly 65,000, and Title VI enrollment was approximately 235,000. This left about 25,000 Title VI sustainment slots to be filled—half of them by people meeting the new eligibility requirements—and 60,000 Title II positions open. Thus, about 85,000 of the 425,000 jobs to be created by March 1978 were in Title II or in the sustainment portion of Title VI.

20. The enrollment figures cited in this section were obtained from the Employment and Training Administration of the U.S. Department of Labor. See Mirengoff, *CETA: An Assessment,* 40-41.

21. The data in Table 4-1 were assembled by William Mirengoff & Associates in their study of public service employment. See *CETA: An Assessment,* 26. The Mirengoff study covered 28 sample prime sponsorships in 14 states. Other important PSE expansion studies were conducted by MDC, in which the authors participated and which investigated 30 sites in 24 states, and by the Brookings Institution, which visited 42 sites in 23 states. See MDC, *The Planning and Implementation of CETA Title VI* and Richard Nathan et al., *Public Service Employment: A Field Evaluation* (Washington, D.C.: The Brookings Institution, 1981).

22. MDC, *The Planning and Implementation of CETA Title VI,* 103.

23. By "direct unemployment reduction" we mean the immediate effect on overall unemployment brought about by hiring people in PSE programs. We are not considering indirect or mutiplier effects of PSE, which refer to the jobs created outside the program because of the economic stimulus PSE provides; any reductions in overall employment that might occur because private income is being taxed to pay for PSE programs; or the administrative jobs established with PSE funds.

24. See Nathan et al., *Public Service Employment.*

25. A variation on the econometric modeling approach developed by the National Planning Association relied on quasi-experimental design techniques. The association's study compared local governments with exceptionally large PSE programs—demonstration sites funded by the Emergency Employment Act of 1971—with other communities that had similar characteristics. The idea was to determine how much the enlarged PSE programs had increased overall government employment in the demonstration sites. The study concluded that 46 percent of the jobs funded by PSE would have been funded without the program. See National Planning Association, *An Evaluation of the Economic Impact Project.*

26. See, for example, Michael Borus and Daniel Hammermesh, "Study of the Net Employment Effects of Public Service Employment: Econometric Analysis," in *An Interim Report to the Congress of the National Commission for Manpower Policy: Job Creation Through Public Service Employment,* Commissioned Papers, vol. 3 (Washington, D.C.: National Commission for Manpower Policy, 1978), 89-149; Michael Wiseman, "Public Employment as Fiscal Policy," in *Brookings Papers on Economic Activity,* no. 1 (Washington, D.C.: The Brookings Institution, 1979), 67-106.

27. Richard Nathan and his Brookings associates report the results of two rounds of field research. The first round, conducted during July 1977, produced an estimated substitution rate of 18 percent. The second round estimate, based

on field work during December 1977, was 15 percent. See Nathan et al., *Public Service Employment,* 15.
28. The categories used by Nathan and his colleagues were defined as follows. See Ibid., 10.
    A. Job Creation
       1. *New programs and services.* Cases in which additional programs or services were provided with PSE funding that would not otherwise have been undertaken.
       2. *Special projects.* New, one-time projects lasting one year or less that were undertaken with PSE funds.
       3. *Program expansion.* Cases in which the level of service was raised or services were improved under existing programs by using PSE funding.
       4. *Program maintenance.* Cases in which PSE employees were used to maintain services that would have been curtailed without PSE funding.
    B. Job Displacement
       1. *Transfers.* Cases involving the transfer of existing state and local government positions to PSE funding.
       2. *Rehires.* Cases in which the government laid off regular employees and then rehired them with PSE funding.
       3. *Contract reduction.* Cases in which PSE participants were used to provide services or to work on projects that had been, or normally would be, contracted to an outside organization or private firm.
       4. *Potential hires.* Cases in which PSE participants were hired to fill positions that otherwise would have been funded with other revenue.
29. See Richard Nathan et al., *Monitoring the Public Service Employment Program, An Interim Report to the Congress of the National Commission for Manpower Policy: Job Creation Through Public Service Employment,* vol. 2 (Washington, D.C.: National Commission for Manpower Policy, 1978), 10. By the second round of the Brookings study, the program maintenance share of sustainment PSE jobs was down to 22 percent. See Nathan, et al., *Public Service Employment,* 13.
30. Enrollment data are from the *Employment and Training Report of the President* (Washington, D.C.: GPO, 1979), 38-47. They do not include the one million youngsters enrolled in the Summer Youth Employment Program each year between 1976 and 1978.
31. See Mirengoff, *CETA: An Assessment,* 94-96, 113-114, and 121-123.
32. The data on people eligible for sustainment PSE, presented in Table 4-5, differ from those displayed in Table 3-4, even though the standards of eligibility are the same. We used a different set of estimates here because the estimates used in Chapter 3 were based on 1975 data, and this new set comes from 1978 data. Population changes between 1975 and 1978 and some minor differences in methodology account for the gaps between the two sets of estimates. The computations with 1975 data estimated a smaller eligible population and larger percentages of women, economically disadvantaged, and welfare recipients than the estimates prepared with 1978 data.
33. Paul Berman, "The Study of Macro- and Micro-Implementation," *Public Policy* 26, no. 2 (Spring 1978): 157-184.

34. Interview with authors, Oct. 5, 1977.
35. See Mirengoff, *CETA: An Assessment,* 104-113, 132
36. Charles O. Jones, "Speculative Augmentation in Federal Air Pollution Policy-Making," *Journal of Politics* 36, no. 2 (May 1974): 438-464.

Implementation by Regulation 5

Until now our story has been about expanding programs with ever burgeoning funds and objectives. In less than three years, CETA's enrollments and expenditures nearly tripled as President Jimmy Carter and Congress established ambitious job creation measures for minority and low-income youths and adults. By 1978, however, a new political and economic climate clouded the fortunes of employment and training policy. The same Congress and president who had once praised CETA now turned an increasingly stern, miserly, and unforgiving face toward it. From that point on, CETA's story would be about the consequences of political failure.

The sprawling employment and training system faced a formidable obstacle in 1978—a reauthorization deadline. Unless Congress acted, CETA was destined for the junk heap of public policies. In 1977 Congress generously funded employment and training programs. Less than a year later, when allegations of widespread waste and abuse had destroyed CETA's reputation, Congress's mood turned ugly. As unemployment abated, inflation became Washington's greatest concern. Demands arose for conservative government spending strategies, and Carter promoted the elusive goal of balancing the federal budget.

Lawmakers reacted to this new environment by overhauling and cutting CETA. The reauthorization preserved the basic employment and training structure but imposed a plethora of rigid administrative rules, ostensibly to correct the abuse and mismanagement perceived by members of Congress and the public. Having lost faith in the value of local control, Congress decided that federal agencies should exercise strict oversight of local operations. Annual funding for employment and training programs peaked in 1979 and thereafter took a nose dive. In 1980 public service employment programs were cut by $3 billion.

Congress's highly prescriptive approach reflected its desire to govern not just the law's objectives but also its day-to-day administration. Having failed to obtain acceptable results with state and local elected officials in charge of most key decisions, Congress would attempt to steer implementation through regulations. Congress's outlook on the employment and training system had come nearly full circle in four years. CETA was heralded originally as a decentralized, flexible block grant that promoted local control and removed onerous federal interference. CETA's reauthorization rejected these principles in favor of a heavy federal hand.

Unfortunately, CETA's root problems were improperly diagnosed. Congress fixated on fraud, waste, and abuse but overlooked the critical cause of CETA's downfall: the White House and Congress had forced state and local administrators to spend too much money, too fast, on too many objectives. One CETA analyst remarked:

> ... Congress set unrealistically high expectations with regard to what was going to be accomplished and when it was going to be accomplished. ... [T]he Department of Labor ... didn't raise a finger and say, "What do you expect to accomplish when you are changing everything every year. We tried to implement an enormous program in record breaking time." [1]

In opting for new restrictions, Congress punished state and local administrators for following congressional mandates.

Ironically, the reforms instituted to rehabilitate employment and training programs generally made matters no better and in many ways made them worse. The revamped law accomplished its main objectives—rooting out waste and corruption, serving the poor, and nudging the system toward the private sector—but these achievements did not silence CETA's critics. Moreover, the new management approach created enemies among elected officials who had once been enthusiastic supporters. Finally, the deluge of procedures, rules, and reports demoralized professionals responsible for delivering services and distracted them from their central mission, helping people obtain jobs. In sum, Congress imposed unrealistic, unworkable, and politically unpopular objectives that contributed to CETA's eventual demise.

The Changing Political Context

Just as employment and training programs prospered from the Carter administration's economic stimulus package, so too did they suffer when the president's agenda changed. In 1977 Carter prescribed large-scale temporary jobs measures as an immediate cure for the economic recession. By 1978 new initiatives were absent from the administration's plans. Instead, the president recommended stable or even slightly reduced domestic expenditures, increased defense spending, and a balanced budget.

Forces at home and abroad altered the domestic policy agenda. The taking of American hostages at the U.S. Embassy in Iran and the Russian invasion of Afghanistan may seem remote from the politics of unemployment, but these events fostered greater defense outlays and helped scuttle plans for larger unemployment programs. Double-digit inflation convinced the president that tight monetary policy and lower government spending were necessary, albeit painful, remedies.

Constraining federal budget growth is no small task. A large portion of the budget—up to 75 percent or more—consists of so-called "uncontrollable expenditures," such as Social Security, Medicare, and veterans' and federal retirees' pensions. These programs are uncontrollable because they entitle eligible individuals to benefits and spending rises in lock step with the cost of living. Laws governing eligibility and benefits can be altered only if Congress is willing to take unpopular action and cut beneficiaries or benefits.

Despite Carter's desire to cut spending, he did not want to offend his political constituencies or abandon his policy objectives. He searched for a strategy that allowed large-scale unemployment programs while holding the line on the budget. The Carter administration proposed cutbacks in mandated cost-of-living increases for Social Security recipients and veterans, but Congress summarily dismissed these ideas.[2] With the option of pruning entitlement programs foreclosed, the administration looked to "controllable" budget items and proposed a freeze on the rate of growth. In 1979, after much political bloodletting, the administration succeeded in reducing federal aid to state and local governments for the first time in more than three decades.

In addition to budget-trimming measures, the president proposed that government should target its limited resources on distressed communities and disadvantaged individuals. For example, the Carter urban policy, unveiled in 1978, reflected the administration's desire to balance efficiency and equity. It contained little additional spending but refocused existing resources on the most hard pressed communities, urged public and private partnerships to solve urban ills, and called for greater coordination among the various elements of the federal establishment. In short, low-cost strategies for serving the "truly needy" were favored over large government spending measures.

Reauthorization Politics

Besides an unfavorable climate for costly domestic programs, the other factor controlling CETA's fate was its unpopularity. When the reauthorization debate began, a bipartisan group of legislators agreed that the perceived excesses of the past would have to be corrected. CETA's supporters were obliged to reshape the program so it could survive.

After prolonged and bitter debate, Congress fashioned a law that was noticeably different from the 1973 version (Table 5-1). Principal operating authority remained with state and local prime sponsors, but the law enlarged federal oversight, levied substantial penalties for misusing funds, imposed detailed restrictions on public service employment, reserved programs exclusively for the long-term unemployed poor, and mandated greater private sector participation. Congress's legislative intent was uncharacteristically clear.

From the outset of the reauthorization debate, it was apparent that CETA was scheduled for radical surgery. The administration's bill set the tone for subsequent deliberations: it reserved jobs and training services for the poor, reduced the number of temporary jobs, and set ceilings on wages. The president's bill also suggested a new strategy—every prime sponsor would appoint a private industry council to advise local administrators on how to prepare the unemployed for private sector jobs. Most of the administration's proposals found their way into the final package, but not before Congress vented its anger.

The principal obstacle to CETA's smooth reauthorization was the House of Representatives, where stories of corruption and abuse engendered great concern. The House Education and Labor Committee was compelled by this unfavorable climate to revise the president's bill. In the committee's version, the Labor Department was given wider authority to curb abuses via audits, investigations, and monitoring.[3] Even though committee members anticipated opposition on the floor of the House, they were not prepared for the buzzsaw that awaited their bill when it came up for consideration in August 1978.

Battered and bruised by several amendments, the bill was withdrawn by its principal sponsor, subcommittee chairman Augustus Hawkins, D-Calif., who complained: "Individual members [were] taking their feelings out on CETA and responding to their emotions." [4] Eventually the House adopted legislation incorporating more severe restrictions than those recommended by the president or the committee.

Reauthorization moved more easily through the Senate but not before more rewriting. The Senate strengthened Labor Department responsibility for preventing abuse and tightened eligibility standards further. Although CETA was roundly criticized in the Senate—Jesse Helms, R-N.C., called it "this massive CETA boondoggle"—no one, not even conservative Republicans, proposed funding cutbacks.[5] Opinions about CETA may have been negative, but Congress was not yet inclined to slash support for the jobless and state and local governments. Compromise between the House and Senate versions of the law was reached quickly, and the reauthorization bill cleared Congress in October 1978.

Table 5-1 Major Changes in CETA Resulting from the 1978
Reauthorization

Issue	Original CETA (1973-1978)	Reauthorized CETA (1978-1983)
Activities and target groups for existing programs	Title I: Training and work experience for the unemployed and economically disadvantaged.	Title IIB, C: Training and work experience programs for the economically disadvantaged.
	Title II: PSE for unemployed in areas with high unemployment.	Title IID: PSE for low-income, long-term unemployed and welfare recipients; money set aside for training programs; wages lowered; tenure limited to 18 months.
	Title IV: Job Corps	Title IV: Job Corps, summer youth, experimental youth programs.
	Title VI: PSE for the recently unemployed. Funds set aside for short-term projects for low-income, long-term unemployed in 1976.	Title VI: PSE for low-income, long-term unemployed and welfare recipients; money set aside for training programs; wages lowered; tenure limited to 18 months.
New programs		Title VII: Private Sector Initiative Program. Training and work experience programs for the economically disadvantaged designed by Private Industry Councils.
		Title VIII: Youth conservation projects.
New administrative provisions		Required establishment of independent monitoring units in each prime sponsorship.
		Added additional prohibitions against substituting federal funds for local funds.
		Added specific definitions of fraud and abuse and specified penalties.
		Made prime sponsorship liable for misuse of funds.
		Increased federal government oversight responsibilities.

Images and the Law

The host of changes mandated by the new law are best explained by Congress's prevailing images of the implementation experience. The perception that CETA was awash in fraud, waste, and abuse overshadowed all other issues. Where did this image come from? In large part, CETA's poor reputation was created by journalists writing in popular news magazines, such as *Time, Newsweek,* and *Reader's Digest,* and in leading newspapers, such as the *Washington Post* and the *New York Times.* One of the most damaging articles appeared in *Reader's Digest* in August 1978, the same month the House debated reauthorization. Entitled "CETA: $11 Billion Boondoggle," the article described several exotic items including a "nude sculpting workshop ... in which naked men and women ran hands over one another's bodies" and body drumming classes, in which inner-city youth were taught "how to slap various parts of their bodies rhythmically." [6] This article and others like it in Washington, D.C. newspapers made strong impressions on legislators and stimulated a flood of letters from outraged constituents.

Reflecting the views of many members, Rep. Robert Cornell, D-Wis., explained why Congress imposed punitive regulations: "The way to show you're against abuse is to be against this program." [7] And so the reauthorized law instructed the secretary of labor to watch over state and local officials carefully, to withhold funds in suspected cases of fraud and abuse, and to withdraw the entire program from offending jurisdictions. The legislation also established new units within the department that were responsible for conducting the anticorruption campaign. A toll-free telephone number was made available so the public could report suspicious activities. Independent monitoring units were created in each jurisdiction to root out problems and report them to chief elected officials or administrative officers. Finally, and most important, prime sponsors were made liable for mistakes—payments to ineligibles would have to be repaid to the U.S. Treasury.

Another concern that fostered legislative action was the matter of public service employee wages. Members of Congress felt that many CETA jobholders got too much money. A former congressional staffer recalled how one member of Congress got this impression:

> I think CETA started having trouble when Jim Corman [D-Calif.], who was then Chairman of the Ways and Means Subcommittee on Unemployment Insurance, flew back to Washington with this guy from California. Corman turned to him and said, "Well, what do you do for a living?" And the guy said, "I'm chief resident engineer for the Los Angeles Environmental Protection Agency. I have a Ph.D. from UCLA." So Corman said, "Oh, that's great, you must do pretty well." And the guy said, "Yes, I am well paid." Corman then learned that the

Los Angeles CETA contributed $12,000 toward this guy's full salary, which was quite substantial. It doesn't take many of those stories to destroy an image of a program in which Congress has some serious doubts.[8]

Many in Congress were suspicious that CETA subsidized skilled professionals who should have been on local government payrolls. And concerns arose that excessive PSE wages made its temporary jobs more attractive than private sector jobs. Rep. Ronald Sarasin, R-Conn., captured the essence of this image: "It is much more attractive to be in this program than to be in the real world."[9]

Congress reacted to these unsavory images by clamping down. A wage ceiling of $10,000 was imposed on PSE jobs, and average wages across all positions could not exceed $7,200. The message was clear: PSE jobs should not pay for engineers and lawyers and should not pay more than similar private sector jobs. People should not be encouraged to hang on to a PSE job indefinitely. Half of the Title VI PSE jobs would be for short-term projects, and no one could hold a PSE job for more than 18 months. The law strengthened the Labor Department's ability to prevent local officials from substituting federal funds for activities normally financed with local revenues. Guilty jurisdictions would forfeit funds.

Congress's dissatisfaction also arose from the belief that CETA had not helped many people get private sector jobs. Members complained that, although 80 percent of all U.S. jobs are with private firms, only 15 percent of CETA's clients received private sector jobs and less than 20 percent of the law's resources were earmarked for training. To local officials these criticisms seemed unjustified because the deployment of funds had been dictated by earlier congressional action. Nevertheless, with unemployment dropping, many in Congress focused on new criteria for assessing employment and training measures. To them, it seemed unwise to commit so much to temporary jobs and income-support programs.

The desire for a greater emphasis on private sector placements fostered important new provisions. A private sector initiative program (PSIP), established as Title VII of CETA, set aside about 4 percent of the law's resources for new programs and called for the creation of an advisory group of private employers, known as a private industry council (PIC) in each jurisdiction. According to Assistant Secretary of Labor Ernest Green, PSIP would "turn the CETA system from its too heavy reliance on the public sector to the much larger private sector where most permanent jobs will be found ... [and] change the direction of the employment and training system...."[10] Indeed, the private sector initiative program served as the forerunner of CETA's replacement, the Job Training Partnership Act of 1982.

Besides establishing a new advisory council and a modest-sized private sector program, the law steered the remaining components toward private sector jobs. For example, an employability development plan (EDP) had to be formulated for every job recipient specifying how he or she might become "job ready." Each EDP was supposed to assess the individual's readiness for work, identify barriers facing that individual, prescribe specific training services, and provide a plan for getting the client a private sector job. The EDP illustrates the kind of control Congress was prepared to exercise. The regulations told local officials not only *what* they should be concerned about but also *how* to implement programs.

Perceptions of CETA's shortcomings also brought about stricter eligibility standards. Under the original legislation, people who were unemployed for only seven days could be served; the new law specified that prime sponsors could enroll in training programs only those people falling below the poverty level and in temporary jobs only those experiencing both low income and long-term unemployment. With unemployment easing, Congress reasoned that resources should be targeted on people who remain jobless even after an economic recovery. Reserving services for the long-term unemployed and poor also might stop the rehiring of recently laid off city and county workers. The Carter administration hoped that people on public assistance might be drawn into training and temporary jobs and break the cycle of welfare dependency.

The 1978 CETA reauthorization reflected new perspectives on employment and training policy. The original CETA was a loosely structured block grant governed by permissive regulations. The public service employment expansion and a potpourri of new initiatives overburdened local administrators and sent CETA into a tailspin. Now Congress resolved to clean up CETA, serve the disadvantaged, and get more private sector placements. Congress was convinced, in the words of Sen. Robert Byrd, D-W.Va., that "the American taxpayers are tired of hearing about the use of their hard-earned tax dollars for programs which are misused, poorly planned, and executed in the name of providing job assistance." [11] The new CETA would operate under strict federal legislation and oversight and become "the most regulated federal government program in the nation's history." [12]

The Federal Role: Eliminating Fraud, Waste, and Abuse

CETA's reauthorization contained emphatic language expressing Congress's displeasure with overblown and poorly managed programs and mandating a much stronger federal role. To curtail embarrassing and illegal uses of funds, the law mandated burdensome administrative procedures for local programs. No distinctions were drawn between the innocent and the guilty. Every jurisdiction would follow the new regimen, and the Labor Department would be Congress's watchdog. Policy makers hoped that with federal bureaucrats in the driver's seat, fraud, waste, and abuse could be curtailed and further political embarrassment avoided.

The reauthorization unleashed an all-out attack against the evils lurking in the system. Now there would be no holding back as there had been in 1976 when Congress scolded Labor Department officials for seeking repayments from local governments that enrolled ineligible people. Local officials now would be held responsible for errors and the Labor Department for enforcing the rule of law. Congress earlier had tried to maintain a delicate balance between federal and local power; now subtle balancing acts were no longer deemed necessary or desirable.

During the period following reauthorization, the department vigorously investigated and audited prime sponsors, searched for abuse, and demanded compliance with federal rules. What did this new strategy produce? From the department's standpoint, the regulations, audits, and investigations fulfilled their mission. Flagrant abuse declined because elected officials and staffs feared the possibility of financial and criminal penalties for enrolling ineligible clients. Prime sponsors were compelled to ensure that ineligible people were barred from their programs.

However, the department's compliance campaign did not allay the doubts of CETA's congressional critics, in part because audits and investigations failed to uncover the expected raft of abuses. In fact, the department's auditors *questioned* only 2 percent of expenditures from 1974 and 1978, and only a third of those ultimately were judged illegal.[13] The "official" illegal expenditure rate, a little more than one-half of 1 percent, seemed to confirm the department's contention that CETA was not as bad as its reputation suggested. These findings put the department at odds with many members of Congress because the audits made the gargantuan compliance effort seem misguided and implied that Congress had exaggerated CETA's shortcomings.

Unconvinced that their perceptions might be wrong, congressional critics accused the department of lax enforcement. Only half of the nation's prime sponsors were audited, and only 38 prime sponsors were investigated.[14] The efforts of the 93 auditors in the Labor Department's inspector general's office and the 52 professionals in the Office of Investigation and Compliance did not satisfy members hell-bent on quashing abuse. During oversight hearings in 1979, Sen. Thomas Eagleton, D-Mo., leveled criticism at Secretary of Labor Ray Marshall:

> ... [W]ith a $10 billion series of programs ... dealing with 400 and some odd prime sponsors and 50,000 ... deliverers, and dealing with four and one-half million individuals ... to have 52 people trying to monitor waste, abuse, and mismanagement seems to me to be very shortsighted.[15]

To some extent, disagreements over the scope and significance of abuse were a matter of semantics. The reauthorization act proscribed more than a dozen potential "abuses" including nepotism, conflicts of interest, failure to keep proper records, kickbacks, political patronage, substitution of funds for regular government or private organization funds, discrimination, embezzlement, knowingly hiring an ineligible person, obstructing an investigation, using funds for religious or political activities, and so on. In practice, however, terms like "abuse" or "waste" mean different things to different people.

Following strict standards of evidence that can be sustained in court or before an administrative law judge, Labor Department auditors reserved the labels "abuse" and "fraud" to activities that clearly violated the law. Congress's investigative arm, the General Accounting Office (GAO), took a broader approach when it criticized local officials for ignoring the law's intent. GAO's comptroller general, Elmer Staats, was said to have remarked: "The more you look at CETA programs, the more abuse you find." [16] Naturally, his opinion undermined the department's claim that it had gotten to the root of the problem. Members of Congress interpreted "waste and abuse" in even broader terms. To them, something might be deemed an "abuse" if it sounded questionable in a news report or a constituent's letter.

Given their varying perspectives and responsibilities, it is not surprising that the department uncovered less abuse than the GAO and much less than Congress expected. Consider the examples cited in *Reader's Digest*, deriding CETA-funded nude sculpting and body drumming classes. However silly and outrageous these seem, a department auditor would not regard them as *illegal* expenditures as long as proper procedures for enrolling people and dispensing funds were followed. The regulations did not outlaw bad judgment. There are limitations on what laws and regulations can do to curtail activities that some find questionable, irregular, or just plain stupid. It is far easier to legislate technically proper programs than it is to legislate good programs.

Despite the skirmishes between Congress and the Labor Department, the new legislation brought about significant changes in the behavior of department officials and state and local operatives. But the federal enforcement effort did not have entirely salubrious consequences. Reflecting the will of Congress, the goal of administrative compliance was placed above all others while other essential program objectives were slighted or ignored. During the expansion of public service employment, the Labor Department may have been occasionally inept and inconsistent, but it justifiably pursued the rapid expenditure of funds to create jobs—a critical *program goal*. During 1979 and 1980 the department focused almost exclusively on *how* local officials managed the system rather than *what* the programs accomplished. Commenting on this phenomenon, a senior Department of Labor official observed:

> The emphasis on eligibility verification and financial accountability . . . for ineligibles [had a] tendency to push prime sponsors to focus on verification as *the single-factor*—to make sure that there is an eligibility check.[17]

The relentless effort to eliminate fraud, waste, and abuse represented a triumph of bureaucratic process over program substance.

An Administrative Nightmare

CETA's reauthorization offered Congress the opportunity to design a better employment and training system. In practice, a "better system" meant "free of fraud, waste, and abuse." The new law and aggressive federal enforcement yielded better-regulated programs that were no more successful in getting people jobs. Just as the emphasis on rapid hiring during the growth of public service employment diverted administrators from other missions, the new regulatory environment shifted staff attention from results to process. When CETA's rules and regulations became rigid and punitive, the interest and support of state and local elected officials declined abruptly. Worse still, the professional managers of the huge, more complex, and highly regulated system were frustrated, angry, and demoralized.

Removing Politics and the Politicians

Whether or not intended, CETA's reformation depoliticized it. State and local elected officials, whose involvement had been earnestly cultivated during CETA's early years, saw their discretion severely eroded under the new law. One participant in the reauthorization debate offered an explanation for Congress's action:

> Congress traditionally doesn't like to hand off money to localities. They just don't like to be out of control of what happens. When you give money to a local elected official, you're giving it to your potential rival. Everybody in a political system is worried about what everyone else's intentions are. Let's say you give money to the mayor of Ann Arbor. Maybe one day he decides to run for Congress and what would be nicer than for him to run for Congress having given out 20,000 jobs.[18]

If Congress was already uneasy about ceding power to political rivals, allegations of widespread abuse in the public jobs component offered an excellent excuse for tightening the reins on the distribution of benefits.

The 1978 version of CETA reduced the political appeal that public service employment had enjoyed during its period of unrestrained growth.

PSE was no longer a political plum but an adminstrative nightmare. Many politicians withdrew from decision making and took their political support with them. The fact that CETA had a distinctly negative reputation in Congress was not lost on local officials. In putting distance between themselves and CETA, many mayors and county executives were reflecting a natural desire to avoid association with a tarnished program.

The exodus of politicians can be traced to several aspects of the law that made public service employment less flexible and therefore less useful to local officials. Referring to restrictions on the duration of enrollment and the caps on wages, one senior Labor Department administrator assessed the scene:

> The 18-month limitation and the average wage limitation have really taken the luster off PSE as far as elected officials are concerned. So they're not all that much interested and they're happy to pass it off to a community based organization or nonprofit corporation. It's not the important issue in the minds of elected officials that it was before.[19]

Ostensibly, these provisions of the law were designed to curb the practice of substituting federal funds for local revenues. Since PSE jobholders could not be paid much or remain with government agencies for very long, the substitution option was considerably less alluring than before. PSE's value was further deflated by the law's eligibility requirements. Fewer skilled workers could be hired so the tasks undertaken by the CETA workforce were less valuable to local governments. As a form of political currency, PSE jobs and projects also suffered. With carefully drawn regulations against abuse and federal officials hovering around, elected officials were loathe to reward friends with jobs or dispense lucrative contracts to favored organizations.

The Lonely Life of the Prime Sponsor Director

With local elected officials moving away from the employment and training business, prime sponsor directors were left holding a political "hot potato." They had to manage a large and badly fragmented set of programs in a heavily controlled regulatory environment without embarrassing their bosses. Staying out of trouble took on great importance. One former prime sponsor director characterized the situation:

> What the prime sponsor director is doing is moving the program responsibility and heat away from the mayor's office or the governor's office. Nobody comes in and tells them how much classroom training they can do, but they do come in and look very carefully at the technical aspects, at the fiscal aspects. . . . That's what the prime sponsor is trying to make sure is clean with the Department of Labor. Nobody wants the inspector general in if they can possibly help it. That can bring heat back at the elected official because that gets attention in the media.[20]

In this environment, it is understandable why compliance issues, such as verifying client eligibility, got more attention than program issues, such as whether vocational training curricula were appropriate to the needs and experiences of participants.

The new law transformed the administrative apparatus of prime sponsors. Staff responsible for reporting, monitoring, and record keeping expanded at the expense of planners and operators. One prime sponsor director estimated that new federal rules doubled the cost of administrative overhead.[21] The emphasis on rules and regulations completed the conversion of local staffs from planners to brokers and overseers who were obsessed with procedures. According to a former staff director:

> Prime sponsors abdicated their management responsibilities. They're not really serious about organizing staff and program design, except for administrative requirements and keeping themselves out of jail. There are exceptions to that, but, for the most part, the prime sponsors seem tied to the administrative arms of the Labor Department. The real decisions are made somewhere else.[22]

What got submerged as the compliance mentality spread was the importance of leadership and program quality. If local staffs were not concentrating on program outcomes, who was?

Unfortunately, in many communities, the answer was "nobody." CETA's reorientation toward more cautious procedures would have been helpful had it not swept aside other essential elements of sound management. Indeed, the fanatic commitment to regulating compliance produced more negative consequences than positive ones. After reauthorization, employment and training programs were more closely regulated than ever before; they were also less likely to contain ineligible participants or suffer from corrupt practices. However important these accomplishments may have been in improving CETA's reputation and mollifying members of Congress, they did not enhance the record of placing people in jobs.

A small group of CETA prime sponsors was able to cope effectively with the difficulties arising out of the new law and rigid enforcement. These communities achieved better results principally because they pursued carefully drawn local strategies while fending off federal bureaucrats. One prime sponsor director explained his approach:

> You don't get bogged down with the department's priority of the day. We have been able to get along through some of these frivolous kinds of initiatives that you know are going to die on the vine. You don't really want to adjust the whole system for these types of initiatives, but just let them die of their own weight over time.[23]

Few staffs possessed the skill and self-confidence to defy the national trends to protect local prerogatives and program quality.

Most CETA staffs were frustrated by their working environment. Compliance activities and Labor Department requirements consumed large chunks of time that many administrators felt was not well spent. For some communities, compliance with the department's rules and regulations amounted to a game of numbers that yielded meaningless reports. One CETA director described her strategy for dealing with federal requests:

> [We get] absolute badgering for reports, for ad hoc reports. "How many gay communities have you talked to this week? How much money have you spent auditing your subgrantees?" You make up the answers. What the department doesn't understand is that the more requests for information, the more devious and soft and inaccurate that data base is and what you are getting is numbers made up.... The changes in requirements are killing the system. Every day it's a new requirement.[24]

Some officials warned that the system would collapse from overregulation. A letter written to the Labor Department by Patrick Moore, prime sponsor director in Salem, Ore., superbly captured the mood of local administrators:

> Please receive this notice of full and unconditional surrender by the Mid-Willamette Valley Consortium! We throw down our arms and beg for the department's mercy.... We have been beaten into submission by a recent attempt to accommodate the department's regulatory paperwork. We offer our plea in the hopes that one of Oregon's most precious resources, its forests, may yet be saved.[25]

The letter went on to say that not only had CETA grown more complex but also that it contained references to some 75 related laws, regulations, executive orders, and Office of Management and Budget circulars to which local officials were bound. Moore concluded: "Quite obviously, every prime sponsor in the country is likely to be continuously out of compliance with some provisions in one or more of these references. . . ."

Equally debilitating from a management perspective was the continuing instability of the employment and training system. After four topsy-turvy years, prime sponsors desperately wanted some calm. But the reauthorization experience contributed to the sense of impermanence. Local staff operated at the mercy of the congressional appropriations process and often were uncertain about how much money they would have, when it would be available, and how it had to be spent.

The Balkanization of CETA

The array of employment and training programs in existence from 1978 to 1982 can be thought of as separate, but contiguous, nation states, each with its own constitution, governing body, and armed forces. CETA was not one, but four programs, each with its own regulations, administrative structures, appropriations, and professional staff. Like the Balkan states after World War I, CETA had been subdivided into discrete and often incompatable entities—a development that complicated the task of implementation and thwarted the emergence of comprehensive services for the unemployed.

At the core of this large and fragmented system were *training and remedial education* programs housed under Title IIB, which had about $2.9 billion, 25 percent of fiscal year 1980 resources. Grafted onto this were private sector, youth, and public service employment components. The *private sector initiative program* (PSIP), under Title VII, supported activities similar to those under Title IIB but had only $325 million, roughly 4 percent of CETA's total funds. Unlike Title IIB, however, Title VII was planned with advice from private industry councils. The $2.1 billion *youth programs,* under Titles IV and VIII represented another quarter of the CETA monies. What distinguished them from Title IIB and Title VII was an exclusive focus on young people and the dominance of part-time, temporary jobs programs, known in employment and training jargon as "work experience." Nearly 4 of every 10 CETA dollars, $3.1 billion, was set aside for *public service employment* programs under Title IID (for the long-term unemployed) and Title VI (for the short-term unemployed). Although PSE was still a significant component of CETA, its share of the pie declined by 13 percent from 1978 to 1980. The remaining funds of the employment and training budget were distributed through demonstration projects and other special efforts administered by the Department of Labor.

Between 1978 and 1982, therefore, CETA consisted of four elements: a core of training programs for youths and adults, special youth programs, a private sector initiative program, and a large, but diminished, public service employment program (eliminated during 1981). All but PSE had similar objectives, clients, and strategies of assistance. Each had been established by special legislation, which encouraged separate operations, duplication of services, confusion, and fragmentation of the delivery system.

Let us consider how CETA's Balkanization manifested itself in Hartford, Conn. In 1980 at least six organizations operated part-time, temporary jobs programs for low-income minority teenagers, including the Hartford private industry council, the Private Sector Employment Assistance Corporation (a subsidiary of the PIC), the Hartford Area Employment and Training Consortium (the local prime sponsor), the Hartford Urban League, the Hartford public schools, and the Hartford community action agency. Each program had separate legislative authority, regulations, and reporting requirements, but the differences among objectives, designs, approaches, and client groups were insignificant.

If the situation in Hartford sounds vaguely familiar, you may be recalling our characterization of the employment and training system of the 1960s. In fact, dissatisfaction with the octopus-like structure of overlapping programs provided the impetus for the Comprehensive Employment and Training Act in 1973. The "comprehensive" in CETA expressed the desire for coordinated, consolidated, and integrated programs. Now, five to six years after the original CETA, the system had fallen into its old habits—a victim of interest group politics and congressional preferences for narrow, categorical aid programs.

Clamping Down on Public Service Employment

From 1979 to 1981 the public service employment program was a hornet's nest of administrative restrictions made worse by dwindling appropriations. Ceilings on the average PSE yearly wage, narrower eligibility requirements, and other regulations made PSE jobs less attractive to potential clients and public agencies. At $7,200, or $3.50 an hour, the average annual wage for PSE jobholders was only slightly above the official government poverty level for a family of four.

The new rules forced realignments in the PSE workforce. Between 1978 and 1979, the percentage of clerical workers, unskilled laborers, and nonprofessional service workers increased from 63 to 73 percent, while professional, managerial, and skilled laborers decreased by 6 percent. Entry-level pay scales in many local government agencies exceeded the PSE wage limits and thus prohibited them from using PSE workers. Instead, a large share of PSE positions were relocated in private nonprofit organizations and educational agencies because they had more flexible job classifications and lower pay scales.[26]

Local administrators claimed that the new PSE regulations had adverse consequences. The remaining PSE jobs did not prepare enrollees for private sector employment because state and local agencies had always sponsored the PSE positions that provided the best stepping stones to unsubsidized jobs. These opportunities declined under the new rules, and the quality of public services suffered because only unskilled workers were hired. In Syracuse, N.Y., for example, the city could not hire entry-level laborers because wage levels determined through collective bargaining exceeded the maximum annual wage ceilings. Instead, the city hired clerks, typists, information aides, and parking checkers. In the staff's opinion, the exclusion of entry-level laboring positions shut off the "positions suited to the skill level of the structurally unemployed." Furthermore, the wages were so low the staff predicted welfare recipients would have no "incentive to leave the welfare system."[27]

A few local officials felt so strongly about the onerous restrictions that they returned portions of their PSE allotment to the U.S. Treasury. The commissioners of Clackamas County, Ore., for example, returned $500,000 saying:

> The alterations in the law (CETA), while perhaps founded in good intent, have worked incredible negative change and reduced not only our [PSE program's] effectiveness, but our program's enrollment.[28]

To add to their difficulties, local administrators also were forced to institute substantial PSE workforce reductions beginning in 1979. Cutbacks in appropriations caused a rapid drop from a peak of 725,000 jobs in mid-1978 to fewer than 400,000 by the end of 1980. Local elected officials and their staffs were put in the unenviable position of handing out pink slips to city, county, and state workers and slashing funds for private nonprofit organizations, undoubtedly reinforcing the dim view that elected officials held toward CETA.

Experimenting with Youth Unemployment

Spending roughly $2 billion a year and serving more than one million young people from 1979 to 1982 were several programs housed under the Youth Employment Demonstration Projects Act (YEDPA). YEDPA was a massive policy experiment to determine how low-income youth might be helped up the economic ladder. Its size and multiple components reflected both the interest group bickering that led to its adoption in 1977 and uncertainty about how to aid unemployed youth. The appointment of Vice President Walter Mondale to head a task force monitoring YEDPA's progress symbolized the law's political significance.

In general, YEDPA stressed short-term jobs in public agencies or nonprofit organizations, supplemented with counseling or remedial education. YEDPA's major components, budgets, and enrollments are outlined in Table 5-2. In some ways, youth employment strategies had barely changed since the Neighborhood Youth Corps in 1965, but YEDPA was much larger and contained new wrinkles. For example, the feasibility of providing youth a guaranteed job in exchange for remaining in school was tested through the Youth Incentive Entitlement Pilot Projects.

The division of YEDPA into discrete entities suited its dual mission. Politicians and interest groups wanted to earmark a pot of money for unemployed youth; evaluators preferred distinct strategies that could be judged independently. From the standpoint of the local prime sponsor staff, however, YEDPA generated undesirable side effects. One prime sponsor director made this assessment: "The Youth Act, more than the 1978 reauthorization of CETA, has done more to turn things back to a fragmented system." [29]

Evaluating the Experiment. The Vice President's Task Force on Youth Employment and the Labor Department sponsored an enormous research effort to assess the effectiveness of YEDPA's many facets. Employment and training programs are usually judged according to how well participants fare in the job market following "graduation." But in the case of youth programs, measuring the postprogram earnings of participants was controversial because fewer than 10 percent of YEDPA's enrollees immediately entered the job market; the rest remained in school or experienced brief periods of unemployment before going back to school or work. Furthermore, from a research standpoint, it was difficult to isolate the effects of YEDPA's short-term temporary job experiences. Evaluators reported few substantial employment or earning gains for those who had participated in YEDPA's work experience programs.[30]

In the minds of some elected officials and evaluators, the failure to help young people attain regular jobs and better wages meant that YEDPA should be eliminated. To others, including members of the vice president's task force, these findings confirmed expectations and proved that youth initiatives must be judged by different criteria. In their view YEDPA provided a modest intervention at a highly volatile period in a young person's life and therefore should have been regarded as one positive element of the cumulative experience that influences a person's employment history.

Government's role in ameliorating youth unemployment has long been the subject of heated debate. Diverse opinions about the causes of youth unemployment lead observers to different conclusions. Liberals assume that young people suffer high unemployment because there are not enough job opportunities and because of discrimination. Government, therefore, should subsidize part-time jobs for them. Conservatives believe that teenagers' attitudes toward work should improve and that government can do little or nothing about that. Conservatives also maintain that federal minimum wage laws force employers to pay too much for teenage employees and that government should lower or eliminate the minimum wage floor. Given these fundamental differences in philosophy, it was inevitable that politicians would not interpret evaluation results in the same way.

Take the findings from the youth entitlement projects, for example. Extensive research conducted by the Manpower Demonstration Research Corporation concluded that youth entitlement projects were by and large successful. The provision of part-time minimum wage jobs in exchange for staying in school attracted thousands of young people to the program, reduced school drop-out rates, and increased the percentage of former dropouts who returned to school. Costs per participant were only a few hundred dollars higher than regular work experience measures, and local

Table 5-2 Activities, Expenditures, and Enrollments in the Youth Employment Demonstration Projects Act (YEDPA), Fiscal Years 1979 and 1980

Program	Program Activity	Expenditures and Enrollments	
		1979	1980
Summer Youth Employment Program (SYEP)	Part-time summer jobs for low-income youth.	$660 million 880,000 youth	$721 million 800,000 youth
Youth Employment and Training Program (YETP)	Part-time year-round jobs for low-income youth; includes counseling, occupational information, linkage with schools.	$556 million 413,000 youth	$695 million 463,000 youth
Youth Community Conservation and Improvement Projects (YCCIP)	Part-time jobs for low-income youth on small-scale public works projects.	$103 million 38,500 youth	$122 million 43,000 youth
Young Adult Conservation Corps (YACC)	Part-time and full-time jobs for low-income youth working on conservation projects in national parks and on other federal lands.	$273 million 51,900 youth	$234 million 66,500 youth
Youth Incentive Entitlement Pilot Projects (YIEPP)	Guaranteed part-time jobs for low-income youth in exchange for their continued enrollment in high school conducted in 17 sites.		$224 million 83,500 youth[a]

[a] Cumulative, over 30-month period of the demonstration project.

Source: *Employment and Training Report of the President* (Washington, D.C.: GPO, 1980) 35-39; and *Employment and Training Report of the President* (Washington, D.C.: GPO, 1981), 35-38.

governments and schools proved themselves capable of managing the complex experiment.[31] Despite this favorable report card, however, the idea of extending the entitlement concept nationwide—at an estimated cost of $1.6 billion—was dead by the time the demonstration ended in late 1980. In a climate of fiscal austerity and skepticism about government interventions, the idea of *guaranteed jobs* for youth was no longer politically feasible.

In the Carter administration's "last major social initiative," the president proposed a "Youth Act of 1980"—a bill incorporating the YEDPA research findings and recommendations from the vice president's task force. Carter's bill consolidated and simplified work experience programs, linked them with remedial education, and promised greater local flexibility. But the coalition of liberal Democrats, education associations, and minority interest groups supporting the bill quickly unraveled.[32] Ronald Reagan's stunning 1980 election victory sealed the Youth Act's fate. Although the House endorsed a $2 billion youth bill during the summer of 1980, it died in the Senate.

Bringing in the Private Sector

The private sector initiative program (PSIP), which operated between 1978 and 1983, proved to be, in the long run, a significant component of the vast employment and training empire. In contrast to the campaign against abuse, PSIP represented a positive effort to improve training programs and place more unemployed people in private sector jobs—the law's original and only enduring mission. While other CETA-funded components also sought private sector placements, PSIP's prime objective was greater private sector involvement in all phases of employment and training policy. PSIP's modest resources belied its potential importance for it presaged the enlarged private sector role mandated by the Job Training Partnership Act of 1982.

Most local staff welcomed PSIP's emphasis on preparing people for private sector jobs but resented the implication that local administrators had a bias against the private sector. The administrators were willing to commit resources to skills training programs as long as the potential for jobs was good and employers were willing to hire successful graduates.[33] From the local viewpoint, sparse expenditures on private sector training programs were caused primarily by Congress's emphasis on temporary jobs programs, such as youth work experience and public service employment, and by the private sector's reluctance to hire the unemployed poor.

Whatever the causes may have been, between 1974 and 1978 CETA gradually *moved away* from training people for private sector jobs and *toward* providing part-time and temporary public sector employment. In 1976, for example, CETA's core "training" title devoted only a third of its resources to classroom training and less than 10 percent to on-the-job training in private firms. CETA's reauthorization took it several steps in the opposite direction. Besides creating PSIP, the law prohibited the use of training monies for public service employment and capped the funds available for work-experience programs.

The new provisions achieved modest success. Training expenditures increased from 16 percent to 24 percent of CETA dollars between 1978 and 1980, work experience and PSE programs declined, and PSIP allocated most of its meager resources to training programs.[34] Although only partially successful, the new training emphasis had a broader meaning. It signaled a growing disillusionment with government-funded temporary jobs as a means for curing unemployment and set the stage for fundamental policy and funding revisions that would come in the near future.

The Politics of PICs. The principal mechanism for bringing business viewpoints into the employment and training arena was the private industry council (PIC). Within each community, a PIC, composed of a majority business membership, was appointed by the mayor or county executive to give advice on the separately funded activities authorized by PSIP, Title VII of CETA. The PICs' recommendations were subject to the review and approval of the prime sponsor's staff and local elected officials. PICs also were permitted to incorporate as private nonprofit organizations and directly operate training or other services. Because PICs were given a good deal of autonomy yet were tethered to the CETA system, the stage was set for competition and conflict between PSIP and CETA staffs. PICs were authorized to carry out programs similar to those already administered by CETA prime sponsors. Consequently, explicit or implicit comparisons between PSIP and the other CETA programs were inevitable.

According to a nationwide study conducted by Ohio State University, three types of PICs—weak, cooperative, and assertive—emerged during PSIP's first three years.[35] In about one-fifth of the study's 25 communities, weak PICs, manipulated by the CETA staff, had only marginal effects on the local delivery system. A prime sponsor staff bent on minimizing the PIC's role could appoint passive members; schedule infrequent, boring, and arduous meetings; and generally discourage the council's initiatives. Weak councils were found most often where the professional staff feared a potential rival and regarded PSIP as "selling out" to the private sector. In other places, PICs never caught fire because the members simply were not interested in employment and training matters.

Cooperative relationships between PICs and regular CETA staffs characterized nearly half of the Ohio State study sites. In these communities, prime sponsor staffs approached PICs positively, established viable councils, involved members in important decisions, and generally promoted healthy interactions. In a few cities and counties, the PICs were influential on a wide range of policy choices.

Assertive PICs that competed with regular prime sponsor staff were evident in a little more than a third of the communities visited by the Ohio State researchers. Such PICs often consolidated power by forming independent private nonprofit organizations, hiring staff with PSIP funds, and disassociating themselves from CETA as much as possible. Distance between the PIC and the rest of CETA could be made even greater by opening separate offices and adopting a different label for PIC programs. Rivalry and distrust were engendered when PIC staff inhabited more elegant office space and received higher salaries than their counterparts on the prime sponsor staff. The desire of many PICs for independence graphically illustrates CETA's dismal reputation in the business community. As one PIC director told us: "We've got to avoid using the name CETA at all costs."

The diverse PSIP experience can be illustrated by briefly examining two communities: Morris County, N.J., and Wayne County, Mich.[36]

Morris County: The Politics of Integration.   Morris County is part of New Jersey's "Sun Belt," where the population is expanding, unemployment rates are well below the national average, and corporations flock to take advantage of a bucolic environment. Prior to PSIP, Morris County's tiny CETA program had little or no traffic with the private sector. Upon receiving a $100,000 PSIP allocation, the Morris County Board of Chosen Freeholders appointed a PIC board to advise the prime sponsor staff. The PIC was integrated closely with the entire prime sponsor operation throughout its life span because the same people planned and operated all components of the CETA system. The PIC offered the CETA staff political support and insights into the needs and concerns of private employers. As a "wholly owned subsidiary" of the prime sponsor, the PIC never caused conflict, competition for resources, or other internecine battles. The PIC acted as an ambassador for CETA and had a modest influence on the design and conduct of local programs for the unemployed.

Wayne County: The Politics of Distrust.   Wayne County, Mich., encompasses Detroit and dozens of smaller cities and towns that suffer from deep economic troubles. Because of their heavy dependence on the ailing automotive industry, the county's residents have one of the highest unemployment rates in the nation. During the late 1970s Wayne County government was mired in one fiscal crisis after another, including near bankruptcies, "payless paydays," and widespread employee layoffs. Under the circumstances, the CETA staff was preoccupied with getting the most fiscal relief afforded by public service employment and relatively uninterested in private sector initiatives. When PSIP first came along, therefore, the staff paid little heed. A compliant PIC was hastily assembled just to satisfy federal rules.

The mess in Wayne County's government prompted CETA's deputy director to abandon ship. He orchestrated the PIC's incorporation and had himself installed as its executive director. The PIC staff moved out of the dingy, renovated city parking garage where the CETA staff worked and into a modern high-rise office building in the suburbs. Thereafter the PIC's new executive director charted an independent and rival course for his organization.

Relationships between the PIC and the CETA prime sponsor staff deteriorated rapidly. The PIC established its own system for enrolling clients, commented negatively and publicly about the prime sponsor's shortcomings, and developed a marketing campaign complete with slogan: "Meet [the] Private Industry Corporation. To Your Profit. As We Should Like To Demonstrate." Although the PIC's $4 million budget came entirely from CETA, neither that acronym nor other references to federal funding were contained in its splashy brochures. Before long, the prime sponsor staff launched a sustained attack against the PIC and threatened to terminate its policy-making authority. The bitter conflicts exacted a heavy toll on the participants and their respective organizations, diverted staff energies, and made the PIC's programs considerably less effective than they might have been otherwise.

Assessing the PSIP Record. The private sector initiative program had three principal objectives: to involve business in the design and conduct of employment and training programs, to encourage innovative, business-oriented programs, and to increase private sector job placements for CETA eligibles. The evidence from thorough studies of PSIP reveals considerable success in achieving the first objective, but limited progress on the other two.[37]

PSIP introduced greater business participation into the employment and training system. Business involvement came in the form of *advice* on training curricula or labor market conditions; *contributions* of office space, personnel, equipment; and *services,* such as running training classes or placing graduates.

Despite increased business participation, however, programs funded under PSIP were similar to those administered solely by prime sponsor staffs. Typically, PICs reworked and refined CETA mainstays such as classroom training, on-the-job training, and job search assistance. PICs were authorized to experiment with "employment-generating activities" ranging from labor market surveys to tax seminars for businesses, but most independent observers doubted the value of these strategies. The absence of innovation or wholesale reform demonstrates the difficulty of finding new solutions to old problems. Handing control for a small portion of CETA over to business did not eliminate the practical obstacles to transforming unskilled and unemployed people into trained and stable workers.

In fact, PSIP's performance was about the same as for programs administered under the regular CETA training system. Data on overall placement rates, private sector job placements, costs per placement, average hourly wages, and average wage gain demonstrate that by fiscal year 1981, the differences between PSIP and the rest of CETA were marginal.[38] The data in Table 5-3 show that PSIP performance was as good as other CETA programs, but certainly not a great deal better.

The PSIP experiment was a political success even if it did not make much difference in program achievement. PSIP brought new people, new ideas, and a new source of political support to the employment and training system, but greater business involvement did not automatically translate into better programs. The PICs heralded an important shift in the thinking of national policy makers. Since the Manpower Development and Training Act of 1962, employment and training measures had been designed around the immediate needs of low-income, unemployed people. As a result, administrators often prescribed short-term, income-producing jobs rather than training courses for their clientele. Beginning with PSIP and culminating in the Job Training Partnership Act of 1982, federal policy and programs shifted toward preparing people to meet the demands of private employers. Notwithstanding a shaky beginning, the next

Table 5-3   Performance Indicators for the Private Sector Initiative Program (PSIP) and Title IIB of CETA, Fiscal Years 1980 and 1981.

Performance Indicators	PSIP		Title IIB	
	1980	1981	1980	1981
Placement rate (percentage of participants who obtain unsubsidized jobs)	23%	35%	26%	30%
Private sector placements (as a percentage of all jobs)	81%	89%	70%	80%
Cost per placement	$7,887	$4,903	$5,134	$5,221
Average hourly wages upon placement	$4.10	$4.57	$3.76	$4.40
Average wage gains upon placement[a]	69¢/hour	60¢/hour	65¢/hour	59¢/hour

[a] Excludes people with no earnings prior to enrollment.

Source: Data supplied by the Employment and Training Administration, U.S. Department of Labor.

governance model for employment and training programs would be founded on the PSIP experience.

Targeting CETA on the Poor

The reauthorization contained an unambiguous message about the intended benficiaries of jobs and training services. Concerned that programs had not reached the truly needy, Congress substantially narrowed the range of people who could partake of CETA's benefits. The decision to tighten up entrance standards was motivated by perceived implementation failures and the national political climate. Stories about well-heeled college graduates occupying CETA-funded jobs were common around Capitol Hill. A growing alarm over budget deficits and the desire to shrink the welfare population made the strict targeting concept appealing to politicians on opposite ends of the ideological spectrum.

The law established poverty as the core standard governing admission to training and work experience programs. The additional test of *long-term unemployment* was applied to public service job applicants. The number of people eligible for federal jobs and training services was cut sharply. *Before reauthorization,* more than 18 million people were eligible for the jobs program and more than 27 million were eligible for training and work experience activities. *After reauthorization,* fewer than 4 million were eligible for temporary jobs under Title IID (where a poverty-level income and 15 weeks of unemployment were used as the entrance standard), and fewer than 6 million could receive jobs under Title VI (where the so-called "lower living standard" and 10 weeks of unemployment served as the eligibility criteria). The eligible population for training programs dropped by more than 50 percent, to around 13 million.[39] As before, there was enough money to serve only a portion of the eligible population, but local discretion was substantially diminished.

The public service jobs expansion episode taught Washington policy makers that legislative eligibility standards are seldom, if ever, self-enforcing. Therefore, they prescribed several stipulations designed to curb the enrollment of ineligible people. Local staffs were required to verify carefully the eligibility of each applicant. If it was later determined that prime sponsors had furnished jobs and services to someone who did not legally qualify then the jurisdiction would be financially liable. To make sure the rules were carried out, the Labor Department vigorously monitored local practices.

What Happened?

The law's principal objectives for program beneficiaries were achieved. Between 1978 and 1980 the enrollment of poor people rose 20 percent in CETA's training components, more than 30 percent in the Title IID PSE jobs and roughly 10 percent in Title VI PSE jobs (Table 5-4). Women, minorities, the young, those with less formal education, and welfare recipients obtained larger shares of federally funded public sector jobs than ever before. Following traditional patterns, the temporary jobs programs enrolled an older and better-educated group than other CETA components, but differences that were once great—in 1975 and 1976, for example—dwindled by 1980.

Significantly, the characteristics of people enrolled in regular CETA training programs, funded through Title IIB, were quite different from the characteristics of people served by new private sector initiatives programs, funded by Title VII. Although the two programs provided similar services, PSIP enrollees were more likely to be older, male, and better educated than their counterparts enrolled in regular CETA training programs and less likely to be public welfare recipients.[40] These findings confirmed suspicions that the private sector program had "siphoned off" the best-qualified people from the eligible population. The chairman of the private industry council responsible for PSIP in Hartford, Conn., had a colorful way of expressing this strategy: "You don't drain a swamp from the bottom." The fact that PSIP sought out and captured these applicants caused resentment among regular CETA staff.

A comparison of people *served* during fiscal year 1980 with the characteristics of the *eligible* population reveals the strengths and weaknesses of the legislative provisions designed to target benefits on the poor (Table 5-5). The gap between those served and those eligible narrowed considerably after reauthorization. For example, the difference between the percentage of females in the eligible population and the percentage of female jobholders was cut in half from where it stood in fiscal year 1977. Nevertheless, women and those with little formal education were still underserved in relation to their presence in the eligible population. In short, the legislation did not guarantee a perfect correspondence between need and the distribution of jobs and services.

There are several explanations for the significant changes in the composition of the groups who benefited from the programs contained in the CETA reauthorization. First, Congress wrote a clear law that identified precisely who should benefit. Second, the law's intent was reinforced by mandating rigorous eligibility determination procedures and by exacting financial penalties for errors. Third, federal overseers aggressively monitored local compliance. Fourth, most local professionals agreed with the new targeting objectives, and elected officials gave up trying to circumvent the process.[41] Finally, a more deliberate pace of enrolling clients and more mature local administrative structures contributed to changes in the groups served. In short, it was a textbook case of successful implementation.

Table 5-4 CETA Participant Characteristics, Fiscal Years 1978, 1980[a]

| Characteristics | Training Programs | | | | Public Service Employment | | | |
| | Title IIB | | PSIP (VII) | | PSE (IID) | | PSE (VI) | |
	FY78	FY80	FY78	FY80	FY78	FY80	FY78	FY80
Females	51%	53%	NA	43%	45%	50%	38%	45%
Nonwhites[b]	52	50	NA	51	37	49	44	49
Less than 22 years old	49	48	NA	36	21	26	21	24
Less than 12 years education	48	48	NA	35	20	33	28	31
Economically disadvantaged	79	98	NA	98	62	96	81	90

[a] Fiscal year 1978 was the last full year before reauthorization; fiscal year 1980 was the first full year after reauthorization.
[b] Includes Hispanics.

Source: *Employment and Training Report of the President* (Washington, D.C.: GPO, 1979) 369; and *Employment and Training Report of the President* (Washington, D.C.: GPO, 1981), 27.

Is a Program Just for the Poor a Poor Program?

Achieving the law's targeting objectives was purchased at a high cost. The process of determining eligibility imposed significant administrative burdens on local staffs. The typical applicant was required to supply 15 items of personal information on a lengthy form. Prime sponsors conducted internal reviews of each application and quarterly verifications of a sample of participants to check their residency, unemployment history, family income, and welfare status.[42] The extra staff working on this arduous task was drawn away from other vital planning and management functions. In addition, the new rules probably discouraged some qualified applicants from applying.

From a political standpoint, the most important change was the denial of services and jobs to *recently unemployed* workers. Many mayors and county executives felt that excluding the newly unemployed and serving only the poor put CETA in the same category as public welfare. No longer would politicians regard CETA as a useful source for public service workers and political patronage. The post-reauthorization experience proved that state and local officials would faithfully implement a program reserved for low-income people, but it also demonstrated that narrow restrictions on eligibility often undermine the political support necessary for survival.

Table 5-5   Characteristics of CETA Participants Compared with the Eligible Population, Fiscal Year 1980

	Training Programs		Public Service Employment			
	Title IIB		Title IID		Title VI	
Characteristics	Partici-pants	Eligibles	Partici-pants	Eligibles	Partici-pants	Eligibles
Females	53%	61%	50%	58%	45%	51%
Nonwhites[a]	50	33	49	44	49	39
Between 22 and 44 years old	46	50	62	64	63	62
12 or more years of education	52	44	67	48	69	53

[a] Includes Hispanics

Sources: Participant data are from *Employment and Training Report of the President* (Washington, D.C.: Government Printing Office, 1981); the eligible populations for Titles IID and VI were taken from special tabulations of the Current Population Survey that appear in William Mirengoff et al., *CETA: Accomplishments, Programs, Solutions*, Appendix A (Kalamazoo, Mich.: W. E. Upjohn Institute for Employment Research, 1982); the eligible population for Title IIB was computed from Bureau of Census, *Current Population Reports: Characteristics of the Population Below the Poverty Level: 1980*, Consumer Income Series P-60, no. 133 (Washington, D.C.: U.S. Department of Commerce, July 1982), 50-54. Eligible population includes everyone below the poverty level between the ages of 15-65, the active working years.

Conclusions

The formulation and implementation of employment and training programs between 1978 and 1981 offer many insights into the relationships among images, politics, and program performance. Experiences during this period also show that policy development tends to be cyclical rather than linear. The directions and turns of the employment and training cycle are determined by the changing political and economic climate and by images of program implementation.

When the unemployment "crisis" of 1976-1977 abated, the Carter administration and Congress cast critical eyes on the $10 billion employment and training system. With publicity about corruption and mismanagement proliferating, the system had to be reformed and redirected. Congress and the president punished state and local administrators for failing to handle the overwhelming tasks of the PSE expansion period and demanded more prudent management and fewer political gaffes. The new framework for federal employment and training programs displayed little sensitivity to the unavoidable problems of implementing massive social policies and a shocking amnesia about the liabilities of overregulation.

As before, immediate political pressures of the day shaped strategies for assisting the unemployed. A flood of strict regulations aimed at correcting some irregular and highly criticized local practices flowed from Washington. To curb the abuses of a few communities, Congress reasserted federal control before the decentralized service delivery model had been given a true test. One seasoned observer of employment and training policy offered this explanation for the seemingly vindictive and capricious behavior of Congress:

> You have to ask the question: why does Congress do these stupid things? If the CETA amendments are so counterproductive, or difficult to implement, why did it happen? The reauthorization changes were the price that had to be paid to retain the system.[43]

Congress's attempt to fashion a tightly governed program helps sharpen our understanding of policy implementation. Convinced that the traditional tools of strong central government control would achieve positive results, Congress wrote an explicit law and ordered watchful federal oversight. Despite the blurred lines of authority in the intergovernmental system, the new urgent national objectives were accomplished. Practical obstacles were overcome by clear rules, incentives, penalties, and enforcement. By the early 1980s, the vast employment and training delivery system was brought under control and refashioned in Washington's image.

Unfortunately, however, success was achieved by focusing on ephemeral objectives. While everyone made sure that the right people were enrolled in programs, that no one was paid too much for a public service job, and that proper forms were completed, too little time and attention remained for constructing effective and efficient programs to get people private sector jobs. The post-reauthorization experience exposed the fundamental weaknesses of a hierarchical management style. Because administrators concentrated on ensuring vertical accountability, local program design and performance goals were often swept aside, and local political support for employment and training initiatives eroded. It is always difficult to achieve the proper balance between uniform national standards and local discretion. If national policy makers get all they demand in the way of compliance, state and local support may evaporate. If national objectives are thwarted by state and local officials, national policy makers may impose counterproductive rules or abandon their commitment to the policy altogether.

The strategies followed during the post-reauthorization period also illustrate the volatile nature of unemployment politics and policy. Fluctuations in the nation's unemployment rate often set off wild swings in government employment measures. The much heralded recession relief packages of 1977 became excess baggage when unemployment rates declined. The prescriptive reauthorization act reflected the feeling that large-scale temporary jobs programs had outlived their usefulness—a rapid betrayal by national policy makers that reveals how tenuous and soft support is for temporary jobs programs to counteract recessions. Although the law stated Congress's intent to tie the size of federal jobs programs to the national unemployment rate, this commitment quickly was abandoned to curb federal spending.

Notes

1. Gregory Wurzburg, formerly of the National Council of Employment Policy, quoted in the transcripts of the CETA Implementation Research Conference, held at the Eagleton Institute of Politics, Rutgers University, New Brunswick, N.J., June 1980. (Hereafter, Rutgers Transcripts.)
2. Timothy B. Clark, "Carter's Election-Year Budget—Something for Practically Everyone," *National Journal*, Feb. 2, 1980, 176-177.
3. "House Panel Rewrites Key Federal Jobs Law," *Congressional Quarterly Weekly Report*, May 27, 1978, 1348-1350.
4. "House Votes Sharp Cuts in CETA Jobs Program," *Congressional Quarterly Weekly Report*, Aug. 12, 1978, 2106.
5. "Senate Extends CETA Jobs Programs, Votes Stronger Fraud Curbs," *Congressional Quarterly Weekly Report*, Sept. 2, 1978, 2371.
6. Ralph Kinney Bennett, "CETA: $11 Billion Boondoggle," *Reader's Digest*, August 1978, 72-76.
7. "House Votes Sharp Cuts in CETA Jobs Programs," 2106.
8. Nathaniel Semple, vice-president, Committee for Economic Development, interview with authors, March 16, 1982.
9. "House Votes Sharp Cuts in CETA Jobs Program," 2107.
10. House Committee on Education and Labor, *Hearings on the Comprehensive Employment and Training Act Amendments of 1978*, 95th Cong., 2d sess., 184-185.
11. Senate Committee on Appropriations, *Special Oversight Hearings: Comprehensive Employment and Training Programs and HEW Consultants— Abuse and Mismanagement*, 96th Cong., 1st sess., 118.
12. Stanley Brezenov, former commissioner, New York City Department of Employment, "Special Seminar on Employment and Training Programs," Eagleton Institute of Politics, Rutgers University, New Brunswick, N.J., March 1980.
13. *Special Oversight Hearings*, 33-34.
14. For a thorough account of the audit and investigations conducted by the

department, see William Mirengoff et al. *CETA: Accomplishments, Problems, Solutions* (Kalamazoo, Mich.: W. E. Upjohn Institute for Employment Research, 1982), 32; *Employment and Training Report of the President* (Washington, D.C.: GPO, 1981), 30-31.

15. *Special Oversight Hearings,* 23-24.
16. Ibid., 34.
17. Richard Haltigan, regional administrator, U.S. Department of Labor, Rutgers Transcripts.
18. Nathaniel Semple, interview with authors, March 16, 1982.
19. Haltigan, Rutgers Transcripts.
20. Robert McPherson, former staff director for the King-Snohomish Employment and Training Consortium, Seattle, Wash., Rutgers Transcripts.
21. Marion Pines, director, Mayor's Office of Manpower Resources, Baltimore, Md., Rutgers Transcripts.
22. McPherson, Rutgers Transcripts.
23. Charles Tetro, director, Penobscot County, Me., Training and Employment Consortium, Rutgers Transcripts.
24. Pines, Rutgers Transcripts.
25. Patrick Moore, director, Mid-Willamette Valley Manpower Consortium, letter to Roberts T. Jones, administrator, Office of Management Assistance, U.S. Department of Labor, Nov. 14, 1979.
26. Mirengoff et al., *CETA: Accomplishments, Problems, Solutions,* 210-211. Mirengoff and his colleagues reported that the share of PSE jobs allotted to private nonprofit agencies jumped from 24 percent to 38 percent between 1977 and 1980.
27. Michael Tierney, manpower coordinator, City of Syracuse, N.Y., letter to authors, Sept. 15, 1979.
28. "Oregon County Protests Restrictions on 'PSE,' Returns $500,000 to 'DOL,' " *Employment and Training Reporter,* Aug. 22, 1979.
29. Pines, Rutgers Transcripts.
30. Robert Taggart, *Youth Employment Policies and Programs for the 1980s: Background Analysis for the Employment and Training Components of the Youth Act of 1980* (Washington, D.C.: GPO, May 1980), 36-37.
31. William A. Diaz et al., *Linking School and Work for Disadvantaged Youths—The YIEPP Demonstration: Final Implementation Report* (New York: Manpower Demonstration Research Corporation, December 1982), 170.
32. *Congressional Quarterly Almanac, 1980,* vol. 36 (Washington, D.C.: Congressional Quarterly, 1981), 440.
33. See, for example, Randall B. Ripley et al., *CETA Prime Sponsor Management and Program Goal Achievement,* R & D Monograph, no. 56 (Washington, D.C.: GPO, 1978), 20.
34. Mirengoff et al., *CETA: Accomplishments, Problems, Solutions,* 81.
35. The study was conducted by Randall B. Ripley and other researchers based at Ohio State and other universities. The authors participated in the two-year study, carrying out field work in four communities. See Randall B. Ripley et

al., "A Formative Evaluation of the Private Sector Initiative Program, 1979-1981." (Report prepared for the U.S. Department of Labor, November 1981.)

36. The observations about Morris County, N.J., and Wayne County, Mich., are based on field research conducted by Carl Van Horn and David Ford as part of the Ohio State PSIP study.

37. See Ripley et al., "Formative Evaluation"; Thomas J. Smith, *Private Sector Initiative Program* (Philadelphia: Corporation for Public/Private Ventures, April 1982); and Grace A. Franklin and Randall B. Ripley, *CETA: Politics and Policy, 1973-1982* (Knoxville: University of Tennessee Press, 1984).

38. Because PSIP began in fiscal year 1979, there were very few programs initiated or completed that year. Therefore, it is appropriate to use the results from fiscal years 1980 and 1981. For a thorough discussion of Title VII performance, see Smith, *Private Sector Initiative Program*, 55-78.

39. These figures were taken from Mirengoff et al., *CETA: Accomplishments, Problems, Solutions*, Appendix A, and computed from the *Current Population Reports: Characteristics of the Population Below the Poverty Level: 1979*, Consumer Income Series, P-60, no. 130 (Washington, D.C.: U.S. Department of Commerce, December 1981), 52.

40. This same basic relationship holds even when youth work experience participants are removed from Title IIB. See *Employment and Training Report of the President*, 1981, 27.

41. Mirengoff et al., *CETA: Accomplishments, Problems, Solutions*, 129-132.

42. Ibid., 137-138.

43. William Mirengoff, Rutgers Transcripts.

Elections, Images, and the Economy

The election of Ronald Reagan to the presidency in 1980 signaled dramatic changes in the nation's approach to helping the unemployed. Reagan brought to the White House traditional conservative preferences for limiting the public sector's role in ameliorating unemployment. What government could do best was to do less and help the unemployed by leaving more money in the hands of investors who could create lasting jobs in the private sector. In the president's view, the principal causes of high unemployment were the "excessive" government spending and taxing policies of the past 30 years.

The 1980 elections also turned control of the U.S. Senate over to the Republican party. Reagan would have at least one sympathetic chamber in the Congress. No Republican president had had such an opportunity since 1953-1954 when President Dwight Eisenhower briefly enjoyed Republican majorities in the House and Senate.

Less than a month after his inauguration, Reagan outlined his plan for economic recovery. Departing sharply from his predecessors, he announced:

> The taxing power of government must be used to provide revenues for legitimate government purposes. It must not be used to regulate the economy or bring about social change. We've tried that and surely must be able to see it doesn't work. Spending by Government must be limited to those functions which are the proper province of Government. We can no longer afford things simply because we think of them.[1]

Job creation and training programs were high on his list of measures that hadn't worked and were beyond the legitimate scope of government. The president proposed to dismantle or diminish the entire system of public service employment programs, public works projects, and training programs for youths and adults that had been built up with bipartisan support since the early 1960s.

Few programs under the broad rubric of employment and training policy escaped the president's scorn. He proposed the immediate termination of the $3.1 billion public service employment (PSE) program, public works projects funded by the Economic Development Administration, and employment tax credits. He also favored a drastic reduction in and phasing out over a five-year period of the remaining job training measures under the CETA umbrella.

According to Reagan, most government strategies for the unemployed were not only ineffective but also counterproductive. He suggested a subminimum wage for youth during summer months, hoping this would encourage employers to hire more young workers. And he vowed to reduce extended unemployment benefits and impose higher taxes on unemployment insurance payments because he felt this might induce beneficiaries to look more actively for employment.

Reagan's proposals for shrinking the government's role in helping the employed were only partially successful. CETA's public service employment component was dropped from the fiscal 1982 budget, and federal unemployment benefits were temporarily curtailed, but the president's other initiatives were not approved. Indeed, less than a year after urging sweeping cutbacks, Reagan reversed positions almost completely. The proposed higher taxes on unemployment benefits were jettisoned, and the president urged continuation of federally funded extended unemployment benefits. He endorsed federal job training programs and backed tax credits for businesses that hire the long-term unemployed. Finally, and most reluctantly, he signed two job creation measures costing more than $10 billion. The only Reagan proposal still on the original list was the lower minimum wage for teenagers, but Congress showed no interest in it.

The president had not changed his mind about how the government should deal with unemployment, but political realities forced him to abandon old positions or suffer embarrassment at the hands of both parties in Congress. Sharply rising unemployment pushed Congress to enact government relief packages, and the president was virtually powerless to stop them. When Reagan took office in 1981, unemployment stood at 7 percent; inflation was around 12 percent and had been in double digits for 2 consecutive years—something that had not occurred for 60 years. The prime interest rate had topped 20 percent and mortgage rates had risen to 15 percent or more, all but halting home purchases. The president's attack on inflation through reduced spending and taxes was received favorably by the public and many politicians.

Less than two years later, the inflation rate had dipped to 4.4 percent, thus removing this issue from the forefront of public consciousness. But unemployment had risen above the dreaded 10 percent barrier in September 1982—the highest level in more than 40 years. Shortly thereafter, during the midterm congressional elections, the president and the Republican party were assailed by Democrats for adopting policies that curbed inflation by inducing higher joblessness. The president claimed credit for reducing inflation but blamed unemployment on decades of Democratic rule in Congress. He implored the nation to "stay the course" of lower taxes and spending and abjured quick fix unemployment programs. Despite the president's pleas, however, his party suffered a substantial defeat at the polls. Most members interpreted the election as a mandate to address joblessness through direct job creation measures.

This chapter examines the twists and turns of unemployment policy from 1980 to 1984. During this period, policy was influenced by broad swings in partisan power and ideology brought about by elections and by changes in the public's and politicans' perceptions of the need to fight unemployment versus the need to curb inflation. This episode also illustrates the importance of political leaders' perceptions of previous government unemployment programs. Images of past successes and failures strongly shape and constrain the policy options considered in Washington.

No More 'Make Work, Dead-end Jobs'

Reagan's diagnosis of the unemployment problem and proposed remedies could not have been more different from those of his predecessor, Jimmy Carter. While Carter believed that the government should spend more federal dollars aiding the victims of economic recession, Reagan believed that too much government spending had brought about high inflation and unemployment. Immediately upon taking office, Carter had proposed ambitious government strategies aimed at stimulating the economy and lowering unemployment. Within months, large Democratic majorities in the House and Senate appropriated more than $20 billion in additional spending, focused primarily on generating jobs. Public service employment was enlarged, public works projects started, special youth employment programs enacted, and antirecession aid for cities provided.

In sharp contrast, Reagan proposed a 30 percent federal income tax cut (Congress approved a 25 percent cutback over three years) and a $53 billion reduction in 1982 federal budget authority. By lowering taxes and spending and ending "unnecessary" economic regulations, the president believed his plan would "create . . . nearly 3 million more [new jobs] than we would have without these measures." [2] According to the president, providing incentives to the private sector and lowering government taxing and spending were "essential to provide the new investment which is needed to make America competitive once again in the world market. These won't be make-work jobs. . . ." [3]

Carter had made federal jobs programs the centerpiece of his economic stimulus package; Reagan moved quickly to cut back or abolish them. Saying that public service employment had "failed as a countercyclical stimulus program," Reagan recommended the elimination of all 300,000 PSE jobs by September 1981.[4] After only token opposition, Congress lowered outlays on public service jobs by $661 million from the already appropriated fiscal year 1981 budget, and wiped out the $3.1 billion for public jobs in Carter's proposed fiscal year 1982 budget.

Given Reagan's economic principles, it is not surprising that he sought an end to federal jobs programs. What may seem surprising is how quickly and easily PSE was dumped. By 1981 federal public job creation programs had been in place for a decade. Millions of people had been put to work in states and local governments and in private nonprofit organizations. Brushing aside vetoes by Republican presidents Nixon and Ford, Congress had funded public service employment even when unemployment was well below where it stood in the spring of 1981.

The swift demise of public service employment was possible because of the political climate in the country and because of the program's weak constituency and poor public image. At·that time, the public regarded inflation as a more immediate threat to prosperity than unemployment. Reagan's election campaign capitalized on the sentiment that the federal budget was out of control. The large liberal Democratic majorities that had enacted and expanded public jobs programs in 1974, 1976, and 1977 dwindled in the House and vanished in the Senate.

Broad changes in the political landscape do not fully explain why public sector jobs died so suddenly. A more important reason is that elected officials at all levels of the federal system had gradually disowned PSE in the aftermath of its massive expansion. During the late 1970s, when enrollments and expenditures doubled, the public jobs programs acquired an unsavory reputation for fraud, abuse, and mismanagement. Writing about CETA's troubles in New Jersey, the *Newark Star-Ledger* observed:

> . . . the mismanagement, favoritism and other abuses, coupled with the administrative foot dragging in pursuing the persons responsible, help to explain why a well-conceived program like CETA has lost public confidence and its termination by the Reagan administration goes unmourned.[5]

In fact, PSE was "on its way out long before President Reagan took office." Consider the observations from a senior congressional staffer about PSE's image:

> I can recall . . . the ill-fated effort by Congressman [Ronnie] Flippo [D-Ala.] to add a billion dollars of new PSE funding in 1978 where his was the only "aye" vote among several hundred. For the remainder of

that session of Congress, whenever anybody stood up and proposed what appeared to be an outrageous amendment, there would be catcalls from the back of the chamber, "Remember Flippo!" [6]

The diminished band of PSE supporters was hard pressed in the budget-cutting environment of 1981 to defend a program that had been so widely and convincingly maligned by the media and on Capitol Hill.

As expected, the Republican controlled Senate agreed with the president's recommendations. Even the Democratic minority that defended jobs programs conceded that public service employment had shortcomings. Sen. Claiborne Pell, D-R.I., commented to his colleagues:

> It is this most recent experience with public sector employment [during the mid-1970s] that has set the tone for the current view in some quarters that the government should no longer play a substantial role in the area of employment and training.[7]

Not only had the public service employment expansion discredited job creation measures, but also it had shaken confidence in other government unemployment programs. Despite the extensive enforcement of regulations designed to rid PSE of corruption, its reputation among politicians remained very much the same between 1978 and 1981. PSE's negative image tainted all programs housed under CETA's broad roof.

Some support for public service employment remained in the House Education and Labor Committee, whose Democratic members staged an unsuccessful effort to salvage it. Refusing to go along with the president's proposed cutoff, the committee's Democratic members argued that temporary jobs programs should not be slashed when unemployment was so high. In the majority's view:

> [R]educing funding for training and temporary employment at this time is short sighted and in direct contradiction to the President's announced intention of putting "America back to work!" ... [T]he savings projected in the proposed PSE elimination are illusory ... between 15 and 25 percent of savings from cutting PSE will show up as costs in the income transfer portion of the budget.[8]

On a straight party-line vote, the committee's Democrats recommended PSE funding at the levels proposed by Carter for fiscal years 1981 and 1982.

Two months later, the full House adopted spending targets for the 1982 federal budget and ordered the House Education and Labor Committee to trim more than $12 billion from its portion of the budget, including $3.1 billion from public service employment, $600 million from youth employment programs, and $200 million from extended unemployment benefits. The committee slashed billions of dollars from programs under its jurisdiction but preserved more than a billion dollars for public service jobs. Chairman Carl D. Perkins of Kentucky complained: "We are meeting with a gun pointed at our heads. The majority of this committee does not want to make these drastic reductions." [9] Nevertheless, under relentless pressure from their colleagues in Congress and the president, the committee ultimately lopped off the entire public service employment program.

Support for public service employment also was in scarce supply beyond the walls of the Capitol. People who were dependent on federal jobs programs were not organized to protect their interests. According to a *Washington Post* editorial, entitled "Requiem for CETA":

> CETA was an obvious first target for the administration because, unlike most social programs, it is not protected by an organized group of professional workers who stand to lose their own jobs. The people who hold CETA jobs don't organize letter writing campaigns. The only way their loss will be detected is in higher welfare and unemployment counts, higher local taxes, and fewer community services. [10]

But, if CETA jobholders were ill equipped to defend PSE, what about government officials whose communities stood to lose funds? The same state and local officials who had assiduously cultivated congressional backing for public jobs programs during the 1970s were conspicuously silent during the spring of 1981. The absence of support from these elected officials stemmed from two facts. First, the proposed cuts in federal spending were broad based, hitting dozens of grant-in-aid programs. There was little time to organize a counteroffensive. The president's strategy of concentrating all the spending cuts in a single "yes" or "no" vote on the budget made it extremely difficult to build support around even the most popular measures on the president's "hit list."

Second, public service employment had lost its luster following the 1978 amendments. The new restrictions imposed by Congress were designed to end questionable PSE expenditures; public sector jobs were targeted on those most in need of help—the low-income and long-term unemployed individuals—and new regulations made it difficult for local officials to substitute federal funds for local revenues. These reforms improved the program from the viewpoint of members of Congress and others who were knowledgeable about PSE, but they made PSE less attractive to elected officials and eroded its base of political support. To be sure, many communities still welcomed federally funded public service jobs, but PSE's political value had been substantially diminished.

The Consequences of PSE's Demise

Anticipating that Congress would approve Reagan's recommended termination of public service jobs, the Labor Department froze hiring nationwide. State and local adminstrators were instructed to phase out approximately 300,000 federally funded workers between March and September 1981. The department announced that it would make every effort to assure that PSE jobholders obtained full-time, unsubsidized employment. Testifying before the Senate Committee on Labor and Human Resources in early March, Albert Angrisani, assistant secretary for employment and training, stated:

> Through this reemployment effort, the vast majority of PSE participants affected by the phaseout of the program will be either placed in an unsubsidized job, training opportunities, or other positive outcomes.[11]

The entire employment and training system—from the state employment service offices to private industry councils—was asked to make placing public service employees into permanent jobs the highest priority.

PSE's sudden death took place on the heels of cutbacks that began in 1979. Enrollment peaked in 1978 when federal funds paid for more than 725,000 jobs nationwide. By 1981 the CETA workforce had dropped to 300,000; by 1982 it would be zero. Consequently, state and local governments were already accustomed to laying off PSE workers when the final blow was dealt. This fact made it no less difficult to maintain public services at the PSE-dependent levels reached during PSE's heyday a few years earlier. As one local official told us, "This last round of cuts has taken the art out of budgeting. We are resigned to a David Stockman approach—cut the hell out of everything." In fact, program managers had only four options. Federally subsidized employees could be 1) absorbed by their employers at a cost to local resources; 2) placed in private sector jobs; 3) transferred to CETA training programs that had not been eliminated; or 4) left unemployed and therefore eligible for various forms of governmental support, including unemployment insurance, food stamps, and welfare.

Studies conducted by the U.S. Department of Labor, the General Accounting Office (GAO), and the Eagleton Institute of Politics at Rutgers University indicate that the results of the reemployment effort were disappointing. As of September 1981, the Labor Department reported that nationwide only 38 percent of the 300,000 laid-off workers had obtained jobs—a level of success roughly similar to the percentage of former PSE jobholders placed in the private sector during the previous two years.[12] Independent studies of 7 jurisdictions by GAO and of 14 New Jersey cities and counties by Eagleton yielded similar findings. GAO reported that 45 percent of the former PSE workers in the communities it studied were employed.[13] The Eagleton Institute reported that only about 33 percent of the more than 7,400 who lost their PSE jobs in New Jersey had found other employment as of September 1981.[14]

The results of the reemployment drive are even less encouraging when the nature of postprogram employment is considered. Of those who found work, only half obtained permanent full-time jobs; the rest were evenly divided between temporary positions and part-time positions.[15] Moreover, a high percentage of the jobs held by former PSE enrollees were not located in the profit-making sector, but with public sector employers or private nonprofit organizations. According to the Eagleton study, two-thirds of those who found new positions were hired by public sector organizations.[16]

Costs to Governments and Reductions in Public Service

The disappearance of PSE jobs was costly to the state and local governments that absorbed people onto their payrolls.[17] The Eagleton Institute estimated that 14 New Jersey jurisdictions spent more than $13 million during the first year alone on 1,500 former PSE workers who were shifted onto local payrolls. The city of Newark, for example, paid more than $2 million to maintain a small portion of what had been its federally funded workforce during 1982.

Virtually all of New Jersey's counties and municipalities were forced to release employees because of PSE's phaseout. Large cities with high concentrations of low-income residents were hardest hit. Newark laid off 1,600 people or 20 percent of its total workforce; Paterson dropped more than 500 employees; and Elizabeth lost 300 workers.

Declining government employment caused public service cutbacks. Reductions occurred in all government departments, but social services, public works, parks and recreation, and health services were most likely to feel the pinch. The social services eliminated or reduced typically included child and adult day care, legal services for the poor, and aid to the disabled and elderly. Municipalities reported delays in scheduled maintenance for roads, bridges, and other public facilities and questioned their capacity to cope with future emergencies. As one manager in New Jersey put it, "My public works department will be all right—if it doesn't snow this year." Because of the withdrawal of full funding for PSE in fiscal year 1981, 14 New Jersey jurisdictions lost nearly $54 million in wages for more than 6,000 PSE workers.

Indirect Effects on Government Spending and Taxes

The indirect impact of killing PSE is nicely illustrated by a story from the weekly newsletter of Rep. Paul Simon, D-Ill. Entitled "Last Year's CETA Workers: Where Are They Now?," the story concerned the experience at the Shawneetown Day-Care Center:

> The day-care center struggled to get by and managed to do so, in part because one CETA employee was assigned to it. When that

CETA employee was cut off, the center couldn't continue. It folded.

The results: The former CETA employee is now drawing unemployment compensation; the four women who were full-time employees of the day-care center are drawing unemployment compensation; four of the women who were able to work because they had a place to leave their children have had to quit their jobs and go on welfare. And so the bottom line: One CETA employee's salary saved and nine added to the welfare and unemployment compensation rolls. Everyone is a loser including the taxpayers.[18]

Getting a handle on the scope of the indirect effects is difficult, but research conducted by the Congressional Budget Office (CBO) and the Eagleton Institute of Politics gives some clues. CBO estimated that in 1981 the savings in direct federal spending derived from eliminating PSE would be decreased by between 16 percent and 29 percent because of lost tax revenues and increased spending in income transfer programs. "In 1982 and beyond, these secondary budget effects would decline to between 7 and 14 percent of the federal cost of the PSE programs. . . ," according to the CBO study.[19] The range of cost estimates was due to uncertainties about the percentage of people who would obtain new jobs after leaving PSE and how many would apply for income support programs.

The Eagleton Institute calculated the indirect cost of laying off PSE workers in New Jersey. Within the first year of PSE's elimination, Eagleton estimated that it might cost $25 million in additional payments to people who could not obtain other employment. Most of this money, about $20 million, would be doled out in unemployment insurance checks; the remainder would be paid out in food stamps and public assistance. The end of PSE jobs also would reduce federal and state tax revenues by approximately $15 million during the first year, according to the New Jersey study.[20] In summary, the short-term costs of cutting PSE were very high in the Garden State.

The 10 Percent 'Solution'

Now that public service employment was "the deadest of doornails in the wake of the Reagan Revolution," the president's fiscal year 1983 budget (presented to Congress in January 1982) took up the task of curtailing and revamping other federal job and training programs.[21] The budget proposed to restructure training programs completely, lumping them into a block grant to the states and slashing funding by two-thirds from their 1981 level—the last Carter budget. Reagan also proposed to cut off community service employment for the elderly and summer jobs for inner-city youth and to decrease spending for the Job Corps. The president's budget stressed broad economic recovery, rather than direct government spending, as the cure for unemployment.

Reagan and his advisers predicted that their strategy of lower taxes and reduced growth in government outlays would lead to lower unemployment during 1982. The president acknowledged that the unemployment rate would not fall as quickly as he had initially expected. His 1982 budget predicted an average rate of 7.2 percent for fiscal year 1983.[22] The 1983 budget proposal adjusted that prediction upward to 8.9 percent but anticipated gradually declining unemployment to 7.1 percent in fiscal year 1984, 6.4 percent in fiscal year 1985, and 5.8 percent in fiscal year 1986.

Instead of declining, however, unemployment shot upward during 1982, from 8.6 percent in January to 10.8 percent in December, for an annual average of 9.7 percent. The nation plunged into a deep recession and experienced the highest unemployment in 40 years. By year's end, an anxious Congress had forced the president to abandon his opposition to job creation and training programs. In October he signed the Job Training Partnership Act (JTPA) to replace what remained of the CETA training programs. In the months that followed, the president would sign several other measures to aid the unemployed.

Round One: Jobs, Jobs Jobs

The body of the ill-fated public service employment program was scarcely cold when Democrats in the House introduced new jobs legislation. Because such measures had little chance of passing at the time and because mid-term congressional elections were approaching, these proposals were regarded as a political ploy to embarrass the president and the Republicans.[23] After all, the president had easily convinced Congress to drop public service employment in 1981. And it seemed highly unlikely that the Senate would support a jobs bill. Finally, even if Congress passed legislation, the president surely would veto it.

Every upward notch in the unemployment rate during 1982 increased the desire of Republican members of Congress to join Democrats in enacting temporary jobs legislation. When the August unemployment rate of 9.9 percent was announced, Republican party strategists began to fear that the Democrats were winning the symbolic battle over the unemployment issue. As one political operative put it, "We have got to focus somehow on jobs, jobs, jobs. . . . That is what the voters want to hear." [24] The picture worsened in September when unemployment crossed the 10 percent threshold and economists of all stripes began predicting that high unemployment could grip the nation for months or even years. Reagan's hopeful assertion that the recession was bottoming out appeared implausible. Although inflation had dropped to a 4.4 percent annual average for 1982, less than half of where it stood when Reagan took office, many people thought the president's view of the economy was overly optimistic because unemployment had jumped from 7 percent to 10 percent and was continuing to rise. Public opinion polls revealed that Americans now regarded unemployment, at a 40-year high, not inflation, as the nation's most pressing problem.[25]

Sweeping aside the concerns of nervous Republicans in the House and Senate, the president stuck to his economic game plan and political strategy. He argued that the country should resist the temptation of stimulative government spending as a path out of economic malaise. Speaking to the nation just before the 1982 congressional elections, Reagan provided his standard characterization of the nation's economic ills:

> You can't solve unemployment without solving the things that caused it—the out-of-control government spending, the skyrocketing inflation and interest rates that led to unemployment in the first place. Unless you get at the root causes of the problem—which is exactly what our economic program is doing—you may be able to temporarily relieve the symptoms, but you'll never cure the disease. You may even make it worse.[26]

The November 2 election results broke the back of Republican resistance to temporary jobs programs. The Republicans held onto their Senate majority, but 26 incumbent Republicans went down to defeat in the House and many others, including House Minority Leader Robert Michel, had close calls. The makeup of the House changed from 243 Democrats and 193 Republicans in the 97th Congress (1981-1982) to 269 Democrats and 166 Republicans in the 98th Congress (1983-1984). The 97th Congress had given the president a working majority in the House when conservative Democrats joined the solid Republican minority; in the 98th Congress, the House Democratic leadership regained policy control.

The way Republicans and Democrats interpreted the results was as important as the new balance of party power. A *New York Times* article assessing the election reported, "Senators and Representatives of both parties said the results of the midterm elections seemed to indicate a public desire for the Federal Government to play a larger and more active role in combating unemployment." [27] That the Democrats demanded unemployment legislation came as no surprise, but the Republican about-face directly contradicted the president's position. Howard Baker, the Senate Republican Leader, broke early. Shortly after the election he remarked: "I think it's almost certain that there will be a jobs program of some sort and there should be." [28] Within a few weeks, House Speaker Thomas P. "Tip" O'Neill and Baker agreed to take up jobs bills during a "lame-duck" session of the 97th Congress scheduled for late November and December.

Despite mounting pressure from the Hill and the release of new figures that put unemployment at 10.5 percent in October, Reagan remained vigorously opposed to what he labeled "make-work, dead-end jobs." At a mid-November news conference, the president denounced temporary government jobs measures. Referring to CETA's public service employment program, he observed:

> The truth is that, over a seven-year period ... the Government has spent $66 billion on the kind of job programs that some of them are talking about now, on the Hill. And that $66 billion got us nothing but an increase in unemployment.[29]

Just a few days later Baker and O'Neill announced their support for a public works bill for rebuilding and repairing some of the nation's highways and bridges and for mass transit projects. The $5.5 billion bill would be financed by a five-cent hike in the federal tax on gasoline and would create about 320,000 temporary jobs. The following day, Reagan endorsed the bill, insisting that it was a highway program, not a job creation measure. Notwithstanding Reagan's views, the bill was widely regarded in the media and among elected officials as a visible response to high unemployment; it quickly won overwhelming bipartisan approval in Congress.

Pressure for temporary employment measures did not abate after the adoption of the highway jobs bill. The House passed another $5.4 billion bill and the Senate a $1.2 billion bill during the closing days of the session. The president forestalled their enactment by threatening to veto any bill containing additional funds for hiring unemployed workers.

Round Two: More Jobs Bills

As the 98th Congress convened, it was clear that the president's last minute roadblock to temporary jobs legislation during the 97th Congress had merely postponed the inevitable. December's unemployment rate of 10.8 percent confirmed that joblessness was continuing to rise, setting post-war records each month. A public opinion poll conducted by the *New York Times* and CBS News found that 74 percent of the American people favored a federal jobs program even if it enlarged the nation's budget deficit.[30]

With the Democratic leadership feeling confident and the Senate Republicans pushing for legislation, the question now was "not whether the federal government should have a job creation program, but what sort of program will work," according to Sen. Dan Quayle, R-Ind.[31] Republicans started sounding more like liberal Democrats. Sen. Mark Hatfield, R-Ore., chairman of the Senate Appropriations Committee, urged his colleagues to press for action during the 98th Congress: "We do not need more soup kitchens, more handouts, more extensions of unemployment benefits. We need to put people to work, not just help them when they are out of work." [32]

Representatives and senators from both parties practically tripped over one another advancing job creation proposals. Quayle offered a $2 billion program; Sen. Edward Kennedy, D-Mass., countered with a $7.3 billion temporary jobs package. Rep. Augustus Hawkins, D-Calif., reintroduced his $5 billion Community Renewal Employment Act, which was modeled on the CETA public service employment program. Representative Simon introduced a $15 billion bill, guaranteeing a public sector job for anyone unable to find work.

Although Reagan expressed strong disapproval of public jobs bills, he was not unmoved by demands for government action. Both his State of the Union message and fiscal 1984 budget proposals departed from his exclusive reliance on private initiatives and recognized the importance of government assistance for the unemployed:

> The Federal Government can play an important role in reducing unemployment. I believe, however, that the government should focus its attention on those groups that will continue to face high unemployment rates even after the recovery has begun.[33]

The president was no longer maintaining that the "rising tide will eventually lift all boats," but that the government should directly assist the structurally unemployed. He pointed proudly to the Job Training Partnership Act—a bill that he had opposed for several months—as a model for government intervention. His new budget proposed extended unemployment insurance benefits, a tactic he had opposed during the summer of 1982, and sought more money for the displaced worker component of JTPA.[34]

Although Reagan shifted ground and offered new initiatives for the structurally unemployed, he rejected Democratic and Republican pleas for jobs legislation. He stated his objections emphatically in the fiscal year 1984 budget message to Congress:

> I remain adamantly opposed to temporary make-work public jobs or public works as an attempted cure for non-youth unemployment.
> ... The cost per "job" created is excessive; we cannot afford major new programs, particularly in our current budgetary straits; the actual number of new jobs "created" is minimal; the jobs created tend to be temporary and of a dead-end nature; and most such jobs do not materialize until after recovery is well underway.[35]

The president criticized the bills under review in Congress as the "Christmas Tree for special interests," and as "pork barrels." [36] Nevertheless, he left open the possibility for compromise. He was willing to speed up already scheduled federal construction projects to stimulate job growth.[37]

Reagan was not alone in opposing federal job creation strategies. A study issued by the nonpartisan Congressional Budget Office criticized federal jobs bills. CBO argued that if jobs programs were financed by government borrowing they might increase the national deficit, drive up interest rates, and retard economic recovery. The study concluded that raising taxes to pay for jobs programs would merely "shift productive activity from the private sector to the public sector, with little effect on overall employment." CBO agreed with the president's contention that jobs programs are very expensive and that short-term measures could benefit only a "small proportion of the unemployed and could only marginally affect the state of the economy at large." [38] Some Democrats in Congress also were critical of jobs bills. For example, Rep. Les Aspin, D-Wis., noted that "if the Federal Government wanted to lower unemployment by just one percentage point, using the most effective and fastest way, a public service program, it would have . . . to put up $13 billion." [39]

Ignoring the advice of liberal and conservative economists who warned that unemployment cannot be lowered quickly and painlessly, the House and Senate leadership forged ahead with their plans. Areas of disagreement centered around the size of the jobs program and whether to fund *public works projects,* such as building construction and water and sewer repair, or whether to enact short-term, labor-intensive *public service employment* programs that usually provide social and health services. Public works projects involve much higher costs for each job created and do not reach the long-term unemployed, but they yield tangible products. Public service employment is more efficient, but less popular politically.

Faced with the certainty of another jobs bill, the president proposed a $4.3 billion public works bill similar to the one backed by the House Democratic leadership. The president and Speaker O'Neill agreed to push this legislation through Congress. Explaining the compromise package of public works projects, accelerated spending for community development, and the repair and rehabilitation of various federal facilities, O'Neill observed: "This is not the best bill we Democrats could write, but it may be the best bill we can enact into law." [40] The Democrats decided they would get the president's support for a bill he would sign immediately and battle for larger jobs programs later.

Reagan and his advisers claimed that funds for his jobs bill would go for useful, necessary work that would have to be done anyway. Forced to choose between what he regarded as two "evils"—a public works bill or a public service employment approach—the president selected a strategy that allowed him to claim he had not abandoned his principles. Whatever varnish he put on the bill, however, Reagan had switched tactics by endorsing government spending to lessen the impact of an economic recession.

In late March, less than two months after the 98th Congress assembled, the House and Senate cleared a $4.6 billion jobs bill that was quietly signed by Reagan.[41] Melding the preferences of the president and House Democrats, who preferred public works, with those in the Senate, who favored public service employment, the law allotted two-thirds of its funds for public works projects and the remainder for social services and humanitarian relief. It authorized supplemental monies for a grab bag of more than 40 existing federal programs, among them the displaced worker program, aid for maternal and child health care, handicapped education, and emergency food and shelter programs. New construction and rehabilitation projects were authorized for highways, urban mass transportation, Amtrak, airports, veterans' facilities, national parks, fish and wildlife areas, watershed and flood prevention, and prison modernization. The largest single component of the supplemental appropriation was $500 million for temporary public service jobs under the Community Development Block Grant program.

The law's funds were doled out through a complex formula using requirements in existing statutes for about a third of the money, the state's overall unemployment rate for another third, and the local area's unemployment rate for the rest. No specific eligibility requirements for potential employees were written into the law. People receiving federal construction jobs, for example, didn't have to be unemployed before they started work on the new projects. For these reasons and because of the law's diverse objectives it was virtually impossible to estimate how many new jobs would be produced by this $4.6 billion appropriation.

The new jobs measure was not without detractors.[42] Some complained that it was too small. Under optimistic assumptions—that each billion dollars would create about 100,000 jobs—the new law could offer relief to only a small percentage of the 12 million jobless Americans. Others argued that it was not directed to those communities and people most in need. They objected to the public works projects because skilled construction workers would be the primary beneficiaries. No matter how much money was spent, it was felt, the long-term structurally unemployed would remain unaided.

Supporters of the law claimed it was the best, or only, alternative that Reagan would sign. Rep. David Obey, D-Wis., summed up the attitudes of many House Democrats: "This is the only turkey you've got to ride."[43] Lawmakers supporting the economic stimulus strategy were concerned about further delays. As Sen. Lowell Weicker, R-Conn., put it: "We all want to get this money out on the streets where it will do some good."[44]

The job creation strategy enjoyed overwhelming bipartisan appeal. It gave members of Congress an opportunity to demonstrate their concern for the plight of the unemployed and assure their constituents that Congress was doing more about unemployment than waiting for the president's promised economic recovery. The law also supplied enough special interest tidbits to satisfy a broad political spectrum of Congress.

Paradoxically, the coalition-building process in Congress and the need for presidential support produced a law that would barely dent the unemployment problem. The public works approach drove up the cost of each job created. If previous experience is a guide and each job costs around $30,000 for wages and construction materials, then the law will add only 100,000 or so jobs to the economy. At $10,000 per job, a public service employment strategy would have been more cost effective and could have been implemented more rapidly. But the widespread disdain for CETA's public service employment program made such an approach politically unsavory and ultimately unsalable.

JTPA: Son of CETA?

With several young people who had benefited from government sponsored training programs looking on, Reagan signed into law the Job Training Partnership Act on October 13, 1982. The president contrasted JTPA with its predecessor, the CETA program: "This is not another make-work, dead-end bureaucratic boondoggle.... It'll make a difference on Main Street. It'll provide help, bring hope, and encourage self-reliance and personal initiative." [45] He was particularly pleased by three aspects of the new law. Unlike CETA, which was supervised by county and municipal government officials, JTPA would be overseen primarily by private sector representatives serving on private industry councils (PICs) appointed by local elected officials. The entire system would be managed by state governments whose responsibilities would be greatly expanded. Finally, JTPA's principal objective would be training people for private sector jobs. Short-term public sector jobs were forbidden, and the payment of stipends or other income support to program participants would be sharply curtailed.

Having opposed federal job training since assuming office, the president switched positions and, in the fall of 1982, endorsed CETA's replacement. The president then claimed credit for JTPA and accused Congress of delaying its adoption. JTPA's congressional sponsors were outraged. Senator Kennedy remarked sarcastically: "We say 'better late than never' and welcome his conversion to the worthwhile idea of job training." [46]

The story of how JTPA became law is more complex than the story of how Congress and the president came to back temporary jobs measures. Like the job creation packages, JTPA might not have existed had it not been for the 10 percent unemployment rate, but its specific content was fashioned during a protracted debate about CETA's accomplishments and failures. The jobs bill debate was waged over the landscape of public opinion, the national media, and congressional elections. JTPA emerged from a less visible battle among members of the employment and training subgovernment. How did JTPA come about? Is it a significant improvement over CETA? Or is it, as one member of Congress remarked, "so far from what we ought to be doing in this nation . . . that it is pathetic"? [47]

Participants and Perceptions

Long before JTPA reached the president's desk, the legislation was gradually molded over a two-year period by the employment and training subgovernment. Although CETA's public service employment components had been dumped in 1981, significant portions of CETA were still around. In fact, remedial education and training programs for the long-term unemployed, worth nearly $3 billion, were operating in state and local prime sponsorships. But CETA's 1978 reauthorization contained a self-destruct clause; unless Congress took action by September 1982, federal job training programs would expire.

The employment and training subgovernment considering CETA's replacement included representatives from the Labor Department, Congress, and various interest groups. (See Table 2-1, page 41.) The struggle over CETA's fate centered in the Senate Subcommittee on Employment and Productivity, chaired by Dan Quayle, and in the House Subcommittee on Employment Opportunities, chaired by Augustus Hawkins. Both subcommittees began working on new legislation in early 1981. Marathon hearings were held throughout the nation, and testimony was elicited from hundreds of witnesses. By early 1982 both subcommittees had prepared draft legislation.

The interest group wing of the subgovernment contained the traditional assortment of organized labor, community organizations, and client groups that strongly support job training initiatives. Also staunchly defending CETA's record were the National League of Cities, the U.S. Conference of Mayors, and the National Association of Counties. Newly prominent were the National Governors' Association and business organizations, such as the National Alliance of Business, the U.S. Chamber of Commerce, and the Committee for Economic Development—groups that were much less visible during the 1973 and 1978 policy deliberations over employment and training legislation. Their presence and clout in 1982 reflected both a heightened concern for employment issues and a sense that whatever bill emerged, states and the private sector would play larger roles in designing and managing programs.

At the risk of oversimplification, the participants in the job training debate can be classified into two factions: *the pro-CETA forces,* which included House Democrats, city and county elected officials, organized labor, and community organizations, and *the anti-CETA forces,* which included Senate and House Republicans, business groups, the National Governors' Association, and the Reagan administration. The pro-CETA forces were more influential in the House; the anti-CETA groups were dominant in the Senate. With the possible exception of the administration, the pro-CETA and anti-CETA forces held in common the desire to enact a federal job training law. During most of the struggle, the administration remained aloof from the fray. Its presence was felt, however, because it was feared that the president would veto legislation containing provisions at odds with his policy.

The pro- and anti-CETA forces articulated very different viewpoints about the CETA experience. Opening the joint hearings on job training bills, Quayle charged:

> CETA is broken and needs to be fixed. What was a modest training program in 1973 . . . grew into an uncontrolled monster by 1977. . . . Though in the past CETA has been fraught with abuses, fraud, and mismanagement, it does not mean we should turn our backs on the plight of the needy and unemployed. I say let's fix it.[48]

Also critical of CETA's shortcomings were senior Labor Department officials. Assistant Secretary Angrisani staked out the administration's position: "I would never defend CETA. . . . When you have in place seven years of mismanagement practices, sometimes it makes more sense to eliminate the processes in place and start over." [49] With the department acting as one of CETA's harshest critics, the pro-CETA forces were at an enormous disadvantage. A spokesperson for the National Association of Counties commented: "The Labor Department began with the assumption that CETA was a failure and they stuck to it. It is very difficult to salvage a program when the federal agency sponsoring it decides to undermine it." [50]

A radically different opinion of CETA was held by some members of Congress and local elected officials. Representative Hawkins set out the pro-CETA perspective:

> Since well-constructed reforms in 1978, the CETA system—despite the fact it has been systematically maligned—has overall produced cost-effective results. . . . Where CETA has not worked, it has not been due to badly conceived programs but instead to administrative problems which . . . could have been corrected by Federal oversight and assistance. We should build on these demonstrated strengths.[51]

Hawkin's affection for CETA's 1978 reauthorization can be readily understood. As its principal author, he naturally found virtue in CETA and fault with federal bureaucrats. Those defending CETA, blemishes and all, did so in part because they suspected that Reagan wanted to kill it. For strategic purposes, pro-CETA groups came to the bargaining table defending the status quo.

Was CETA "broken" and a "failure" or a "cost-effective" program upon whose strengths a better approach could be built? CETA was one of the most thoroughly studied programs in the history of American domestic policy. The House and Senate subcommittee members heard from hundreds of expert witnesses; subcommittee staffs examined dozens of government-funded research reports, but there was still considerable disagreement and uncertainty about which employment and training strategies worked best. Part of this disagreement stemmed from the nature of the research process, which often yields cautious and equivocal answers. Some of the disagreement reflected differences in political philosophies.

Students of public policy typically observe that research results rarely alter the adversarial nature of the process, especially in Congress.[52] Instead, research is used by advocates to back up their own points of view. A former staff member on the House Education and Labor Committee neatly summed up the role of evaluations in policy debates:

> Data are used in politics just like they are used everywhere else—to support preconceived, predetermined political positions. I think that if the data show a fantastic track record, they still wouldn't change people's basic fundamental attitude about CETA.[53]

Even though research findings alone did not determine the shape of the new law, the thorough body of evidence suggesting that CETA programs had worked was used effectively by CETA's defenders. Had this evidence not existed, it would have been difficult, it not impossible, to build support for continuing federal job training programs.

The principal research results were that people enrolled in CETA-funded training programs had better employment records and made more money than similar people not enrolled in such programs. The findings were detailed and rather complicated, but CETA's supporters seized upon some presentations supplied by a group of independent researchers, who dubbed themselves the National Council on Employment Policy. The council expressed CETA's record in simple cost-benefit terms. For every *dollar* invested the following benefits were produced:

For on-the-job training programs:	$2.28
For classroom training programs:	$1.14
For work experience programs:	$ .50

In other words, two of CETA's major strategies returned more to society than the government had invested.[54] The administration and congressional Republicans also took comfort from the findings because they supported the view that federal dollars were more profitably invested in training programs rather than in part-time work experience positions.

Systematic research discredited claims that CETA was a bust, but it did not alter the fundamental perception that CETA should be retailored. A former congressional staffer summed up CETA's liabilities:

> In political terms it has failed. The current data suggest that the CETA system as such, right now, is not so bad. Why change it? It's the perception. The perception of CETA is that it is bad. There are only a few people in this ball game that know the system—what is good and what isn't. There is no way to offset the perception that people have that the program is a ripoff.[55]

Democrats in the House and Senate and other pro-CETA groups recognized that CETA would have to be changed substantially to satisfy the Republicans. Thus, by the March 1982 joint hearings on replacement legislation, the pro- and anti-CETA forces had agreed on five fundamental changes. First, private sector representatives would be more involved in designing and managing programs. Second, state governments would be more important. Third, program results would be more carefully evaluated. Fourth, programs would prepare people for private sector jobs and not provide temporary public employment. Finally, the long-term unemployed and economically disadvantaged would remain the principal clients, but displaced workers, who might not otherwise be eligible, also could be helped.

The new direction of job training policy had been established, but how far and exactly where it would go were still subject to hard bargaining between the House and Senate. Three central policy disputes remained. First, there was considerable disagreement about how the private sector role should be defined. House Democrats, representing the interests of mayors and county officials, wanted an equal partnership between the private sector and local elected officials. The administration and many Senate Republicans wanted complete autonomy for private sector representatives. Second, there were differences about the role of state governments. The pro-CETA forces sought strong federal oversight and alleged that states were "the weakest links in the [CETA] system." [56] Senate Republicans and the administration argued for unequivocal state control over training programs. Although these issues were troublesome, they reflected disagreements over governance matters rather than over fundamental objectives.

The third issue provoking dispute—whether to allow the payment of wages, stipends, or allowances to enrollees—proved much more difficult to resolve. The administration wanted to outlaw such payments. Secretary of Labor Raymond Donovan, testifying before the joint House and Senate hearings, pointed out that, under CETA, stipends and wages "consumed about 44 percent of available resources." [57] Quayle asserted that many of CETA's problems stemmed from the fact that

> it lost its character as a job-training program and became, instead, an income-transfer program. It provided people with public service jobs and with allowances to help them with their living expenses, but did not train them for permanent work. It became a good program to get into—instead of being a good program to get out of. . . .[58]

House Democrats and CETA administrators favored retaining the option of payments. In their view, stipends and wages for trainees helped keep people in programs. Moreover, studies had shown that work experience programs, which pay wages for part-time work, had been most effective for the least job-ready participants. Critics of the administration's position on payments to enrollees also complained that an outright prohibition was "too prescriptive" and "ridiculous." [59]

The Legislative Compromise

The Job Training Partnership Act was forged from the House and Senate bills summarized in the box, page 178. The Senate version, known as the Quayle-Kennedy bill, incorporated most of what the Reagan administration wanted. Private industry councils would oversee the program; state governments would manage the system; and the payment of allowances, wages, or stipends was forbidden.

The House bill reflected positions favored by CETA operatives. Elected officials and private representatives together would develop community training strategies. Governors would have greater responsibility than under CETA, but the federal government would still review plans and monitor performance. Finally, allowance payments to participants were permitted.

By all accounts the conference committee deliberations that ultimately yielded the Job Training Partnership Act were very arduous. The House and Senate bills contained more than 300 differences, including several fundamental ones. House Democrats felt abused and frustrated. According to Hawkins: "We've done all the giving up so far. . . ." [60] The Senate Republicans were instructed by the White House to make no concessions.

The art of compromise was very much in evidence in resolving the state government and private sector issues. Governors would divide up their states into "service delivery areas," but communities with 200,000 or more residents would be guaranteed a program. The precise relationship between each private industry council and local government officials would not be "settled" by the law but rather decided by local politics and preferences. Elected officials and private industry councils would jointly

Final House and Senate CETA Replacement Bills

Issue	Senate Provisions	House Provisions
Role of the private sector	Private Industry Council (PIC) develops plan, designates program administrator; PIC plan must be reviewed by local elected officials; disagreements between PIC and elected officials appealed to governor.	Local elected officials and PIC jointly develop plan, designate program administrator; disagreements between PIC and elected officials appealed to the U.S. secretary of labor.
State role	Governor designates service delivery areas; approves local plans, monitors local programs, and may adjust performance standards.	Governor develops programs for displaced workers and little else.
Federal role	Allocates funds to the states and little else.	U.S. secretary of labor approves local plans, monitors local programs, prescribes and applies performance standards.
Restrictions on uses of program funds	Prohibits payment of allowances, wages, or stipends, except in summer youth program; requires that 70 percent of all funds be used for training.	Permits the payment of allowances for work experiences (on the basis of need); requires that 70 percent of all funds be used for training, but work experience and supportive services may be charged to training costs.

establish programs and make organizational arrangements.

The allowance payment dispute was more troublesome. House conferees would not accept the Senate prohibition, and the Labor Department insisted that permissive language would cause a presidential veto. With their patience worn thin, the House managers provoked a confrontation. Senate conferees were informed that the House planned to enact a simple extention of existing CETA programs unless compromise was forthcoming. Sen. Orrin Hatch, R-Utah, immediately compromised. The Senate lifted its outright ban on paying wages, allowances, and stipends to trainees and permitted the payment of work experience wages if such programs were coupled with classroom or on-the-job training. The House Democratic conferees accepted this gesture.

House and Senate Republican sponsors huddled with the president's advisers at the White House and informed them that the compromise bill was the best possible package. But Assistant Secretary Angrisani was in no mood to compromise. He urged the senators and representatives to uphold the administration's proposed prohibition on allowances and payments. David Stockman, director of the Office of Management and Budget, argued that the president should not oppose a job training bill during an election campaign with unemployment at 10 percent. The White House also had received messages of strong support for the new training bill from influential business organizations. The president's advisers consented to the compromise bill—the impasse was broken, and JTPA sailed through the House and Senate.

JTPA's basic provisions are summarized in the box, pages 180 and 181, and compared with the 1978 version of CETA. Looking back on the legislative process, one of its key participants, Rep. James Jeffords, R-Vt., observed that he had never heard people "groan, bitch, and moan" so much as during the consideration of JTPA, "and then everybody ran out and took credit for it." [61]

Images, Myths, and Ideologies

The new policy approaches adopted in JTPA were a product of the images, myths, and ideologies held by the legislation's key proponents, particularly Reagan administration officials and Senate Republicans. These new directions—increased private sector involvement, state government management, training instead of income-maintenance—stemmed from perceptions of CETA's deficiencies and convictions about how they might be remedied.

Take the issue of private sector participation, for example. JTPA's supporters argued that private employers were alienated from CETA training programs, that private sector job placements were woefully inadequate, and that CETA's experimental private sector initiative program was superior to the rest of it. JTPA's framers also believed that prime sponsor organizations were inefficient at best and corrupt at worst. Reliance on private sector representatives was in line with conservative Republican principles. Finally, the fact that some groups representing the business community, such as the National Alliance of Business, actively sought a private sector role helped foster movement along those lines.

The elimination of stipends and the emphasis on training also stemmed from images as well as political realities. CETA research reports supported the conclusion that training was more cost effective than short-term work experiences. The curtailment of stipends grew out of a desire to move job training away from being a social service program and toward serving the private sector's need for competent, trained employees.

	Key Provisions of JTPA...	
	The Job Training Partnership Act (October 1983-present)	CETA (April 1979 to September 1983)
Target groups	Low-income and long-term un-employed; 60 percent adult, 40 percent youth; 10 percent "window" for the nonpoor; includes dislocated workers.	Low-income and long-term un-employed; no specific program for dislocated workers.
Program activities and restrictions	On-the-job training, classroom training, and other activities that lead to jobs in the private sector; 70 percent of funds must go for training; restrictions on the use of funds for work experience; public service jobs prohibited; payment of stipends or wages to trainees restricted	Work experience, on-the-job training, classroom training, supportive services, remedial education; no restrictions on the use of funds to pay wages or stipends to program enrollees.
State role—governor	Responsible for overall program coordination and monitoring of state and local programs; approves or disapproves local plans; determines the areas that will deliver local programs; administers state level programs for older workers, dislocated workers; appoints state advisory council.	Administers programs in areas falling outside CETA prime sponsorships; administers special grants programs; appoints statewide advisory council.

CETA's opponents persuaded Congress that the balance between helping the jobless and satisfying the employer had tipped too far on the side of providing temporary income support for the unemployed. Finally, the reduction in stipends meant that more people could be enrolled for less money.

Placing responsibility for federal job training programs at the state level was motivated by a variety of perceptions. Many members of Congress believed that both the federal government and local prime sponsors had failed miserably as stewards of CETA. Enhancing the state role also accorded with the president's "New Federalism" proposals through which he hoped to bolster state governments. States should administer training measures, it was argued, because the states were

... Compared with CETA

	The Job Training Partnership Act (October 1983-present)	CETA (April 1979 to September 1983)
Service delivery areas	Units of local government in partnerships with PICs, with a population over 200,000 or serving a substantial area of the labor market.	Units of local government with population of 100,000; remainder in balance of state.
Local program management	PICs composed of representatives from the private sector, as the majority partner; from labor, education, and other groups; appointed by local elected officials; plans must be approved jointly by PICs and local elected officials.	Chief elected official of the local political jurisdiction; local advisory councils, appointed by elected officials, offer advice but do not approve or disapprove plans.
Federal role	Promulgation of national performance standards; management of research and demonstration projects; management of national programs for Indians, migrant workers, the Job Corps.	Principal responsibility for oversight of the system, including review and assessment of activities and delivery of technical assistance; research and demonstration projects; management of national programs for Indians, migrant workers, youth, the Job Corps, and other programs.

already responsible for closely related policies, such as education, economic development, and public assistance.

Perhaps major reforms in federal job training were inevitable because of CETA's horrible public reputation. But the Job Training Partnership Act's actual content was determined primarily by perceptions of what was wrong with the old system and the Reagan administration's political philosophy. That some of the system was preserved relatively unchanged is a function of the critical role played by CETA's defenders on Capitol Hill. While the administration succeeded in having its principal objectives incorporated into the new law, CETA's sympathizers constituted a modest, but significant, barrier against wholesale change or abandonment.

Early Readings on the JTPA Experience

Although the Job Training Partnership Act was signed in October 1982, provisions were made for a lengthy transition to the new system, and, indeed, the process took nearly two years. CETA programs were continued during fiscal year 1983 (October 1, 1982, to September 30, 1983) while the administrative transition to JTPA was under way. Not until October 1, 1983, were new clients enrolled in JTPA. Because preparing for JTPA was difficult and complicated, the new system initially bore striking resemblance to the old CETA one.

The real transition to JTPA took place after October 1, 1983, as staff and PIC members prepared for the first full program year, which began on July 1, 1984. At this point, it is impossible to make firm judgments about a program that is just starting up. There are some signs, however, about the shape of the new system, the legacies from CETA, and the promises for the future.[62] These policy issues and how they develop will receive careful scrutiny in the years to come.

Legacies from CETA

It is perhaps not surprising, at this early stage in its evolution, that the JTPA system contains many reminders of CETA. The new geographical divisions, called Service Delivery Areas, are remarkably similar to the old prime sponsorships. More than 80 percent of the areas served under JTPA are either identical to the areas served under CETA or hybrids of two or more CETA prime sponsorships. Only 20 percent are altogether "new" areas, lacking prior administrative experience. While the number of units handling JTPA programs has increased—from 470 to 596—there has not been wholesale change in the makeup of the system.[63]

Paralleling the geographical stability is an even more important legacy. The agencies and people responsible for JTPA are for the most part the same as for CETA. Despite the fact that private industry councils and local elected officials were given wide latitude to designate *new* organizations and to hire *new* professional staffs, nearly 8 in 10 chose to locate JTPA with the same state or local government agency that had been responsible for CETA operations. Moreover, only 15 percent of the PICs opted to run programs themselves.[64] The operations personnel also have remained. Senior staff continuity from CETA to JTPA is very high across the nation. In three states—New Jersey, New York, and Florida— where we examined the question of staffing carefully, the senior administrators responsible for JTPA are, with few exceptions, the people who ran CETA.[65] In short, the organizations and people behind employment and training programs have not changed.

The old CETA staffers carry some heavy baggage into the JTPA system. Attitudes and preferences about programs, beneficiaries, and methods of operation that developed during their CETA experience will not die quickly or easily. Take the controversial issue of allowance payments, for example. Most CETA operatives regarded allowance payments and stipends as necessary building blocks for training programs. It is not a simple matter for these professionals to revise their opinions and adjust to a new regime where allowance payments are sharply curtailed. Problems with enrollment and drop-out rates are already being blamed on the lack of allowance payments. Staff members claim that the JTPA system cannot succeed without stipends for trainees, and many are seeking creative devices to circumvent the new restrictions.

The former CETA administrators also carry with them a deep fear of financial liability. They painfully recall how the promise of local autonomy made during the early days of CETA turned out to be hollow when the Labor Department and Congress cracked down after 1978. As a result, many local JTPA administrators are skeptical of state government overseers who urge them not to worry about questions of accountability. More important, seasoned staffers warn new PIC members that program approaches that depart from accepted practice are risky ventures. Innovation may well be dampened by the fear of failure and its financial and political consequences.

Prospects for Change

Although there are many familiar features in the new system, several portents of change are already emerging. The most striking and definitive changes have occurred in the realignment of governance structures. The federal government's role in oversight and management, which hit a high-water mark after the 1978 CETA reauthorization, has receded sharply. While this change was indicated in the new law, the Labor Department has interpreted the legislation in a way that lessens its influence even further.

Consequently, the emerging state role is quite important. For the first time in most states, governors, senior state government staff, and even some state legislatures are seriously addressing the issue of job training for youth and adults and getting deeply involved in management and policy issues. Many states are considering how job training programs for the long-term unemployed relate to other state programs.

While the initial implementation of JTPA at the state level is generally positive, there remains great diversity. Some states have aggressively pursued issues such as program performance standards and have insisted on close coordination between the JTPA system and other state and local programs. Other states are much less involved in charting policy directions for local communities, preferring to dispense funds and track local performance.

Diversity among states in the administration of federal programs is commonplace. States vary in their interests, capacities, and performance in all aspects of public management. But the broad range of state management approaches in the JTPA system also was encouraged by the compromises made during the law's formulation. On the one hand, the law clearly calls for state-level leadership in the design and conduct of job training programs for the unemployed. On the other hand, the law also says that state policies "shall not affect local discretion concerning the selection of eligible participants or service providers." In short, different interpretations of the proper balance between state leadership and local autonomy are bound to emerge from a public law that contains support for both positions.[66]

The other principal change in employment and training governance is the public/private partnership brought about by the creation of private industry councils. The planning and management of JTPA programs is now a joint responsibility of private sector representatives and local elected officials. The average PIC consists of about 25 members, more than half of whom are representatives of the business community. Of these PIC members—about 11,000 business volunteers throughout the country— *three out of four are new* to employment and training programs and have little experience with the issues and history of government sponsored programs in their community, according to a nationwide survey of PICs.[67] The impact of private sector participation has been limited thus far because of truncated planning periods, inexperienced PIC boards, and professional staff held over from the CETA system. But the presence of private sector representatives as planning and management partners has already influenced the job training system, and that influence may increase.

Important changes in the shape of employment and training programs are taking place in the new system. The survey of PICs found a significant increase in on-the-job training programs, job placement efforts, and short-term training programs.[68] Longer training programs and work experience activities that were favored under CETA are being replaced. Reformulations of the program mix are caused by a combination of legislatively mandated restrictions on activities and changed attitudes about the fundamental purpose of job training. The law placed sharp restrictions on payments to participants and the use of support services, such as day care. At the same time, the law's performance standards stress the importance of helping program graduates find private sector jobs. These elements in the legislation convinced many local operatives that longer training programs with potentially higher rates of failure no longer could be tolerated.

Just as important as the legislative changes, however, were the new attitudes ushered in by JTPA. CETA was based on the premise that programs should be built around the needs of low-income, long-term unemployed people. Critics charged that insufficient attention was paid to results, that too little effort went into getting people jobs. JTPA operates on the premise that federal job training programs must have two groups of clients—the low-income, long-term unemployed *and* the employer community. The system should prepare competent employees to fill available job openings. The needs of the private sector must be fulfilled along with the needs of unemployed individuals. Some say this brings a healthy balance to government training programs; others think it is wrong and mean spirited. But nearly everyone agrees that substantial alterations in program orientation have already occurred.

The changes could have profound implications for the types of people who benefit from JTPA training and services. Although the eligibility standards for admission have changed little from CETA to JTPA, analysts predicted that JTPA programs would serve the least disadvantaged segment of the eligible population. JTPA has funds sufficient to serve only a tiny portion, perhaps 4 percent, of the eligible population. Many observers have concluded, therefore, that new restrictions, more short-term training and on-the-job training programs, and the emphasis on preparing job-ready applicants for the private sector will bring about a different mixture of job training enrollees.[69] The national survey of PICs reported, for example, that 35 percent expected a change in the participant mix under JTPA and that 25 percent expected their programs to skim off the best available applicants.[70] In sharp contrast, some local administrators have complained that JTPA applicants are more likely to be welfare recipients and others who are not as well qualified to enter training programs than the people who applied for CETA programs. Lack of stipends and new intake procedures are being blamed.[71]

Is JTPA Better than CETA?

JTPA solves some problems, ignores a few others, and creates some new ones. By wiping the slate clean—changing the law's name and modifying its governance structure—JTPA provided a new lease on life for federal job training strategies. Some of CETA's principal liabilities were swiftly jettisoned. JTPA's focus on a more narrow agenda and on measuring results are positive steps. CETA suffered from constantly shifting and multiplying objectives meted out by Congress. JTPA's task is more manageable, more modest, and in many ways different from CETA's.

Bringing the private sector into a partnership with local elected officials should be regarded with optimism at this juncture. Despite differences in emphasis, all earlier federal job training programs aspired to prepare people for private sector jobs, but employers played almost no meaningful role in program design or management. Equally important, private sector representation in the employment and training environment may create a more solid base of political support on both the local and the national levels.

The enhancement of state government participation under JTPA seems to be a positive step. State governments have managed and often funded the nation's principal education, income support, and economic development programs. JTPA holds out the as yet unfulfilled promise that remedial job training programs can be effectively integrated into a network of human service and economic growth strategies at the state level.

On the negative side, the employment and training system may not be paying sufficient attention to the needs of the most disadvantaged. It is possible that federal dollars may be poorly invested by training people who could obtain employment without federal assistance while others, unable to find work without this kind of assistance, remain on public welfare, food stamps, and other forms of dependency. Clearly, a balance between the needs of employers and the unemployed must be found, but, if the balance swings too far in the direction of helping employers, the system could become terribly inefficient.

The legislation contains the usual handful of unresolved conundrums and creates some new dilemmas. The passage of JTPA did nothing to "solve" the fundamental problem faced by employment and training professionals: how can the low-income, long-term unemployed be helped to become self-sufficient, productive members of the labor force? The new legislation added few new tools for handling this old problem. In fact, the reduction of allowance payments and support services may make the task more difficult than ever, creating a new set of obstacles that will require creative strategies. The first few years of JTPA's implementation are likely to be fraught with difficulties.

The early readings of JTPA contain signs of warning and signs of promise. If private sector representatives make strong commitments to JTPA's success, if governors develop effective management and leadership strategies, and if Congress resists the temptation to tinker with the law for at least a few years, then it is possible that JTPA will prove a better strategy than CETA for helping the long-term unemployed and low-income people obtain jobs. The individuals and organizations that have inherited the nation's job training system face a formidable task.

Notes

1. Ronald Reagan, "A Program for Economic Recovery—Address by the President of the United States," *Congressional Record,* 97th Cong., 1st sess., Feb. 18, 1981, H-513.
2. Ibid., H-511.
3. Ibid., H-513.
4. *Budget of the United States, Fiscal Year 1983,* 5-121.
5. "CETA Showdown," *Newark Star-Ledger,* Dec. 7, 1981, 14.
6. Nathaniel Semple, letter to authors, Nov. 10, 1983. Semple served as counsel to the minority, U.S. House of Representatives, Education and Labor Committee.
7. *Congressional Record,* 97th Cong., 2d sess., Feb. 2, 1982, S-246.
8. House Committee on Education and Labor, *Report to the Committee on the Budget of the U.S. House of Representatives,* 97th Cong., 1st sess., March 20, 1981, 23.
9. "Over $11 Billion Cut from Social Program," *Congressional Quarterly Weekly Report,* June 13, 1981, 1030.
10. "Requiem for CETA," *Washington Post,* March 29, 1981, B6.
11. General Accounting Office, *Implementation of the Phaseout of CETA Public Service Jobs,* HRD-82-48, Appendix I (Washington, D.C.: GPO, April 14, 1982), 8.
12. Ibid., Appendix I, 14; Appendix III, 37.
13. Ibid., Appendix III, 3.
14. Carl E. Van Horn and Henry J. Raimondo, *The Impact of Reductions in Federal Aid to New Jersey* (New Brunswick, N.J.: Eagleton Institute of Politics, Rutgers University, May 1982). The results of this report are summarized in "Living with Less: New Jersey Copes with Federal Aid Cutbacks," Carl E. Van Horn and Henry J. Raimondo, *Public Budgeting and Finance* 3 (Spring 1983): 41-56.
15. General Accounting Office, *Implementation of the Phaseout,* Appendix I, 17.
16. Van Horn and Raimondo, *The Impact of Reductions,* 13.
17. Ibid., 13-15.
18. "A CETA Story," *New York Times,* Jan. 22, 1982, A16.
19. Congressional Budget Office, *Effects of Eliminating Public Service Employment* (Washington, D.C.: GPO, June 1981), xi.
20. For details on the procedures used in arriving at these estimates, see Van Horn and Raimondo, *The Impact of Reductions,* 15-17 and Appendix B.
21. "Republicans, Democrats Start Struggle for Position over 'Jobs, Jobs, Jobs,'" *Employment and Training Reporter,* Nov. 17, 1982, 281.
22. "FY 1983 Budget Slashes Employment and Training Funds in New Program," *Employment and Training Reporter,* Feb. 10, 1982, 556.
23. "House Democrats Press $1 Billion Jobs Plan," *Congressional Quarterly Weekly Report,* Aug. 28, 1982, 2124.
24. Steven R. Weisman, "Reagan Tiptoes Around Some Economic Liabilities," *New York Times,* Sept. 26, 1982, E4.

25. *Gallup Poll Report,* Sept. 1982, 6-7.
26. "Transcript of Reagan's Speech to Nation on G.O.P. Policy and the Economy," *New York Times,* Oct. 14, 1982, B14.
27. Robert Pear, "Congress to Consider Job Program to Curb Unemployment Rise," *New York Times,* Nov. 7, 1982, 1.
28. "Elections Could Boost Job Creation, Slow Implementation of Training Act," *Employment and Training Reporter,* Nov. 10, 1982, 259.
29. "Transcript of President Reagan's News Conference," *New York Times,* Nov. 12, 1982, B6.
30. "The New York Times/CBS Poll," *New York Times,* Jan. 25, 1983, B4.
31. "Quayle Hearing Explores Designs for Job Creation Program that 'Will Work,'" *Employment and Training Reporter,* Jan. 19, 1983, 541.
32. Robert Pear, "Helping the Unemployed Is the First Priority But It's Expensive," *New York Times,* Jan. 2, 1983, E4.
33. "Reagan's Economic Report," *Congressional Quarterly Weekly Report,* Feb. 5, 1983, 298.
34. For details on the president's proposals, see Ibid. and "Text of Reagan Proposals on Structural Unemployment," *Congressional Quarterly Weekly Report,* March 19, 1983, 579-581.
35. "Reagan's Fiscal 1984 Budget Message," *Congressional Quarterly Weekly Report,* Feb. 5, 1983, 296.
36. "Interest Withholding Dispute Stalls Senate Jobs Bill Action," *Congressional Quarterly Weekly Report,* March 12, 1983, 491; "Text of Reagan Press Conference," *Congressional Quarterly Weekly Report,* Jan. 8, 1983, 73.
37. Hedrick Smith, "Reagan's Stronger Hand," *New York Times,* Feb. 5, 1983, 7.
38. Congressional Budget Office, *Strategies for Assisting the Unemployed,* (Congressional Budget Office, Washington, D.C., Dec. 8, 1982, Photocopied).
39. Pear, "Helping the Unemployed Is the First Priority," E4.
40. "Reagan, Democrats Move on Jobs Plan," *Employment and Training Reporter,* Feb. 16, 1983, 688.
41. For a detailed description of the law, see "Congress Votes $4.6 Billion For Jobs and Recession Relief," *Congressional Quarterly Weekly Report,* March 26, 1983, 638-642.
42. For a summary of these criticisms, see Steven V. Roberts, "Many See Jobs Proposal as Merely a First Step," *New York Times,* Feb. 22, 1983, A14.
43. "Recession Aid Bill Makes Progress with Bipartisan Support, Criticism," *Employment and Training Reporter,* March 2, 1983, 723.
44. "Congress Votes $4.6 Billion," 638.
45. Administration of Ronald Reagan, *Weekly Compilation of Presidential Documents,* Oct. 13, 1982, 1302-1303.
46. John Herbers, "President Asserts Economic Policies Prove Effective," *New York Times,* Oct. 14, 1982, B15.
47. "House Passes Scaled-down Job Training Measure, 356-52," *Congressional Quarterly Weekly Report,* Aug. 7, 1982, 1895.
48. Sen. Dan Quayle, "Opening Statement Before the Joint Hearings on Job

Training Legislation," Press release, March 12, 1982, 2.

49. Quoted in "Life after Death—CETA's Demise Won't Mean the End of Manpower Training," William J. Lanouette, *National Journal*, Feb. 6 1982, 241.

50. Nancy ReMine-Trego, interview with authors, Oct. 25, 1982.

51. Rep. Augustus Hawkins, "Introductory Remarks, Joint Hearings of the House Subcommittee on Employment Opportunities and the Senate Subcommittee on Employment and Productivity," Press release, March 12, 1982, 7.

52. See, for example, James Sundquist, "Research Brokerage: The Weak Link," in *Knowledge and Policy: The Uncertain Connection*, Laurence Lynn, ed. (Washington, D.C.: National Academy of Sciences, 1978).

53. Nathaniel Semple, interview with authors, March 16, 1982.

54. These results were reported in "CETA's Results and Their Implications" (National Council on Employment Policy, Washington, D.C., September 1981, Photocopied).

55. Nathaniel Semple, interview with authors, March 16, 1982.

56. "Management of Remedial Employment and Training Programs in the 1980s," (National Council for Employment Policy, Washington, D.C., January 1982, Photocopied).

57. Raymond J. Donovan, "Statement Before the Subcommittee on Employment and Productivity and the Subcommittee on Employment Opportunities," Press release, March 15, 1982.

58. Quayle, "Opening Statement," 2.

59. Nathaniel Semple, interview with authors, March 16, 1982.

60. Quoted in *Employment and Training Reporter*, Aug. 25, 1982, 1321.

61. Quoted in *Employment and Training Reporter*, Nov. 13, 1982, 241.

62. Visits to statewide meetings of JTPA program administrators in New Jersey, New York, and Florida were conducted during the fall of 1983 and early winter of 1984. Interviews also were conducted in Washington, D.C., in March 1984 with Susan McGuire, House Subcommittee on Employment Opportunities; Burt Carlson, National Governors' Association; Rod Riffel, National Conference of State Legislatures; and Nathaniel Semple, Committee for Economic Development. Also interviewed were Ed Dement and R. C. Smith of MDC, Inc., who participated in the independent sector analysis of JTPA in conjunction with Grinker-Walker Associates and Syracuse Research Corporation.

63. MDC, Inc. "Tracking the Transition (Round II): A Report on the Status of State and Local Preparations for Implementation of the Job Training Partnership Act," (National Commission for Employment Policy, Washington, D.C., 1983, Photocopied), 6.

64. National Alliance of Business, *An Overview of the New Job Training System*, Survey Report 1 (Washington, D.C.: National Alliance of Business), 10-12.

65. Interviews with program administrators in New York, New Jersey, and Florida, December 1983 and January 1984.

66. MDC, Inc."Tracking the Transition: Summary and Analysis: Early State-level Preparations for JTPA Implementation," (National Commission for Employment Policy, Washington, D.C., 1982, Photocopied), 23.

67. National Alliance of Business, *Overview of New Job Training,* 9.
68. Ibid., 20.
69. MDC, Inc. "Tracking the Transition (Round II)," 19-20.
70. National Alliance of Business, *Overview of New Job Training,* 20.
71. Interviews with JTPA program administrators in New Jersey and Florida conducted during January and March 1984.

Policy and Politics 7

Unemployment has been a vexing public problem for decades. For the entire generation of Americans who lived through the Depression of the 1930s, massive unemployment and its consequences left an indelible impression. The jobless rate has never again climbed to Depression-era levels, but the reality and fear of unemployment are still with us. Despite the enormous growth of the U.S. economy over the last 40 years, high levels of unemployment have accompanied economic recessions, which occurred with increasing frequency during the 1970s and 1980s. Unlike many public issues that are debated in Washington, unemployment genuinely concerns the average citizen. The performance of the economy and the rise and fall of the unemployment rate are widely reported each month. People can readily judge the nation's "misery index" for themselves.

Policy makers have been groping for effective strategies to curb unemployment for more than 50 years, but the problem has proven difficult and very expensive to treat. After decades of trial and error, programs to aid the unemployed remain highly controversial. In this chapter, we review the record to determine what years of experimentation and billions of dollars have accomplished. We also examine the politics of unemployment and consider whether its characteristics are unique or commonplace in the policy process. Finally, we describe the contemporary debate over new unemployment initiatives and assess their prospects in the latter half of the 1980s.

Reviewing the Record

In characterizing contemporary programs and reviewing several decades of policy change, we will apply the political scientist Lawrence Brown's distinction between "breakthrough" policies and "rationalizing" policies.[1] Breakthrough policies are major new government objectives and approaches. The New Deal, the War on Poverty, the Clean Air Act, and the

Civil Rights Act were breakthroughs because they charted new policy directions. Rationalizing policies revise and attempt to improve policies created by breakthroughs. Fundamental questions are no longer central; instead policy makers try to reform the delivery of government services and respond to implementation problems. Breakthrough politics are partisan, ideological, contentious, and visible. Rationalizing politics are less partisan and contentious and concern relatively few citizens or interest groups. Debates about rationalizing policies focus on program results, rather than on ideological preferences.

Like most policy domains, unemployment programs are marked by few breakthroughs and by ongoing efforts to rationalize past decisions. However, the struggle to rationalize unemployment policy breakthroughs has been unusually contentious and ideological. Since the 1930s, there have been just two major unemployment program breakthroughs.[2] The first and most important occurred during President Franklin D. Roosevelt's first term in office, when the federal government for the first time explicitly adopted the goal of direct aid to the jobless through unemployment insurance and job creation programs.

After several decades, unemployment insurance remains by far the largest and most durable government strategy for helping the jobless. Expenditures from the unemployment insurance fund have skyrocketed. Between 1974 and 1983, millions of unemployed workers were paid an average of $16 billion dollars annually from the fund, nearly $33 billion in 1983 alone. Eighty-five percent of all federal dollars devoted to ameliorating unemployment were funneled through this system during the 1980s.

Federal job creation strategies have been embraced and rejected periodically by U.S. politicians over the years. The New Deal's public works projects vanished during World War II and did not reappear until the 1960s. During the 1970s and early 1980s, federal jobs programs were funded under the Emergency Employment Act and the Comprehensive Employment and Training Act (CETA). Currently, public works projects are popular again. In late 1982 and early 1983, with 10 percent of the workforce unemployed, Congress allocated more than $10 billion to hire the jobless and to keep others employed on public projects.

The second major breakthrough came during President Lyndon B. Johnson's War on Poverty. During the 1960s federal lawmakers committed the government to aiding a portion of the long-term structurally unemployed through job training programs. Since then the government has supported a "second chance" training system for thousands of people who do not obtain adequate education and training in the public schools.

Job training programs have been overhauled several times. During the 1960s youth and adult training programs operated under the Manpower Development and Training Act and the Economic Opportunity Act; in the 1970s and early 1980s they were administered under CETA; and since 1983 such programs have been housed under the Job Training Partnership Act (JTPA). Although there have been many twists and turns, the fundamental objectives of job training programs have remained stable—to help the unemployed and disadvantaged obtain jobs and escape poverty. The price tag for job training has not changed either. The $2 billion spent in 1984 is roughly the same amount allocated to similar programs a decade ago.

Despite the absence of recent major breakthroughs, unemployment programs continue to generate a great deal of conflict in the political system, and, consequently, the program environment has been very unstable. Presidents, Congresses, state and local officials, and interest groups have been locked in almost constant wrangling over the size, shape, and very existence of federal job training and job creation programs. Rationalizing politics for unemployment programs are atypical because fundamental questions are continually raised. Only unemployment insurance has thus far escaped sustained scrutiny and major revamping.

Given the obstinate, complex nature of unemployment and the large and diverse political system in which strategies are planned and implemented, it would be difficult to administer even the best-designed programs. Clearly the conditions surrounding the formulation of unemployment policy have not been conducive to optimal implementation. Before explaining why policy formulation and implementation have been difficult, however, let us briefly review the performance of these programs.

The accomplishments and shortcomings of employment and training programs can be examined by looking at three aspects of implementation: federal leadership, professional capacity, and program results. *Federal leadership,* in this case, refers to efforts by the Labor Department (acting on behalf of the president and Congress) to steer implementation and to achieve national objectives. *Professional capacity* refers to the abilities of state and local governments and other organizations to deliver services in an effective and efficient manner. The term *program results* refers to how well the services aided unemployed people.

Federal Leadership

The federal government's leadership of unemployment programs was rather disappointing. A large share of the problems experienced by the employment and training system during the last decade originated with federal policy and were exacerbated by inept federal management. Insensitivity to the concerns and responsibilities of "street-level bureaucrats" was often displayed by federal administrators. No sooner were state and local officials handed one set of tasks than they were given yet another mission, higher or lower spending targets, or stacks of new regulations.

Much of the federal government's ineffectiveness was a direct result of changing political objectives. The Nixon administration assumed a lenient federal posture; President Carter adopted a more aggressive federal presence; President Reagan turned control over to state officials; and Congress regularly sent confusing signals. Given changing statutes and a volatile environment, the Labor Department was unable to follow a clear and consistent strategy of federal oversight, management, and leadership. The Labor Department successfully promoted several national objectives that later proved troublesome. It stimulated a rapid expansion of public service employment (PSE) and youth programs during the mid-1970s, but the fixation on speed, rather than quality, turned out to be politically costly. The department also enforced the restrictions in CETA's complex 1978 reauthorization but, in doing so, lost the program many of its supporters.

Overall, federal government administrators were shortsighted and in some instances misguided. Narrow questions of accountability, such as adherence to spending and reporting schedules, were stressed instead of more important matters, such as the development of strong state and local organizations and the management of effective programs. The department carried out precise national objectives that demanded strict compliance to rules, but this "no-risk management" strategy was not beneficial to the system as a whole. Federal officials were too responsive to the transient political concerns of Congress. Political criticism was temporarily avoided, but other more important objectives were sacrificed. In the process, the reputations of both employment and training programs and the Labor Department suffered severe damage.

Professional Capacity

For programs to succeed, agencies responsible for implementation must develop and improve their professional capacity. The most important participants in the delivery system are the administrators, teachers, and counselors who deal with the needs of unemployed people in their communities. Unfortunately, the federal government gave little or no help to local professionals. In fact, several federal practices inhibited the development of effective service delivery. Nevertheless, when shortcomings in job training and job creation measures were identified, the president and Congress blamed state and local administrators and exonerated themselves. Insult was added to injury.

Given this rather hostile climate, the accomplishments of state and local administrators must be judged sympathetically. These professionals competently provided basic services to the unemployed in most communities. With little advance warning or assistance, they expanded youth and public jobs programs during the mid-1970s and phased them out again in the 1980s. They mounted large-scale summer jobs programs for young people each year. They planned and managed training programs for the long-term unemployed. State and local implementers acquired indispensable experience and knowledge about how to make programs work. The early evidence suggests that many of these experienced operatives are involved in the new Job Training Partnership Act system, but some communities and states were forced to start fresh, without benefit of seasoned professionals.

Notwithstanding the accomplishments of many communities, the record reveals serious deficiencies. The decentralization of programs from the federal government to states and local governments under CETA did not fulfill its basic promise—coordinated and effective programs. Still worse, some elected officials used federal funds to balance local budgets or to reward favored groups and organizations—a development that prompted a counterproductive federal crackdown. Even in communities where political considerations were not paramount, significant reform rarely materialized. Most agencies were too preoccupied with national goals such as the public jobs expansion or elimination. Only a few elite organizations successfully integrated employment and training strategies into their community's social service and economic development programs.

The establishment of new institutional responsibilities and relationships under the Job Training Partnership Act again holds out the promise of more effective and efficient programs. State governments have inherited an important leadership role. It is too early to tell whether they can achieve what the federal government and a locally centered system failed to do. Perhaps state governments and local public/private partnerships will give more attention to the design and delivery of effective unemployment programs than was given by national policy makers during the last decade.

Program Results

When assessing employment and training programs, one is reminded of the old adage: Where you stand depends on where you sit. To many observers, especially the unemployed people who obtained temporary jobs or received training assistance, unemployment programs were a godsend. In many communities, federal aid, in the form of job creation measures, salvaged public services. But, for those who worry about the size of the federal budget or who think that unemployed people don't want to work, the performance of job training and job creation programs merely confirms the suspicion that money was wasted on questionable enterprises. When programs are evaluated by politicians, expectations and perceptions are almost always more powerful than objective results.

Over the years, scores of researchers have attempted to sort out and assess the economic impacts of employment and training programs on unemployed people.[3] Most studies reached a similar conclusion: remedial classroom and on-the-job training programs are beneficial public investments. More is returned to society, in the form of greater participant earnings and reduced welfare and unemployment insurance outlays, than is spent for the programs. On-the-job training is particularly efficient from a cost-benefit perspective. Part-time temporary work experience programs, in contrast, usually do not have positive cost-benefit ratios, but can be effective when coupled with training and job development services. The considered judgment of the research community is that remedial job training programs are reasonably effective strategies for helping the long-term unemployed attain a better life. These results are cause for modest optimism about the value of unemployment programs because the results were achieved during a period of considerable turbulence.

Because of their high costs, job creation measures are considered less effective than training programs. However, CETA public service jobholders realized long-term benefits in the form of increased employment and earnings.[4] Under optimum conditions, PSE functions as an on-the-job training experience that prepares people for permanent public sector jobs. People with limited skills perform needed public services and gain useful experience. Unfortunately, these optimum conditions were seldom present in federal job creation programs, and the potential benefits were diminished. In particular, the rapid expansion, alteration, and contraction of public jobs programs during the last decade greatly limited movement of program participants into unsubsidized jobs.

The primary recipients of job training programs have been the poor, the long-term unemployed, minorities, and people with limited education. In the early 1970s permissive entrance standards in public service employment programs allowed many nondisadvantaged individuals to obtain jobs. Subsequent changes in eligibility requirements effectively targeted job programs on the long-term unemployed poor. The implementation experience of the 1970s proves that clearly written laws and federal enforcement practices can ensure that the least advantaged are helped. The patterns of benefit distribution also reflect the consensus of professionals at all levels of the federal system that the disadvantaged should be the principal participants in federal training programs.

Contemporary job training programs reflect the lessons of the past two decades of experimentation; job creation programs do not. The Job Training Partnership Act strikes a good balance between strict entrance standards and flexibility. Most programs are directed at people with the longest unemployment and the least financial resources. The law also permits the enrollment of people who do not meet these criteria, but soon would if help were not forthcoming.

Eligibility standards for the latest round of temporary public works programs are a different matter. The Transportation Assistance Act of 1982 and the emergency jobs appropriation of 1983 are likely to provide many federal jobs to people who were already employed elsewhere or who would have gotten private sector jobs rather quickly without government help. Not only has the net job-generating potential been substantially reduced, but, more important, the long-term unemployed with limited skills and experience will receive few federally financed jobs and therefore remain dependent on income transfer programs.

A Fragile Consensus

The record of federal employment and training programs is mixed. Modest success in aiding jobless Americans has been achieved, but unemployment measures have been plagued by serious problems. Their turbulent history is marked by unstable policies and by abundant implementation failures. During the last decade alone, dozens of new programs have been enacted and then swiftly discarded. Not only have there been radical shifts in objectives, funding, and delivery systems but also ambiguous and conflicting statutory provisions—in short, every kind of administrative nightmare. Why were so many policies adopted and then abandoned, and why did the implementation experience so often go awry? Are these kinds of cycles, consisting of policy formulation, implementation, and reformulation, typical of U.S. politics?

Unemployment strategies exist at the forefront of social and political change in the United States. Contemporary policies reflect a fragile consensus over when and how the government should assist the nation's unemployed. This weak and ephemeral consensus is the central condition that explains government policy actions. Debates over unemployment programs expose fundamental philosophical disputes about the proper responsibilities of the government, the private sector, and the individual. Within American political culture, government job training and job creation programs are regarded as significant public interventions in the private economy.

Nowhere is conflict more apparent than in the formulation and implementation of temporary jobs measures. These programs tread on the constantly shifting (and imaginary) line that divides liberals and conservatives over public and private sector responsibilities. The fact that many unemployment programs are aimed at low-income citizens makes them even more controversial. Collecting federal tax dollars from the *employed* to help the *poor* and *long-term unemployed* is bound to upset many groups and citizens.

Deep-seated disagreements about the nature and extent of government aid for the unemployed produce fluctuating objectives and spending levels. Policy changes are caused by the swinging balance of partisan power and by other major political and economic events. As control of the White House changes, as the national economy prospers or falters, and as public opinion shifts, so too do the fortunes of job creation and training programs.

The unemployment rate has a powerful influence on political calculations and policy decisions. The reality of unemployment and the fear that one might become unemployed shape public attitudes.[5] When the unemployment rate is rising, people who have jobs become concerned that they might become part of the statistic. As unemployment and concern over it rise, public support for government action increases. Presidents and members of Congress worry that they will be blamed for not taking action. That is why President Reagan endorsed temporary public works measures in 1982 and 1983 after opposing them for his entire political career. Such programs had become political necessities to both Republican and Democratic lawmakers.

When unemployment rates drop, however, the public eventually becomes less fearful of economic disaster and focuses on other national problems, such as inflation. The absolute level of unemployment may remain quite high, but as long as the *direction* is downward, most people seem to be reassured. The public's concern over unemployment declined sharply during 1984, even though the unemployment rate of more than 7.5 percent was well above levels that had caused alarm in earlier recessions. Because unemployment had fallen from its post-World War II high of 10.8 percent in 1982, the fear of joblessness vanished for many Americans.

The balance of partisan power, the fluctuating economy, and shifting public opinion not only account for unstable unemployment policies but also explain why public laws are often vague. Partisan disagreements and uncertainty about which strategies are most effective produce laws that are full of rhetoric but often lacking in specific and clear objectives. Because policy makers cannot agree on precise solutions, the laws that are enacted reflect temporary agreements over broad purposes. The hard choices and difficult decisions, more often than not, are delegated to program implementers. Unemployment programs are striking examples of Congress's propensity to enact ambiguous statutes that foster implementation problems.

Implementation Images

Unstable policy and subsequent administrative confusion also occur because elected officials are quick to alter policies when they suspect that programs are performing poorly. These assessments are fundamentally political and shaped by a mixture of ideology and perceptions about how well or how poorly the law's objectives have been fulfilled. Thus, even when political and economic events do not affect the calculations of elected officials, implementation images may provide the stimulus for change. Politicians' images of the implementation experience have a strong influence on their actions.

In the continuous process of policy making, negative implementation images lead concerned policy makers to adjust and revise existing strategies.[6] But if policies are altered frequently, policy makers have less time and opportunity to assess the value of each round of innovation, and administrators have less chance to develop the capacity to carry out the initiatives. Clearly, weaknesses in program design and administration should be corrected periodically by lawmakers, but repeated modifications will improve matters only if there is a firm consensus on ultimate objectives and an accurate diagnosis of policy problems. Unfortunately, these conditions were rarely present in the unemployment policy domain. All too often the wrong remedy was applied to a problem or the wrong problem was identified.

Contemporary job creation measures illustrate the powerful effect of negative imagery on the design of public laws. During the "unemployment crisis" of 1982 and 1983, polls indicated that the citizenry was anxious for government action to ameliorate joblessness. Republicans and Democrats alike agreed that the government should respond to these concerns. Two expensive public works programs were authorized, but they could provide jobs for only a small segment of the unemployed. Congress rejected the public service employment approach to job generation, even though it would have produced jobs faster and at less cost. Public service employment programs had fallen into disfavor under CETA. The stories of corruption and abuse, which represented the extremes rather than the norm, were never effectively countered. A potentially viable approach for helping the unemployed was discredited by a negative implementation image.

Policy Reformulation

Policy formulation, implementation, and reformulation cycles are becoming increasingly significant in U.S. politics. Heightened concern over massive federal budget deficits, large commitments for national security, and rapidly rising outlays in existing entitlement programs make it extremely difficult to enact large new domestic programs. Presidents, members of Congress, the bureaucracy, and interest groups are likely to devote more attention to scrutinizing and revising existing policies and programs. When opportunities for dramatic policy innovations become scarce, improving old policies may be the only way to gain political credit. Presidents and Congress may be tempted to alter policy just to demonstrate "responsiveness," thus increasing the danger that the revisions will not be entirely salubrious and that programs may become even more difficult to administer.

To the extent that our expectations are borne out, the constant reworking of policies could have implications for relationships among presidents, Congresses, and the bureaucracy. Presidents may have fewer opportunities to provide domestic policy leadership as they find themselves unable to initiate new approaches. As Congress spends more of its time reconsidering existing policies, it could decline even further as a forum for debating fundamental principles. The ascendence of rationalizing politics is likely to make bureaucracies even more of a negative symbol that politicians will exploit, and thus administrators will become more wary, defensive, and ineffective.[7]

In our view, these trends are already apparent in the politics of unemployment. Since Lyndon Johnson's War on Poverty, presidents have made no sustained policy breakthroughs in unemployment strategies. The most recent history of federal employment policy is marked by repeated episodes of new policy initiatives, followed by disappointment and reformulation. Jimmy Carter enlarged public jobs programs during the early months of his presidency, but public and political support for aggressive government action ebbed quickly when the unemployment rate declined and federal budget deficits rose. Carter gained neither electoral rewards nor historical recognition for his unemployment initiatives, despite the fact that they were among his principal domestic policy accomplishments.[8] Reagan attempted to reverse the unemployment strategies adopted by the Johnson and Carter administrations but failed, for the most part.

Constant attempts to rationalize past decisions have characterized the politics of unemployment in Congress. New programs, objectives, resources, and organizations have been authorized frequently. Revisions have been justified by the need to resolve political problems or by attacking the performance of the Labor Department and state and local governments. Under these circumstances, it is not surprising that program administrators became defensive and demoralized.

Making proper and useful revisions in law and administrative practice depends on first making correct assessments about the underlying problems. This has seldom occurred in the unemployment policy area. Both policy design flaws and implementation problems plagued the system during the 1970s and early 1980s. Overall, the fundamental deficiencies were not caused by the refusal or inability of state and local implementers to carry out national objectives. Rather the most important miscues stemmed from poorly constructed laws that were too frequently overhauled and expanded by impatient national lawmakers.

Fragmented Institutions

The problems created by unstable, vague, and poorly designed policies are made even worse by the fragmentation of American political institutions. The separate power bases of national political institutions and state and local governments inhibit comprehensive action on major social problems. The political system does not consider far-reaching and complex issues like unemployment as a whole. Instead, various aspects of the problem are addressed by different subgovernments. The integration of strategies designed to expand the economy, create jobs, and train the workforce is either ignored entirely or delegated to those without the authority to do the job—federal bureaucrats and state and local officials.

The byproducts of fragmentation are poorly coordinated and partially conflicting programs that are considerably less effective than they might be. Dozens of government programs directly and indirectly affect unemployment, but they are not connected with one another during the formulation process or during implementation. Unemployment insurance is not tied to training programs; secondary schools often have little connection with federal job training for youth; economic development strategies seldom are related to the employment and training system; public welfare programs are isolated from employment measures; and the list of shortcomings continues.

Significant obstacles stand in the way of anyone who might want to consolidate and coordinate the nation's unemployment strategies. The structure of the American political system and the nation's political culture undermine the strong central authority that would be required to move disparate agencies and governments in a coordinated fashion. Moreover, many politicians and interest groups prefer the status quo. Politicians benefit because fragmentation creates opportunities to frame discrete policies and to claim credit. Interest groups benefit because they can exert more influence when policies are subdivided than when they are enacted through sweeping initiatives.

Comprehensive unemployment policy can be brought about only by a widespread consensus that is thus far conspicuously absent in the political system. Paradoxically, politicians are unlikely to work toward more comprehensive strategies unless they perceive a public consensus and demand for action, and the public is unlikely to achieve that consensus unless mobilized by elected officials.

The Struggle over the Unemployment Agenda

Heated debates over the nature and scope of federal programs for the unemployed continue. Existing strategies have been assailed by both liberal and conservative lawmakers. The fragile consensus about government strategies is even less firm today than it was during most of the 1970s.

Contemporary concerns about unemployment were heightened by conspicuous signposts in 1982 and 1983—the highest unemployment rates in more than 40 years. But people may be even more worried about what the unemployment rate indicates about the future of the U.S. economy. Because the average unemployment rate has remained higher after each recession since 1969 and recessions have occurred more frequently, there is an increasingly widespread feeling that the nation's economic health is in jeopardy. In addition, the overall measure of prosperity—the gross national product—has shown a slower growth rate. There is fear that the United States is no longer competitive in the world economy and that our trading partners in the industrial world, especially Japan, are poised to ruin our economy if we do not somehow check their intervention in our market and improve our productivity. Severe weaknesses in the automobile and steel industries have prompted concerns that many more jobs in manufacturing and heavy industry will be lost.

The current debate centers around the definition of the problem. How serious are the economic obstacles? What are the underlying causes of unemployment? What is government's role, if any, in ameliorating these problems? Not surprisingly, Democrats and Republicans make very different suggestions about the nature and extent of government action. The policy landscape is crowded with proposed remedies for unemployment. During the past few years alone, dozens of new initiatives have been advanced. A sampling of major ideas follows:

—revamping trade policies to restrict imports or increase exports
—repairing and expanding the nation's infrastructure
—enhancing industrial productivity through expanded educational and training programs and through improved management/labor practices and relationships
—developing new public/private ventures for commercial and industrial growth
—increasing the regulation of businesses to curb the relocation of capital and facilities to foreign countries
—establishing a national system of mandatory public service for youth to work in national, state, and local governments for small stipends
—directing public and private investments toward new high technology industries and encouraging their growth
—abolishing the minimum wage for teenage workers
—enacting plant-closing legislation that would require advance notice to workers and provide training or relocation assistance to displaced workers

—creating a national program entitling all low-income youth to a part-time job in exchange for their participation in education and training activities

A comprehensive discussion of these proposals is far beyond the scope of this book, but we will briefly examine the major approaches that are likely to receive close scrutiny during the latter half of the 1980s. The various strategies can be grouped as follows: the expansion and improvement of existing programs, the establishment of a comprehensive industrial policy, and reliance on private market forces. The first two alternatives have been advanced primarily by Democrats; the third is held primarily by Republicans. The distinctions are not perfectly neat, but they characterize the situation generally.

Expand and Improve Existing Programs

The underlying concern of those favoring increased government action is that contemporary unemployment programs are inadequate. They are convinced that the federal government should be more involved in developing human capital and in stimulating economic growth through public investment. The group we call the "reformers" are disgruntled with the current structure and size of the unemployment insurance system, job training programs, and job creation programs.

The central weakness of unemployment insurance, according to the reformers, is that it is a passive income-maintenance system rather than an active program for upgrading the workforce.[9] People receiving unemployment benefits are encouraged to remain idle while they wait to return to work. But what happens if their employers go out of business or if their occupational skills are unmarketable? They probably will exhaust their unemployment compensation before seeking other employment, usually without benefit of retraining.

To rectify these deficiencies, the reformers would encourage unemployment insurance recipients to enroll in training or retraining programs. Money for programs would come from employers' and employees' payments into "individual training accounts." These accounts would be used to pay companies offering on-the-job training or to pay vocational education schools.[10] Reformers also argue for uniform unemployment insurance payments so that benefit levels are not determined by where people live, but by how long they have been employed.

Reformers also criticize contemporary job training programs. With funds sufficient to train fewer than one million people annually, the system cannot adequately serve the unemployed. The Job Training Partnership Act is targeted primarily on low-income, unskilled workers. Critics point out that there are millions of employed people who need training services but cannot now receive them under JTPA.

Reformers would substantially expand the $2 billion Job Training Partnership Act system so that more of the long-term unemployed and disadvantaged could be served. Funds for retraining dislocated workers also would be raised. Finally, the tax code would be restructured to encourage companies to retrain their older workers *before* they join the ranks of the unemployed.[11]

Many reformers are also displeased with contemporary job creation strategies. First, they argue that the jobs bills enacted in late 1982 and early 1983 will serve only a tiny portion of the unemployed. Second, they complain that the jobs bills are tilted toward skilled construction workers and exclude the unskilled and women. Finally, some reformers are distressed that the public works projects funded by the jobs bills will not comprehensively address the nation's needs in this area.

Ambitious job creation programs have been advanced by several groups. Some reformers urge a federal effort to rebuild and upgrade the nation's infrastructure—highways, bridges, railroads, waterways, tunnels, ports, subways, and water and sewer lines. They maintain that investments in public facilities are a necessary condition for private sector investment and economic growth. Massive infrastructure repair and construction programs, patterned on the Public Works Administration of the 1930s, would employ millions of workers.[12]

Another group of lawmakers and academics want to enlarge short-term jobs programs for young people. In their view, the United States will inherit an entire generation of unskilled and inexperienced workers unless bold government action is taken to reduce youth unemployment, especially for minority groups. A national service corps has been proposed in which teenagers would work in minimum wage, public sector jobs.[13] Such a system would provide an alternative to military duty, expand public services at low cost, and offer teenagers valuable experience.

A different strategy for ameliorating youth unemployment is contained in companion bills already introduced in the House and Senate. Based on an experimental approach initiated during the late 1970s, all unemployed low-income youth between the ages of 16 and 19 would be guaranteed a part-time, government-subsidized job in the public or private sector provided they remain in school or return to school or training programs. Approximately 1 million eligible young people could be served at a cost of $2 billion annually.[14]

Finally, some reformers favor a return to CETA-style public service employment, where young people and adults work in federally funded jobs with state and local governments and community organizations. People with limited skills could gain experience while public services were delivered at low cost. A bill based on these ideas passed the House of Representatives in late 1983. Known as the Community Renewal Act, it would provide jobs for roughly 500,000 people every year at a cost of $3.5

billion. Chances of this bill becoming law were considered slim, unless unemployment were to rise sharply again.[15]

Establish a Comprehensive Industrial Policy

A substantially different strategy for attacking unemployment and promoting economic growth is advanced by a group of lawmakers, presidential candidates, and academics known as "industrial policy advocates." Their perceptions of the unemployment problem and their solutions are significantly different from those of the reformers. While they agree with reformers that U.S. employment and training policy needs to be reshaped and expanded, they go several steps further. In their view, the federal government should substantially increase its role in directing and managing the private economy. Federal policy makers should embark on an unprecedented effort to create a more competitive and prosperous economy.

According to these advocates, the government already has a haphazard industrial policy that consists of a tangled web of tax code policies, trade agreements, and loan guarantee programs. They complain that contemporary policies are "inconsistent, inadvertent, ineffective, and very expensive." [16] In their view, current approaches simply are not adequate to address the serious problems facing the U.S. economy in the late 20th century.

What are these problems? Generally, industrial policy advocates agree that the U.S. economy is "deindustrializing" as the nation's manufacturing sector diminishes.[17] Moreover, in many industries the United States has fallen behind other technologically advanced countries. Industrial policy supporters claim that the private sector is "not capable of making the transition that modern technology is forcing upon the nation—the shift from older heavy industries to the new computer-based, high-tech industries." [18] Profound structural problems, such as declining productivity, insufficient investment, poorly coordinated research and development activities, and a deteriorating infrastructure, could lead to an economy that produces fewer jobs, lower quality jobs, and, in general, a lower standard of living for Americans.

The advocates have not yet agreed on what a comprehensive industrial policy should be. While they emphasize different problems and solutions, industrial policy advocates hold in common a deep concern about the long-term health of the American economy and do not believe that either standard government macroeconomic policies or traditional employment and training programs will meet the challenge.

A variety of industrial policy proposals have been advanced during the the early 1980s.[19] A Senate Democratic caucus committee headed by Edward Kennedy, the House Subcommittee on Economic Stabilization, the AFL-CIO, the Center for National Policy, the Office of Technology

Assessment, and a number of leading economists in academia all endorsed industrial policy schemes. The leading contenders for the 1984 Democratic presidential nomination, former vice president Walter Mondale and Sen. Gary Hart, also advocated various forms of industrial policy.

At the risk of oversimplifying the situation a bit, we can divide the strategies into two categories. One group of advocates places primary emphasis on revitalizing declining industries, such as automobiles and steel. This approach could be labeled "protecting the losers." For the steel industry, for example, higher tariffs could be imposed on foreign steel. Manufacturers of steel-based products could be encouraged (through tax policy) or required (through regulations) to use U.S.-produced steel. The government might grant low-interest loans and tax incentives to steel companies that modernize their facilities and retrain their workers. And, air quality standards might be relaxed temporarily until steel manufacturers became more competitive internationally.

Another cadre of advocates is more concerned about stimulating growth in expanding sectors of the economy, such as service industries and high-tech firms. This approach could be labeled "picking the winners." Instead of reviving weak industries, government would help out rapidly developing growth sectors so they could compete better against foreign firms. For example, the government might make large investments in research and development in the computer industry, provide large subsidies and loans for expansion, and offer .tax incentives for worker training programs.

Obviously, a comprehensive industrial strategy would include both support for ailing industries and aid to stronger elements of the economy, but this may prove fairly difficult to achieve. Organized labor unions are among the leading supporters of government aid for declining industries. They favor a number of "protectionist" measures, such as high tariffs and domestic content requirements, that other elements of the Democratic party and most Republican lawmakers strongly oppose.

The free-trade wing of the industrial policy movement prefers subsidies, incentives, and regulatory relief that will help the private sector become more competitive in the world economy. They seem willing to sacrifice existing labor contracts to make firms more efficient and to let other industries decline or even expire. A major challenge for those who favor a comprehensive strategy is the need to reconcile the protectionist inclinations of organized labor and some Democrats with free trade principles.

How would an industrial policy be structured and administered? The House Subcommittee on Economic Stabilization has proposed the establishment of a "council of industrial competitiveness," consisting of representatives from business, labor, academia, and the federal government.[20] The council would provide a forum for developing national industrial policy recommendations. Its views would represent a broad consensus that could then be communicated to government, labor, and business leaders.

The subcommittee's bill also would establish an $8.5 billion "bank for industrial competitiveness." Modeled after the Reconstruction Finance Agency of the New Deal era, the bank would loan capital to mature industries in need of revitalization and to innovative firms at early and risky stages of their development. In the words of Lester Thurow, a leading industrial policy advocate: "We need a national equivalent of a corporate investment committee. . . . Major investments decisions have become too important to be kept to the private market alone. . . . Japan, Inc. needs to be met with U.S.A., Inc." [21]

Finally, the subcommittee bill calls for the creation of an "advanced technology foundation." It would foster the application of research and development to generate new products and work to improve productivity in existing firms. In summary, government resources would be marshaled on behalf of selected industries in the hope that such strategies ultimately would produce a more vital economy.

Rely on Private Market Forces

The "private market forces" group have distinctly different views on unemployment problems and the federal government's proper role. While many of these advocates support modest training programs and unemployment insurance, they do not believe the federal government can create jobs efficiently. Unlike the industrial policy advocates, they do not believe the federal government can or should play a central role in revitalizing the economy. They maintain instead that the private sector should be the primary designers of American industry and commerce.

The private market advocates recognize weak spots in the economy, many of which they blame on excessive government intervention. They are not convinced that the economy suffers from deep structural problems. In their view, the high unemployment and the unfavorable trade balances, thus far evident during the 1980s, eventually will be solved by a resurging private sector and by the Reagan administration's economic policies. Government's role should be to slow its budget growth, decrease regulation of the private sector, reduce taxes on businesses and individuals, and hold down inflation.

Government spending to "create" jobs is scorned by the private market group. Stimulative policies that further swell the federal budget deficit or temporary employment programs that enlarge the public sector are seen as misguided.[22] In their judgment, such policies siphon money away from the private economy where it can be more efficiently invested and where it could stimulate employment of a lasting nature.

Most policy makers in the private market group do not actively oppose government education and training programs for the structurally unemployed. They acknowledge the possibility that such training programs will lead to a more qualified and productive workforce. They *would not* like to see job training programs substantially expanded, however. They favor lowering minimum wage levels for young people, and tax incentive programs that reward employers who hire the unemployed. In short, they prefer methods that preserve the autonomy of the private sector rather than enhance the power of government agencies.

Finally, the notion that government entities could revitalize private industry is firmly rejected by the private market adherents. They are convinced that the private marketplace is a more efficient mechanism for allocating scarce resources. Industrial policy proposals, such as a bank for industrial competitiveness, meet with their disapproval. According to Edwin Harper, former Reagan assistant, "Industrial policy has all the potential of becoming a bureaucratic nightmare." In his view the government cannot effectively "savage one industry and salvage another." [23]

An Intractable Problem

No government strategy can ever hope to end unemployment. The strategies for reducing unemployment and coping with its side effects are as numerous as the causes of the problem. The principal emphases of U.S. government policy for the past 20 years have been financial relief for the short-term unemployed and training programs for the long-term unemployed. The size of the federal commitment has been large in absolute terms but modest in relation to the number of jobless Americans.

Government sponsored training measures tackle an enormously difficult task. In simple terms, they seek to transform chronically unemployed people into steady, productive workers. Most of the people served by the current job training system have not been successful in school, have only limited skills, and may exhibit personal characteristics that make them unattractive to private employers. Their jobless status may be just one manifestation of a broad and deeply rooted set of problems.

To some observers, the magnitude and complexity of unemployment and the modest success of previous government strategies suggest that further interventions are doomed to fail. Others are convinced that unemployment must not be regarded as a private problem. They point out that many people already have benefited from employment and training measures, but that programs can be improved. They argue that it is the government's responsibility to search for better approaches.

In many ways, the history of employment and training policy provides an object lesson in how *not* to design and implement public policy. A fundamental prerequisite for effective policy is a process in which policy makers learn from experience. Only when past mistakes and accomplishments are clearly understood will improvements emerge. Unfortunately, the knowledge that might be gained from even successful experiences is often lost or ignored. Unemployment policies and programs are formulated under highly conflictual conditions that make careful and effective policy making almost impossible. Changing political and economic conditions virtually assure that today's policies will be replaced by others. Uncertainty and instability guarantee trouble for program implementers.

Before substantially better unemployment programs can emerge, present strategies must be refined and improved. Stronger leadership from the employment and training subgovernment may be necessary. Many political scientists emphasize the negative aspects of subgovernment power in American politics.[24] Subgovernments are accused of serving narrow group interests and entrenched inefficient federal bureaucracies, but they are the principal arenas in which policies are formulated and reformulated. Subgovernment participants are just about the only people engaged in the policy process who could potentially rise above rhetoric, symbolic politics, and ideology and reach pragmatic solutions. They have the potential to use their experience and knowledge to assess the strengths and weaknesses of programs and to incorporate these lessons into policy modifications.

The struggle over unemployment programs and policies has intensified. The issues of long-term economic growth, competitiveness, productivity, and job security are receiving more attention now than at any time since the end of World War II. Despite all this attention, the federal government's basic strategies for addressing unemployment problems so far have remained essentially unchanged. Are we on the verge of a major breakthrough in unemployment policy?

Whether new strategies will be adopted during the late 1980s depends mainly on three factors: the outcome of the 1984 presidential and congressional elections, the level of unemployment among Americans, and assessments of contemporary employment and training programs. High levels of unemployment or increased Democratic strength in Congress or a Democratic takeover of the White House would likely lead to an expansion of existing programs and several new initiatives. Lower rates of unemployment and Republican strength in Congress and the White House would have the opposite effect.

Recall that when Reagan entered office he declared that the federal government should not fund temporary jobs programs and that he wanted job training programs either eliminated or reduced. It was only after unemployment exceeded 10 percent and congressional Republicans rebelled that the president endorsed job training programs and supported public works job bills. During a second term, unless unemployment were to rise sharply, Reagan would resist major enlargements of current unemployment measures.

No matter who is in power, the multi-billion dollar unemployment insurance system is likely to come under scrutiny. While the system's image is basically positive, Republican and Democratic lawmakers complain that people who do not need help are subsidized and that others are discouraged from seeking retraining. Policies aimed at strengthening incentives for recipients to find jobs and to obtain additional training probably will be added to the system.

The implementation of the Job Training Partnership Act has not generated much controversy thus far. JTPA has not acquired the same negative reputation that hounded CETA for nearly a decade. Members of Congress seem sensitive to the need to leave JTPA alone: the prospects for program stability are reasonably good. Major shake-ups will occur if JTPA fails to aid the structurally unemployed effectively or if an attempt is made to place the expanded youth and adult training programs under the JTPA umbrella.

The future of federal job creation programs is clouded. A second Reagan administration can be counted upon to oppose jobs programs. Concern over the size of the federal deficit is likely to dominate policy debates during the 1980s. Public works projects could be scorned as budget busters by many Republicans and Democrats. Unless unemployment rises sharply to levels near or above 10 percent, Reagan will successfully oppose additional spending on unemployment measures.

Nevertheless, public works projects are politically popular and may be difficult to erase. Members of Congress have always liked public works because they produce visible and tangible benefits for unemployed people and communities. The claim that the nation's infrastructure must be repaired and strengthened also will make large-scale public works schemes very appealing.

The prospects for a comprehensive industrial policy are dim, even under a Democratic president. Major new initiatives are unlikely if the Republicans retain control of the Senate. But even if the Democrats capture the White House and a majority in both chambers, the establishment of a far-reaching industrial policy is improbable. A more likely outcome would be that a few of the industrial policy proposals having strong appeal for key constituencies would be enacted.

For many politicians, the concept of a government led economic renaissance runs against the grain of American political culture. It strikes them as an attempt to substitute "rational" planning for politics and the private marketplace. This is unappealing because it detracts from their ability to take credit for delivering tangible benefits to constituents and because they are skeptical about significant government participation in economic development. Many Democrats would join Republicans in blocking or watering down any broad measures for centrally planned industrial development.

Strong presidential leadership and sustained economic decline could produce consensus around fundamentally different and comprehensive approaches to coping with unemployment. Without this combination, the nation's approach to aiding the unemployed is very likely to remain fragmented and unstable. Government spending will expand when unemployment is uncomfortably high and rising and when the public is anxious about the economy. Government programs will contract when unemployment drops to politically tolerable levels and the perception of serious threats to prosperity subsides. The shape of specific programs will be determined by images of implementation successes and failures. An optimistic, but not unrealistic hope is that policy makers will improve their ability to learn from experience as they design the unemployment strategies of the future.

Notes

1. Lawrence D. Brown, *New Policies, New Politics: Government's Response to Government's Growth* (Washington, D.C.: Brookings Institution, 1983), 11.
2. The Employment Act of 1946 was a very important policy statement and consolidation of the government's macroeconomic policy-making apparatus; however, we have not labeled it a "breakthrough" here because it did not establish any new *programs* for aiding the unemployed. See Stephen K. Bailey, *Congress Makes a Law: The Story Behind the Employment Act of 1946* (New York: Columbia University Press, 1950).
3. Most of the observations on program impact are drawn from Robert Taggart, *A Fisherman's Guide: An Assessment of Training and Remediation Strategies* (Kalamazoo, Mich.: W. E. Upjohn Institute for Employment Research, 1981). For an excellent summary of employment and training research, see Michael Borus, "Assessing the Impact of Training Programs," in *Employing the Disadvantaged,* ed. Eli Ginzberg (New York: Basic Books, 1980).
4. The postprogram earning gains for public service jobholders were $261 a year after leaving the program and $326 two years later. Comparable figures for job training programs are $347 and $442. See Taggart, *A Fisherman's Guide,* 57 and 130.

5. For an excellent discussion of unemployment and public opinion, see Kay Lehman Schlozman and Sidney Verba, *Injury to Insult: Unemployment, Class, and Political Response* (Cambridge: Harvard University Press, 1979).

6. For a discussion that offers a similar perspective, see Daniel A. Mazmanian and Paul A. Sabatier, *Implementation and Public Policy* (Glenview, Ill.: Scott, Foresman & Co., 1983), 7-9.

7. Brown, *New Policies, New Politics,* 18-46.

8. Jimmy Carter, *Keeping Faith* (New York: Bantam Books, 1982).

9. See Robert B. Reich, *The Next American Frontier* (New York: Times Books, 1983), 209.

10. See, for example, "House Group Backs Bill Giving G.I. and 'IRA'-type Benefits to Job Training," *Employment and Training Reporter,* March 7, 1984, 704-705; and Richard Corrigan and Rochelle L. Stanfield, "Casualties of Change," *National Journal,* Feb. 11, 1984, 252-264.

11. Reich, *The Next American Frontier,* 241.

12. Patrick Choate, *America in Ruins* (Washington, D.C.: Council of State Planning Agencies, 1980); U.S. House of Representatives, Democratic Caucus Committee on Party Effectiveness, *Rebuilding the Road to Opportunity: A Democratic Direction for the 1980s* (Washington, D.C.: National Legislative Education Foundation, September 1982).

13. See, for example, Franklin A. Thomas, *Youth Unemployment and National Service* (New York: Ford Foundation, April 1983).

14. "House, Senate Bills Boost JTPA With Youth Jobs Tied to Continued Schooling," *Employment and Training Reporter,* March 7, 1984, 703-704.

15. "Jobs Bill for $3.5 Billion Passes House But Faces Uncertain Future in Senate," *Employment and Training Reporter,* Sept. 28, 1983, 64-65.

16. "Democrats in House, Senate Call for New Economic Policies to Revive U.S.," *Employment and Training Reporter,* Nov. 30, 1983, 333.

17. Barry Bluestone and Bennett Harrison, *The Deindustrialization of America* (New York: Basic Books, 1982).

18. Charles L. Schultze, "Industrial Policy: A Solution in Search of a Problem," *California Management Review* 25 (Summer 1983): 5-15.

19. A sample of industrial policy discussions and proposals would include: Reich, *The Next American Frontier;* House Subcommittee on Economic Stabilization, Committee on Banking, Finance, and Urban Affairs, *Forging and Industrial Competitiveness Strategy,* 98th Cong., 1st sess. (Washington, D.C.: GPO, 1983); U.S. Senate Democratic Caucus, *Jobs for the Future: A Democratic Agenda,* Nov. 6, 1983, Photocopied; and Center for National Policy, *Promoting Economic Growth and Competitiveness* (Washington, D.C.: Center for National Policy, 1984).

20. "Democrats in House, Senate Call for New Economic Policies to Revive U.S.," 333-335.

21. Quoted in Sidney Blumenthal, "Drafting a Democratic Industrial Plan," *New York Times Magazine,* Aug. 28, 1983, 41.

22. For other criticisms of job creation measures, see James O'Toole, *Making America Work: Productivity and Responsibility* (New York: Continuum, 1981), Chap. 8; and Congressional Budget Office, *Strategies for Assisting the*

Unemployed (Washington, D.C.: Dec. 8, 1982, Photocopied).

23. Quoted in Blumenthal, "Drafting a Democratic Industrial Plan," 59; Richard Corrigan, "Let the Market Choose Winners and Losers, Says White House's Harper," *National Journal,* July 2, 1983, 1395.
24. See, for example, E. E. Schattschneider, *The Semi-Sovereign People* (Hinsdale, Ill.: Dryden Press, 1960); Theodore J. Lowi, *The End of Liberalism,* 2d ed. (New York: W. W. Norton, 1979); Roger H. Davidson, "Breaking Up Those 'Cozy Triangles': An Impossible Dream?" in *Legislative Reform and Public Policy,* eds. S. Welch and J. G. Peters (New York: Praeger Publishers, 1977).

For Further Reading

Overviews of the Policy Process

Anderson, James E. *Public Policy Making*. 2d ed. New York: Holt, Rinehart & Winston, 1979.

Dolbeare, Kenneth M. *American Public Policy*. New York: McGraw-Hill, 1982.

Dye, Thomas R. *Understanding Public Policy*. 4th ed. Englewood Cliffs, N.J.: Prentice-Hall, 1981.

Jones, Charles O. *An Introduction to the Study of Public Policy*. 3d ed. Monterey, Calif.: Brooks/Cole Publishing Co., 1984.

Lindblom, Charles E. *The Policy-Making Process*. 2d ed. Englewood Cliffs, N.J.: Prentice-Hall, 1980.

Lineberry, Robert L. *American Public Policy*. New York: Harper & Row, 1977.

Wildavsky, Aaron. *Speaking Truth to Power: The Art & Craft of Policy Analysis*. Boston: Little, Brown & Co., 1979.

Policy Making in American National Government

Bailey, Stephen K., *Congress Makes a Law: The Story Behind the Employment Act of 1946*. New York: Columbia University Press, 1950.

Davidson, Roger H., and Walter J. Oleszek. *Congress Against Itself*. Bloomington: Indiana University Press, 1977.

Dodd, Lawrence C., and Richard L. Schott. *Congress and the Administrative State*. New York: John Wiley & Sons, 1979.

Edelman, Murray. *The Symbolic Uses of Politics*. Urbana: University of Illinois Press, 1964.

Fiorina, Morris P. *Congress: Keystone of the Washington Establishment*. New Haven, Conn.: Yale University Press, 1974.

Heclo, Hugh A. *A Government of Strangers*. Washington, D.C.: Brookings Institution, 1977.

Lowi, Theodore J. *The End of Liberalism*. 2d ed. New York: W. W. Norton, 1979.

Ripley, Randall B. *Congress: Process and Policy*. 3d ed. (New York: W. W. Norton, 1983.

Ripley, Randall B., and Grace A. Franklin. *Congress, the Bureaucracy, and Public Policy.* 3d ed. Homewood, Ill.: Dorsey Press, 1984.

Schick, Allen, ed., *Economic Policy Making in Congress.* Washington, D.C.: American Enterprise Institute, 1983.

Wildavsky, Aaron. *The Politics of the Budgetary Process.* 3d ed. Boston: Little, Brown & Co., 1979.

Policy Implementation

Bardach, Eugene. *The Implementation Game.* Cambridge, Mass.: MIT Press, 1977.

Bullock, Charles S., III, and Charles M. Lamb. *Implementation of Civil Rights Policy.* Monterey, Calif.: Brooks/Cole Publishing Co., 1984.

Edwards, George C., III. *Implementing Public Policy.* Washington, D.C.: CQ Press, 1980.

Mazmanian, Daniel A., and Paul A. Sabatier. *Implementation and Public Policy.* Glenview, Ill.: Scott, Foresman & Co., 1983.

Nakamura, Robert T., and Frank Smallwood. *The Politics of Policy Implementation.* New York: St. Martin's Press, 1980.

Ripley, Randall B., and Grace A. Franklin. *Bureaucracy and Policy Implementation.* Homewood, Ill.: Dorsey Press, 1982.

Van Horn, Carl E. *Policy Implementation in the Federal System.* Lexington, Mass.: D. C. Heath & Co., 1979.

Williams, Walter, ed. *Studying Implementation: Methodological and Administrative Issues.* Chatham, N.J.: Chatham House, 1982.

Public Policy Case Studies

Bailey, Stephen K., and Edith K. Mosher. *ESEA: The Office of Education Administers a Law.* Syracuse, N.Y.: Syracuse University Press, 1968.

Bauer, Raymond A., Ithiel de Sola Pool, and Lewis A. Dexter. *American Business & Public Policy.* 2d ed. Chicago: Aldine Publishing, 1972.

Derthick, Martha. *New Towns In-Town.* Washington, D.C.: The Urban Institute, 1972.

Fritschler, A. Lee. *Smoking and Politics.* 3d ed. Englewood Cliffs, N.J.: Prentice-Hall, 1983.

Jones, Charles O. *Clean Air: The Policies and Politics of Pollution Control.* Pittsburgh, Pa.: University of Pittsburgh Press, 1975.

Pressman, Jeffrey L., and Aaron B. Wildavsky. *Implementation.* 2d ed. Berkeley: University of California Press, 1979.

Employment and Training Programs

Davidson, Roger H. *The Politics of Comprehensive Manpower Legislation.* Baltimore, Md.: Johns Hopkins University Press, 1972.

Employment and Training Reporter. Weekly journal published by the Bureau of National Affairs, Washington, D.C.

Franklin, Grace A., and Randall B. Ripley. *CETA: Politics and Policy 1974-1982.* Knoxville: University of Tennessee Press, 1984.

Haveman, J., and L. Palmer. *Jobs for Disadvantaged Workers.* Washington, D.C.: Brookings Institution, 1982.

Levitan, Sar A., Barth L. Mangum, and Ray Marshall. *Human Resources and Labor Markets.* New York: Harper & Row, 1972.

Levitan, Sar A., and Robert Taggart. *The Promise of Greatness.* Cambridge, Mass.: Harvard University Press, 1975.

Mirengoff, William. *The New CETA: Effect on Public Service Employment.* Washington, D.C.: National Academy of Sciences, 1980.

Mirengoff, William, and Lester Rindler. *CETA: Manpower Programs Under Local Control.* Washington, D.C.: National Academy of Sciences, 1978.

Mirengoff, William, and Associates. *CETA: An Assessment of Public Service Employment.* Washington, D.C.: National Academy of Sciences, 1980.

Mirengoff, William, et al. *CETA: Accomplishments, Problems, Solutions.* Kalamazoo, Mich.: W. E. Upjohn Institute for Employment Research, 1982.

Nathan, Richard P., Robert F. Cook, V. Lane Rawlins, and Associates. *Public Service Employment: A Field Evaluation.* Washington, D.C.: Brookings Institution, 1981.

Unemployment

Anderson, Bernard E., and Isabel V. Sawhill, eds. *Youth Employment and Public Policy.* Englewood Cliffs, N.J.: Prentice-Hall, 1980.

Bluestone, Barry, and Bennett Harrison. *The Deindustrialization of America.* New York: Basic Books, 1982.

The Economic Report of the President. Annual report to Congress, U.S. Government Printing Office, Washington, D.C.

The Employment and Training Report of the President. (Formerly *The Manpower Report of the President.*) Annual report to Congress, U.S. Government Printing Office, Washington, D.C.

Garraty, John A. *Unemployment in History.* New York: Harper & Row, 1978.

Ginsberg, Eli, ed. *Employing the Unemployed.* New York: Basic Books, 1980.

Goodwin, Leonard. *Do the Poor Want to Work?* Washington, D.C.: Brookings Institution, 1972.

Scholzman, Kay Lehman, and Sidney Verba. *Injury to Insult: Unemployment, Class and Political Response.* Cambridge, Mass.: Harvard University Press, 1979.

Index